D1164424

Food and Agricultural Policy for the 1980s

A Conference Sponsored by the American Enterprise Institute for Public Policy Research

Food and Agricultural Policy for the 1980s

Edited by D. Gale Johnson

American Enterprise Institute for Public Policy Research
Washington and London

Library of Congress Cataloging in Publication Data

Main entry under title:

Food and agricultural policy for the 1980s.

   (AEI symposia ; 81G)
   Proceedings of the Conference on Food and Agricultural Policy
for the 1980s, held in Washington, D.C., Oct. 2–3, 1980.
     1. Agriculture and state—United States—Congresses.
2. Food supply—International cooperation—Congresses.
I. Johnson, D. Gale (David Gale), 1916–
II. Conference on Food and Agricultural Policy for the 1980s
(1980 : Washington, D.C.)   III. Series.
HD1755.F66   338.1'9'73   81-7965
ISBN 0-8447-2217-0   AACR2
ISBN 0-8447-2216-2 (pbk.)

AEI Symposia 81G

Printed in the United States of America

1/4008

Contributors

Peter M. Emerson
Principal Analyst
Congressional Budget Office

Bruce Gardner
Professor, Department of Agricultural Economics
Texas A&M University

W. E. Hamilton
formerly of American Farm Bureau Federation

Dale E. Hathaway
Under Secretary of Agriculture
U.S. Department of Agriculture

Dale M. Hoover
Professor and Assistant Head
Department of Economics and Business
North Carolina State University

D. Gale Johnson
Chairman, Department of Economics
University of Chicago

Timothy Josling
Professor, Food Research Institute
Stanford University

John Mellor
International Food Policy Research Institute

William R. Pearce
Cargill, Inc.

J. B. Penn
Deputy Administrator for Economics
Economics and Statistics Service
U.S. Department of Agriculture

John A. Schnittker
Schnittker Associates

G. Edward Schuh
Professor and Head
Department of Agricultural and Applied Economics
University of Minnesota

Phillip F. Sisson
Director of Agricultural Economics
Quaker Oats Company

Luther Tweeten
Regents Professor, Department of Agricultural Economics
Oklahoma State University

*This conference was held at
the American Enterprise Institute for Public Policy Research
in Washington, D.C., on October 2–3, 1980*

Contents

Foreword

D. Gale Johnson

A Conference on Food and Agricultural Policy was sponsored by the American Enterprise Institute on October 2 and 3, 1980, and held at its offices in Washington, D.C.—three years after a similar conference was held.[1] This conference was in response to requests from a number of policy makers who expressed the belief that a conference similar to the earlier one would make a contribution to the preparation of agricultural legislation that was required during the early part of 1981. The Food and Agriculture Act of 1977, which covers most of the legislation directly affecting farm prices, supply management, and reserves, expires with the 1981 crop year.

The conference was attended by approximately seventy people of varied backgrounds. They came from universities, business, farm organizations, the U.S. Department of Agriculture, and staffs of congressional committees and of the Congressional Budget Office. The discussion was lively and constructive.

The conference was organized into three major groups of presentations. The first group included two papers, one concerned with economic developments affecting food and agriculture in the United States during the 1970s and the other with various consequences of the farm policies followed during the 1970s. The second session consisted of two papers that made an effort to look ahead: one emphasized potential developments in world food production, consumption, trade, and farm policies and how they might affect U.S. agriculture; the other considered possible changes in the structure of U.S. agriculture. The third session was concerned with the future of U.S. farm policy, especially major issues of legislation concerning agricultural policy.

In this foreword I highlight some of the important points that were made and the significant areas of both agreement and disagree-

[1] *Food and Agricultural Policy* (Washington, D.C.: American Enterprise Institute, 1977).

ment concerning the appropriate policy directions for the 1980s. The major papers were summarized by their authors, and one participant had been asked to serve as a critic and discussant for each paper. Each of the three major sessions was followed by lively discussion and comments from the audience.

The first paper, presented by J. B. Penn, was about the major economic developments that shaped U.S. agriculture during the 1970s. His paper is a major work, worthy of careful study by anyone interested in understanding the major economic changes in American agriculture during the past decade. The first part of the paper presents a concise summary of farm sector developments, and the second part provides a profile of the farm sector as the 1980s begin. A brief final section draws out some of the major policy implications of the two previous sections.

The first of the farm sector developments discussed by Penn is "the emergence of relative resource equilibrium in the sector." He notes that, as we entered the 1970s, the symptoms of the farm problem were still evident—large stocks of grain in governmental hands, high program costs, and a large amount of cropland idled by government programs. Penn argues, however, that certain changes, largely unnoticed at the time, resulted in a striking change in the economic setting for agriculture. One was the rapid growth in demand for U.S. agricultural exports due to significant growth in income and population in many developing countries. Other significant changes included the transformation of the centrally planned economies from net food exporters to net importers, the devaluation of the dollar, and the modest shortfall in world grain production in 1972. Penn points out that changes on the supply side had gone largely unnoticed, although he was kind enough to give me credit for having argued in early 1973 that there no longer existed significant excess resources in agriculture. He concludes that the slowing down of net out-migration from agriculture, the emerging near equality of the per capita incomes of farm and nonfarm people, and the full utilization of the readily available cropland strongly support an assertion that "the farm sector is now in near equilibrium and perhaps has been for several years."

Penn discusses trends in land in farms, in the uses of that land, and in the distribution of ownership of the land. He notes the uncertainty concerning the amount of additional land that could be brought under cultivation. The decline of the farm population, which had fallen by half between 1940 and 1960 and by almost 40 percent during the 1960s, slowed during the 1970s. The slowdown in migration from farms may be attributed to the significantly improved income of farmers. He discusses the uncertain state of our knowledge concerning the growth of productivity in agriculture, especially whether the rate of such growth has slowed during the 1970s. If productivity growth is slowing and if land and labor resources continue to disappear, "the prospects for *output expansion* in the future are not bright, absent a major breakthrough in production technology."

The second part of Penn's paper provides an illuminating profile of the farm sector as we enter the 1980s. The topics covered include farm numbers and sizes, the economic well-being of farm people, and the economic viability of farms. Penn emphasizes that the income of farm operator families from farm sources alone gives a misleading picture of their well-being. He presents data showing the importance of off-farm income, which has exceeded farm operator income since 1965. For farms with value of sales greater than $40,000, off-farm income during 1975–1978 equaled 25 percent of net farm income. One consequence of the growth of off-farm income has been a significant narrowing of income disparities within agriculture. In his discussion of the economic viability of farms, he compares the rate of return on equity investments from agriculture, common stocks, and long-term bonds. He finds that since 1965 the combined returns from current income and real capital gains from farm assets have significantly exceeded returns from either common stocks or long-term bonds.

The variability of farm prices and income was found to have increased significantly during the 1970s. During 1972–1978 farm prices were six times as variable and farm income was approximately three times as variable as they had been in 1955–1971. Nonfarm income, however, was quite stable during the 1970s as well as during the earlier years. Penn concludes that price and income variability during the 1980s is likely to be much greater than during the 1960s.

In summarizing his paper, Penn notes that the problems facing American agriculture are significantly different from those of the past several decades. After stressing the points referred to above, Penn emphasizes the potential growth in foreign demand for our farm products. He notes that the future may well bring forth increasing prices of farm products rather than the surpluses that our farm programs have been designed to deal with.

In his paper, "Consequences of Farm Policies during the 1970s," Bruce Gardner notes that during the 1970s commodity programs were modified toward increased market orientation and that the "importance of government in determining farm incomes, asset prices, and labor returns declined." He argues, however, that there were two areas in which governmental intervention increased, namely, in trying to deal with instability of prices and income and in protecting farmers and consumers against natural hazards and middlemen.

Gardner analyzes the view that farm programs of the 1970s were more market oriented than in earlier years. If the criteria are a significant decline in the real (deflated) levels of price supports and reduced efforts to control production, there was a clear increase in market orientation. Gardner argues, however, that if the criterion is the difference between average prices received and loan or support prices, the picture is less clear. Only in the cases of cotton and soybeans were the differences larger in the 1970s than in earlier years, and for the other major farm products there was no apparent increase in the differential. By another criterion of market orientation—the reduction in quantities of price-supported commodities owned by the government—there was a significant increase in such orientation for the major farm products except for dairy products. By still another criterion, the amount and importance of government payments, the programs were much more market oriented after 1973 than before.

Gardner argues that the farmer-owned reserve program is an example of reduced market orientation. He notes that there seems to be an effort to use the program for short-term price stabilization. In pursuing that objective, frequent changes in such important variables as price supports and release and trigger prices have been required. Gardner argues that the reserve program has done little to stabilize wheat and corn prices, primarily because it has not had much effect on the quantities of grain in storage.

Commenting on Penn's paper, Phillip Sisson notes that the United States bears the brunt of variations in world supply and demand. He also observes that for several countries, especially Japan and Germany, the import prices of our corn and soybeans in their currencies increased hardly at all during the 1970s because of the sharp decline in the dollar exchange rate. The consumer prices of major food importers should reflect international market conditions. If they did, Sisson remarks, international market prices would be less variable.

W. E. Hamilton notes that Gardner's emphasis upon the difference between the average price received by farmers and the support price has significant limitations as a measure of the degree of market orientation. He points out the substantial differences among the various commodity programs: In some cases loan rates are mandated by legislation while in others there is administrative discretion. For soybeans the loan rate is entirely discretionary, and for the 1970s the rate was substantially below market prices.

One of the conference participants raised a pertinent question in response to Penn's paper: What is the justification for a 1981 farm bill if farmers' incomes are equivalent to those of nonfarm residents? Penn responded that the rationale for intervention can be different from what it was in the past; the strongest rationale for new farm legislation may well be to deal with the problems of instability in prices and incomes.

Another participant asked whether it was U.S. policy to maximize exports. The response was that we had policies that permitted agricultural exports to grow and that the most accurate way of describing our programs as they relate to exports is that all we are doing is standing aside and letting the market function.

In his paper "World Food Production, Consumption, and International Trade," Timothy Josling describes the dramatic growth in U.S. agricultural exports during the 1970s, emphasizing the shifts in export markets by region and commodities. He notes that although the value of agricultural imports from the United States to Eastern Europe and the Soviet Union grew by 41 percent between 1970 and 1978, by 1978 that region accounted for a little less than 10 percent of all our agricultural exports. The two most important regional markets, each with about a third of the total in 1978, are Western Europe and Asia. Japan alone took 15 percent of our farm exports. By commodity groups, grains and oilseeds and products accounted for more than two-thirds of the value of our agricultural exports in 1978.

Josling argues that the sharp price increases that occurred in 1973 and 1974 had little impact on governmental policies affecting agriculture. It does not appear that such policies were modified in either the developing or the developed economies; he found no evidence that development priorities were shifted toward food production. Nor does he find that the 1970s brought any significant change in policies affecting trade in agricultural products. Self-sufficiency remains a strong priority in many countries. Developed countries continue to protect inefficient agricultural production.

The growth of U.S. agricultural exports depends on both the growth of demand and the degree of competition from other countries in providing the export supply. Josling concludes that U.S. agriculture is in a relatively favorable position compared with many other export sectors of the economy and that the potential threat to the U.S. export position "comes as much from the subsidized exports of countries with high levels of agricultural protection as from the more regular and more soundly based production of commercial exporters." He notes that two countries—Brazil and Argentina—stand out as having considerable export potential.

In spite of the lack of progress toward reducing barriers to trade in agricultural products or achieving greater stability of international prices, Josling concludes that exports of U.S. agricultural products will continue to grow. He argues that the United States must do two things to ensure that growth: (1) ensure that market information and marketing facilities are adequate and (2) ensure that domestic market and income support policies are consistent with overseas trade realities. The latter point was emphasized by both G. Edward Schuh and me in our policy discussions.

In recent years there have been an increasing interest in and concern about agriculture structure. The extended and perceptive analysis by Luther Tweeten supports the view that trends in U.S. farm structure have had significantly more benefits than negative outcomes. He notes the following positive elements: incomes of farm people have improved relative to those of persons in the rest of the economy; the incidence of poverty in the farming sector has fallen dramatically; increases in farm productivity have permitted the growing demand to be met with a constant level of farm inputs; consumers have continued to spend a declining percentage of their incomes on food; and drudgery has been largely eliminated from farm work.

Tweeten expresses pessimism about the long-term outlook for the traditional family farm. He estimates that the required growth in size of family farms to keep farm incomes growing at the same rate as nonfarm incomes will need to be greater during the remainder of the century than for the past four decades. He also emphasizes that inflation puts particular pressure on agriculture, especially family farms, since only a part of inflation is passed on through higher product prices.

A striking point made by Tweeten is that farmland is not overpriced in relation to its prospective earning capacity. Current earnings on farmland have averaged about 4 percent per year since World War II. In addition, the value of farmland has increased faster than the rate of inflation by at least 4 percent per year in recent years. Thus farmland has been an excellent investment, and Tweeten expects it to continue to be. He does note that, since the current rate of return on farmland is significantly below recent interest rates on farm mortgages, recent purchasers of farms have been faced with severe cash flow problems.

Tweeten draws a number of important conclusions from his analysis. For example, commodity programs have had little effect on the number and size of farms; the increasing cost of energy will not improve the comparative advantage of small farms; the optimal size of farms will continue to increase; and the "social and economic vitality of many rural towns and small cities has declined but on the whole has been maintained remarkably well in the face of declining employment on the farm."

The third part of the conference included three papers that addressed the agricultural policy issues for the 1980s. G. Edward Schuh stresses policy alternatives given that U.S. agriculture is a part of an interdependent world and the world's largest trader in agricultural products. His paper is based on two major premises: in the 1980s we should move to even greater dependence on market forces, and we should recognize that general economic policies are now more important to the welfare of agriculture and rural people than farm commodity policies. Schuh includes monetary and fiscal policies, exchange rate policy, labor market policy, and trade policy among general market policies.

Schuh gives particular emphasis to the role of science and technology as a factor in agricultural productivity. He notes some evidence that the rate of growth of productivity in agriculture has declined, although he adds that the choice of base period affects the conclusion. More important, he observes, is that federal support for agricultural research has remained constant since 1965. The case for increased support of agricultural research turns on the benefits that result from such research; most of the benefits go to consumers either directly through lower food prices or indirectly as a result of large exports. Increased exports improve the foreign exchange value of the dollar, which reduces the dollar costs of our imports.

Schuh gives considerable emphasis to price instability, as does John Schnittker. In Schuh's view, the commodity policies did not perform well in limiting price instability during the 1970s. Giving freer reign to market forces was desirable, but the market and the commodity programs were not "able to cope with the basic source of the instability, which has been the monetary and fiscal instability of the past decade." Schuh notes, as does Gardner, that the farmer-owned reserve program added little to price stability, in part because of the politicization of the system and its failure to add significantly to the total quantity of grain stocks.

Schuh supports a continuation of the evolution of the 1973 and 1977 legislation in the direction of a free market commodity policy. He does believe, however, that there should be an "actuarially sound but subsidized income insurance program that could be developed by extending and improving the crop insurance program." This program should replace the current disaster payments program, which has encouraged crop production in high-risk areas and has transferred income to many who are relatively well off.

Both Schuh and I call attention to enormous budget costs and economic waste associated with the production of alcohol from farm products. The gasohol program, if carried through as announced, could reach an annual subsidy level by 1990 of $10 billion, dwarfing the costs of all farm commodity programs. In addition, the gasohol program could pose a threat to the world's food supply.

In my paper, "Agricultural Policy Alternatives for the 1980s," I emphasize the continuity in the evolution of farm commodity programs during the past two decades. During this period there was a gradual movement toward increased market orientation. This increase in market orientation was followed by the large upsurge in agricultural exports and the gradual elimination of the excess resources in agriculture. I discuss what I consider the major policy issues relevant to the 1981 agricultural legislation and argue that price supports for the major crop products should be kept at levels that will permit the market to allocate the available supplies freely between domestic and foreign use. The primary purpose of price supports should be to assist farmers in the orderly marketing of their products by providing prompt and easy access to credit. I point out that, unlike the crop products, dairy products benefit from high price supports, which have a major influence on domestic prices. As Gardner notes, the price supports for dairy products have not declined in real terms but, contrary to the experience with all other price supports, have increased during the past two decades.

I oppose the use of cost of production as the criterion for establishing target prices. Target prices have been set substantially higher, in relation to past market prices, for wheat, barley, and grain sorghums than for corn. I argue that target prices should bear approximately the same relationship to price support levels for each of the crops and should not be used to affect the allocation of resources significantly.

Though critical of the numerous changes that have been made in the support, release, and trigger prices for the farmer-owned reserve storage program, I do favor the retention of the program. In particular, I believe that the farmer-owned reserve program is superior to the previous control over stocks by the Commodity Credit Corporation. As I argue in my paper, the current supply management tools have not been very effective in limiting agricultural production; but since there is likely to be a rough balance between the growth of demand and of supply for U.S. farm output during the 1980s, I do not favor instituting more effective supply management tools in the 1981 legislation. I do favor continuing our present export policies and strongly oppose the replacement of the private trading system by a federal board or agency.

John A. Schnittker presents a scenario of future developments in supply and demand for U.S. farm products that differs significantly from the assumptions underlying the policy proposals made by Schuh and me. In consequence, Schnittker gives primary emphasis to policy instruments other than price supports, target prices, and deficiency payments. Schnittker argues that managing shortages of agricultural resources and commodities will probably become the focus of food and agricultural policy during the 1980s.

Schnittker supports the conclusion that the demand for agricultural products will be strong during the 1980s by referring to prospective circumstances in the developing countries and the centrally planned economies. Some developing countries that produce oil will neglect their agriculture; other developing countries will consume whatever agricultural successes they may have because of income and population growth. Schnittker believes that the centrally planned economies will continue to demand more grain, largely for livestock feeding, than they can supply. "Real prices of agricultural products seem likely to rise under such circumstances." He does not indicate how much real prices may increase, but apparently it will be enough to generate quite radical changes in our agricultural policies.

Schnittker views the role of loan levels during the 1980s as that of determining how grain reserves will be accumulated and used; the role of target prices will be negligible when market prices are usually above direct production costs and acreage limitations are not in effect. The main policy problem he discusses is that of managing the volume of grain exports to maintain adequate supplies for all domestic users at "reasonable and competitive prices." If U.S. and world demand outpaces production or poor world grain harvests dissipate reserve stocks in the years ahead, such limitations might be justified. This latter circumstance is likely in view of "the anticipated large decline in feed grain reserve stocks in 1981."

Schnittker suggests that we might develop a number of arrangements with importing nations under which the United States would agree to supply a certain volume, though not unlimited quantities, of agricultural exports; he notes that the 1975 grain agreement between the United States and the Soviet Union "may well become a pattern for future bilateral trade agreements with our large customers." Schnittker recognizes that general use of bilateral arrangements to control agricultural exports "would constitute a fundamental modification of our policies and our rhetoric on free and unlimited exports." He adds that, if significant limits were imposed upon our exports, it might be necessary "to think the unthinkable and to design procedures for selling our products into a very demanding world market at a premium over prices prevailing in the United States." To do so, he adds, would not require a federal export board or corporation.

After the three policy papers were presented, there was considerable discussion and disagreement concerning the prospective trend of real farm prices. J. B. Penn and John Mellor supported the view that real farm prices and real export prices for agricultural products would be likely to increase during the 1980s. Both Schuh and I disagreed with this view. Schuh emphasized three points in support of his view: (1) more developing countries will change their domestic farm policies because of balance-of-payments difficulties; (2) the developing countries will soon produce more farm products as a result of international research centers; and (3) the real value of the dollar in terms of foreign currencies will increase since the U.S. economy has made many adjustments, including increasing domestic energy prices and recognizing the need to improve productivity.

William Pearce agreed with Schnittker that the prospects were good for a high degree of price instability. If all countries played by the rules of market price equality, then international prices would not be unduly variable. Given the domestic price polices of most of the trading nations, however, it was agreed that, unless reserves were very large, we could look forward to substantial international price instability during the 1980s. There did not appear to be general agreement on the desirability of our controlling exports as a means of offsetting the effects of international price variability upon our domestic markets.

Commenting on my paper, Dale Hathaway emphasized that the creation of the farmer-owned reserve program was the major policy innovation of the 1970s and that over a broad range of demand and supply conditions, it is that program, and not simply the price support levels, that affects storage and other decisions. He also observed that the release price rather than the support price had been the important policy variable. He further argued that it was nonsensical to assume that there is no relation between cost of production, political factors, loan rates, and release and call prices. He supported the higher level of target prices for Great Plains crops because the variable costs had increased more than the similar costs for crops grown in the Corn Belt. Hathaway urged that target prices can be based on any of three criteria—a reasonably definite criterion such as some concept of cost of production, judgment, or current political pressures. His preference was for the reasonably definite criterion.

Don Paarlberg noted that the 1977 legislation was drafted at a time when it was uncertain what the price trends were to be. That legislation, he emphasized, was a two-track bill that provided for moderate price supports, deficiency payments, and supply management if farm prices remained low and for the phasing out of supply management and the elimination of most income transfers if farm prices increased. There appeared to be general agreement that the 1981 legislation should provide for sufficient flexibility to meet whatever underlying price pattern may emerge. In any case, there was no support for sharp increases in either support prices or target prices because of the expectation that real farm prices would be substantially higher during the 1980s than in the 1970s. It remains important that support prices be at levels that will permit our exports to be competitive and that target prices not encourage output expansion.

Several reservations were expressed about the potential effectiveness of the farmer-owned reserve in minimizing price instability. Some argued that there had been too much tinkering with the reserve while others expressed the view that the reserve simply did not significantly increase total stocks. The general, though not unanimous view, however, seemed to be that the farmer-owned reserve merited further trial.

Food and Agricultural Policy for the 1980s

Edited by D. Gale Johnson

Part
One

Economic Developments in U.S. Agriculture during the 1970s

J. B. Penn

In this paper, I review the significant economic developments in U.S. agriculture during the 1970s that are especially relevant to prescriptive policy discussions. My paper has three sections. In the first I examine some of the major developments reflected in characteristics of the farm sector as a whole: the emerging resource equilibrium, the land in farms, the rural and farm population, the productivity of agriculture, and the growing importance of international markets. In the second section I develop a profile of the farm sector and look behind the aggregate sectoral data at the nation's farms—their numbers, sizes, types, incomes and wealth positions, earnings, and relative efficient sizes. The third section contains some summary observations.

Farm Sector Developments

Equilibrium in Agriculture. Perhaps one of the most significant developments in agriculture during the 1970s was the emergence of relative resource equilibrium in the sector. The symptoms of the decades-old farm problem were still very pronounced as we entered the 1970s. We began the decade with huge stocks of surplus grain under government ownership, high program costs, and a large proportion of cropland idled by government programs. At the same time forces were converging from two fronts—from the domestic and global economies and from the farm sector itself—that went largely unnoticed. In the world economy, several forces were gradually evolving to create a much closer balance between demand and the output of America's farms. Rapid growth in global population and incomes, together with a heightened

The views expressed are the author's and do not necessarily reflect views and policies of the U.S. Department of Agriculture. The assistance of colleagues in the Department of Agriculture in preparation of this paper is gratefully acknowledged.

sensitivity to hunger and malnutrition, were leading to increased demand for U.S. agricultural output. Further, the concurrent shift of some countries with centrally planned economies from being net food exporters to net importers worked to the same effect. Meanwhile, however, U.S. farm output was rising less rapidly, with the rate of crop yield increases in the very early 1970s falling behind the impressive gains of the 1960s.

Accompanying these long-run developments were several unique events in the early 1970s that resulted in the abrupt change in the balance of supply and demand for food. Foreign exchange rates were first realigned in 1971, increasing the competitiveness of U.S. products in foreign markets; wage and price controls were imposed on the domestic economy; adverse weather brought poor harvests to parts of the world; and the policies of some major countries, particularly the Soviet Union, toward food shortages changed abruptly.

This convergence of long-term forces coincided with the more abrupt events in 1972. The surreptitious entry of the Russians into our grain market was first revealed in midyear. This signaled the beginning of a tumultuous period for U.S. agriculture, which stripped away trappings to reveal conditions of even greater significance over the long run.

For the next three years, 1973–1975, parts of the agricultural sector enjoyed nearly unparalleled prosperity; record volumes of exports pushed crop commodity prices to record-high levels while farmers' production costs lagged considerably, significantly increasing profit margins. Real net farm income for the sector reached the highest level since World War II. Although incomes were down sharply from that peak in 1974 and 1975, they remained well above the average of the previous decade.

But this economic boom was not without its undesirable side effects—on the farm sector itself and on the national economy. This prosperity was not uniformly shared across the farm sector. While crop farmers prospered, the domestic livestock industry was buffeted by the volatile grain markets and forced into one of the most unprofitable periods in its history. Further expectations of permanent prosperity were created in the farm community, expectations that were not to be realized and that were to be of policy significance later. Many young people entered farming during this period; many existing farmers expanded their capital investment in land and machinery; and land prices were bid up substantially. Both groups contracted large debt at the inflated asset prices—based on expectations of what were to prove to be unsustainable conditions.

Domestic food prices also increased sharply during this period, exacerbating inflationary pressures and severely affecting low-income consumers. The concerns about domestic inflation led to commodity export embargoes that severely strained relations with many of our longstanding trading partners.

On a second front, fundamental changes in the farm sector itself had been occurring before the 1970s. These, too, had gone largely unnoticed, undoubtedly because of the large carry-over commodity stocks and large acreages withheld from production. (It is ironic that in the year of the initial disruption, 1972, 62 million acres, nearly one-fifth of the nation's cropland and the second largest acreage ever, were idled by programs.) Because of the overhang of surplus stocks on the market, grain prices had remained depressed, no doubt masking the more fundamental changes that were occurring, changes bringing supply conditions into closer accord with the demand side.

It is now rather widely accepted that the resource disequilibrium was passing in the early 1970s but was obscured by the remaining vestiges of the farm problem. One of the early persuasive arguments of this view was advanced by D. Gale Johnson in a monograph appearing in 1973.[1] Johnson argued that:

> Most of the resources that had been retained in U.S. agriculture during the early 1950's and early 1960's had been eliminated, primarily through adjustments in the labor market and the significant abandonment of farm land. The labor market adjustment prior to 1950 had occurred primarily through migration away from farms but starting in the 1950's part-time nonfarm employment played an increasing role in labor adjustments in agriculture. In 1960, the first year for which we have data, 42 percent of the income of farm operator families came from off-farm sources; by 1970 the percentage had increased to 55 and in 1976 and 1977 to 62 percent. In large part as a result of the reduction in the number of farm workers and the increase in off-farm income, the per capita disposable income of farm relative to non-farm people increased from less than 50 percent in the latter part of the 1950's to about 75 percent in 1970 and 1971. Given the characteristics of the data and the fact that capital gains are not included in the income data, farm per capita disposable income that is 75 to 80 percent of nonfarm is probably not far from an equilibrium level. By equilibrium level I mean one which provides approximately the same return to farm resources, both labor and land, as is received by comparable nonfarm resources.[2]

[1] D. Gale Johnson, *Farm Commodity Programs: An Opportunity for Change* (Washington, D.C.: American Enterprise Institute, 1973).

[2] D. Gale Johnson, "Agricultural Policy for the 1980s," speech to the Chase Econometrics Agricultural Outlook Seminar, Arlington, Va., April 16, 1980.

The subsequent evidence—the slowed net labor out-migration from the farm sector, the emerging equality of per capita incomes of farm and nonfarm people, the essentially full utilization of the readily available cropland, and the continued strong demand for U.S. products in foreign markets—strongly supports an assertion that the farm sector is now in near equilibrium and perhaps has been for several years.[3]

This does not in any way imply, however, that a static state has been reached or that there will not be times of supply-demand imbalances resembling former periods. There may well be, but these will undoubtedly be transitory. Most likely they will arise from brief, consecutive periods of favorable global weather, rather than reflect any chronic imbalance as in previous decades.

The early seventies, preoccupied with shortages rather than with surpluses, was probably not an aberrant time. This tumultuous period may well have presaged the conditions that will be the norm in the 1980s. The implications of sectoral resource equilibrium, when combined with the likely future economic environment (treated in the section "A Profile of the Farm Sector"), have significant meaning for the domestic farm sector and the structure of policies appropriate for that future.

Land in Farms. The portion of the total land area of this country encompassed in farms has changed relatively little in the twentieth century (see table 1). Land development was still being encouraged early in the century (for example, by the 1902 Reclamation Law), and nearly 150 million acres were added to farms in the next three decades. The land in farms continued to increase slightly, reaching a peak in 1950, and then declined slightly in the succeeding decades.

The total land in farms is used in various ways—for crops, pasture, fallow, forests, lots, and the farmstead itself. Total land used for crops was greatest just after World War II (in 1949) and was least in

---

[3] Four years later, addressing what he called "the new macroeconomics of agriculture," Schuh reinforced the Johnson argument, citing the significant changes that occurred in the economic environment of agriculture in the early 1970s: reduced labor out-migration from agriculture, stagnating growth in productivity, the shift to floating exchange rates, and changes in the international economic environment. Drawing one of the implications of this combination of changes, he stated: "The secular income problem in agriculture is now largely behind us. The emerging equilibrium in the labor market is of major significance in this respect. When this equilibrium is combined wth the decline in the rate of productivity growth, the release of most of the idled land back to production, and the shift to the right in the demand for agricultural products as a result of devaluation, the result is an almost total disappearance of the excess capacity that existed at prevailing price ratios for such a long period of time." (G. Edward Schuh, "The New Macroeconomics of Agriculture," *American Journal of Agricultural Economics*, vol. 58, no. 5 [December 1976], pp. 802–11.)

TABLE 1

Land in Farms, 1900–1974

Year	Land in Farms (millions of acres)	Percentage Change
1900	839	—
1910	879	+4.8
1920	956	+8.8
1930	987	+3.2
1940	1,061	+7.5
1950	1,159	+9.2
1954	1,158	−0.1
1959	1,120	−3.3
1964	1,110	−0.9
1969	1,062	−4.3
1974	1,017	−4.2

Source: U.S. Department of Agriculture, Economic Research Service, *Economic Tables*, June 1975, and U.S. Bureau of the Census, *Census of Agriculture, 1974*.

the late 1960s and early 1970s, when large acreages were idled by government programs (table 2). Interestingly, the total land used for crops in 1979 was essentially the same as in 1929. The total cropland base (excluding pasture land) is slightly larger than the total used for crops in any one year, suggesting that some additional acreage (undoubtedly of lower quality) may be available for cropping if economic conditions warrant.

While there is general agreement that there is some relatively small additional acreage that could be brought into production rather quickly, there is much less agreement on the quantity of land that could eventually be used for crops. The estimates range from a few to several million acres of varying capabilities. It is clear, however, that the larger the amount, the greater the investment required to make that land suitable for sustained production. This investment, of course, will occur when economically feasible, that is, when the expected future stream of real returns to agricultural production justifies the commitment of the capital to this particular use.

While land is the major farm input, greater awareness in recent years of the fragility of the entire natural resource base and its interrelation with the quality of the environment has made the future productive capacity of American agriculture a much more immediate

7

TABLE 2: MAJOR USES OF CROPLAND, 1924–1979

(millions of acres)

Year	Harvested	Crop Failure	Fallow	Total Used for Crops	Idle	Pasture	Total Excluding Pasture	Idled by Programs
1924	346	13	6	365	26	n.a.	391	0
1929	356	13	10	379	34	n.a.	413	0
1934	296	64	15	375	40	n.a.	415	0
1939	321	21	21	363	36	n.a.	399	0
1944	353	10	16	379	24	n.a.	403	0
1949	352	9	26	387	22	69	409	0
1954	339	13	28	380	19	n.a.	399	0
1959	317	10	31	359	33	66	392	22
1964	292	6	37	335	52	57	387	55
1969	286	6	41	333	51	88	384	58
1972	289	7	38	334	51	n.a.	385	62
1973	316	5	31	352	32	n.a.	384	19
1974	322	8	31	361	21	83	382	3
1975	330	6	30	366	n.a.	n.a.	n.a.	2
1976	331	9	30	370	n.a.	n.a.	n.a.	2
1977	338	9	30	377	n.a.	n.a.	n.a.	0
1978	331	7	31	369	n.a.	n.a.	n.a.	18
1979	342	7	30	379	n.a.	n.a.	n.a.	12

NOTE: n.a. = not available.

SOURCE: Adapted from U.S. Department of Agriculture, Economics, Statistics, and Cooperatives Service, *Changes in Farm Production Efficiency, 1978,* Statistical Bulletin no. 628, January 1980; U.S. Department of Agriculture, Agricultural Research Service, *Major Uses of Land in the United States, 1950,* Technical Bulletin 1082 (Supplement) (January 1953); and published reports in the land use series since 1950.

public concern than it was a decade ago.[4] Other issues, somewhat separate from capacity, also surround the nation's resource base and the use of resources. One of those issues is the ownership and control of the land resource and the effects of emerging patterns on agriculture. A recent survey revealed that landownership was highly concentrated. Table 3 shows that 1 percent of the landowners own 30 percent of the farmland area and 5 percent own 48 percent.

The distribution of farmland ownership is an important consideration in developing farm policy given that much of the benefit of past farm programs has been capitalized into asset (primarily land) values and hence has accrued to the owners of the farmland. The implications are even more significant because of the growing trend toward separation of ownership and operation of farms (the progressive emergence of part ownership and tenancy: just under one-half of the cropland is farmed by someone other than its owner).

The Farm Population. While there are many meaningful ways to identify people associated with agriculture, the most popular identifiers are farm residence and occupation. The populations formed by these bases, however, are not identical. Some farm residents are engaged in nonagricultural occupations and, conversely, some persons employed in agriculture do not live on farms.

When the farm population of the United States was first separately enumerated in 1920 it was found to be 32 million, constituting 30 percent of the total population (figure 1). It has declined almost continuously in the ensuing six decades, generally corresponding to the decline in the number of farms. In 1979, the most recent year for which data are available, the number of persons living on farms in rural areas was 6.2 million (table 4). Thus only one person in thirty-three, or about 3 percent of the nation's 220 million persons, resided on a farm. This estimate is based on the new definition of a farm introduced in 1978, under which the farm population consists of all persons living in rural territory on places with sales of agricultural products of $1,000 or more. Under the previous definition, the farm population consisted of all persons in rural areas on places of ten acres or more with at least $50 worth of agricultural product sales or places of less than ten acres with at least $250 worth of sales. The estimate of the 1979 farm population under this previous definition is 7.5 million. The change in

---

[4] The potential productive capacity of American agriculture, with special emphasis on the land resource, is more fully explored in a paper by Velmar Davis, "American Agriculture: Its Capacity to Produce in the 1980's," mimeographed (U.S. Department of Agriculture, Economics, Statistics, and Cooperatives Service, National Economics Division, September 1980).

9

TABLE 3

DISTRIBUTION OF LANDOWNERSHIP BY AGE OF LANDOWNER, 1978

(percentage of acreage)

Region	Holdings of Largest 5 Percent	Holdings of Largest 1 Percent	Holdings by Age of Landowner				
			Under 35	35–49	50–64	65–74	75 and over
Northeast	34.2	13.8	7.8	29.1	38.4	16.3	8.4
Lake states	24.2	8.4	9.6	31.3	36.0	15.2	7.9
Corn Belt	24.6	7.9	6.2	25.1	37.4	18.5	12.8
Northern plains	32.7	14.9	6.4	24.0	39.9	19.5	10.2
Appalachian	39.1	17.0	6.5	24.1	37.5	20.5	11.4
Southeast	49.2	27.1	4.3	22.1	42.1	20.4	11.1
Delta	45.8	23.0	5.2	25.1	37.2	22.2	10.3
Southern plains	53.6	33.4	4.7	20.1	39.6	21.3	14.3
Mountain	67.2	37.6	5.0	26.5	43.6	17.9	7.0
Pacific	71.0	43.0	4.3	23.1	42.4	18.2	12.0
United States	48.1	30.3	5.9	24.6	39.8	19.1	10.6

SOURCE: U.S. Department of Agriculture, Economics, Statistics, and Cooperatives Service, *Land Ownership Survey*, 1978.

FIGURE 1

FARM POPULATION, 1920 TO 1977

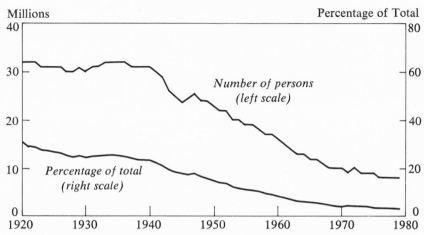

SOURCES: U.S. Department of Agriculture and U.S. Department of Commerce.

farm definition thus reclassified approximately 1.3 million persons from farm to nonfarm residents. Given the nature of the change in definition, all persons reclassified as nonfarm were on places with farm product sales under $1,000.

The total agricultural employment, of course, was not affected by the definition change. The number of persons employed primarily in agriculture in 1979 was 3.3 million. This work force is now about equally divided between farm and nonfarm residents. Persons self-employed in agriculture—farm operators—are, however, mainly farm residents. Of the 1.6 million self-employed agricultural workers, 1.1 million, or two-thirds, lived on farms. The rest lived in town or in rural nonfarm homes. On the other hand, agricultural laborers are more likely to live off the farm and commute to work. Of the 1.4 million agricultural wage and salary workers employed primarily in agriculture in 1979, only about a fourth lived on farms.[5] Unpaid family farm workers, who numbered about 390,000, were predominantly farm residents.

[5] Another widely quoted estimate of the hired farm labor work force is 2.7 million. This estimate is based on the Hired Farm Working Force Survey, conducted in 1979 but not in 1978. The estimate is the total number of people who worked at least one day on a farm during the 1979 calendar year. The estimate of 1.413 million is an average of quarterly estimates of people who list agricultural work as their primary occupation. Neither estimate takes account of undocumented aliens, variously estimated to number as high as one million workers.

TABLE 4

SELECTED POPULATION CHARACTERISTICS, 1920–1979

(thousands)

Year	Total Resident Population[a]	Rural Population[b]	Farm Population[c]	Total Agricultural Employment[d]	Agricultural Wage and Salary Workers[e]
Current definition					
1979	220,099	55,000[f]	6,241	3,297	1,413
1978	218,228	55,000[f]	6,501	3,342	1,418
Previous definition					
1979	220,099	55,000[f]	7,553	3,297	1,413
1978	218,228	55,000[f]	8,005	3,342	1,418
1977	216,400	n.a.	7,806	3,244	1,330
1976	214,680	n.a.	8,253	3,297	1,318
1975	213,051	n.a.	8,864	3,380	1,280
1974	211,389	n.a.	9,264	3,492	1,349
1973	209,859	n.a.	9,472	3,452	1,254
1972	208,219	n.a.	9,610	3,452	1,216
1971	206,219	n.a.	9,425	3,387	1,161
1970	203,810	53,887	9,712	3,462	1,152
1960	179,323	54,054	15,635	5,458[g]	1,762
1950	151,326	54,479	23,048	7,160	1,630
1940	132,166[g]	57,459	30,547	n.a.	n.a.
1930	122,755	54,042	30,529	n.a.	n.a.
1920	105,711	51,553	31,974	n.a.	n.a.

NOTE: n.a. = not available.

[a] Estimate as of July 1 each year.

[b] Persons outside urban areas in open country, on farms, and in places with a population less than 2,500.

[c] Current definition: persons on places with at least $1,000 of agricultural sales. Previous definitions: since 1960 persons on places of ten acres or more with at least $50 of agricultural sales and on places under ten acres with at least $250 of agricultural sales; before 1960 farm residence was based essentially on self-identification of the respondent.

[d] Sole or primary agricultural employment of persons sixteen years old and older. The data are not strictly comparable over time because of definitional changes. Data are annual averages.

[e] Persons sixteen years old and older.

[f] Estimated.

[g] Denotes first year Hawaii and Alaska included in the data.

SOURCES: U.S. Bureau of the Census, *Decennial Census of Population* and *Current Population Reports*, various issues; and U.S. Department of Labor, Bureau of Labor Statistics, *Monthly Labor Review*, various issues.

Farm residence was once strongly associated with farm employment, but this is no longer the case. Today farm people are almost as likely to work in nonagricultural industries as to work on the farm. Of the 3.3 million farm resident work force in 1978, 44 percent were not employed in agriculture. Employment in nonagricultural industries, however, is more prevalent among farm females than farm males. In 1978 about seven of ten employed farm females were engaged solely or primarily in nonagricultural pursuits; among males living on farms, only four of ten were so employed.

This examination of the population characteristics of rural America and the farm sector leads to some summary observations.

• The total population of the country has almost doubled since 1920, but the rural population has remained constant in absolute numbers (at 54 to 55 million in the last several decades). Of course, as a proportion of the total population, it has declined from about 45 percent to about 25 percent.

• The farm population, a subset of the rural population, has declined by 80 percent over the six decades. That is, for every ten people in the farm population in 1920, there are only two today.

• The total agricultural labor force (regardless of residence) has declined by 60 percent, the largest decline being in self-employed owner-operators. The hired farm worker labor force (a subset of the total agriculture work force) has declined since 1950 by about 13 percent but has been relatively stable in the 1970s, actually increasing slightly from the low point recorded in 1970 (taking no account of undocumented workers).

• The extent of the out-migration of people from agriculture over the past fifty years was tremendous, very clearly emphasizing that farm sector earnings today are distributed among a much smaller number of people, with important implications for per capita income comparisons across sectors of the economy.

From this review, the impression is quickly gained of a farm sector in a rural setting so amorphous, so heterogeneous that it severely limits generalized description. Some farmers live in town; some people employed in the nonfarm sector live on farms; farm household members often have nonagricultural employment. This situation is far different from the once much more easily identified group of farm people whose well-being was an objective of a major element of our national public policy.

Productivity in Agriculture. The process of economic development in societies has historically been characterized by changes in sectoral productivity accompanying the release of labor from food production for subsequent employment in the nonfarm economy. This has been true for the United States, where technological innovations and their adoption have released large numbers of people from farming while growth in the nonfarm economy has at most times been sufficient to ensure their rapid absorption. This emergence of excess labor in agriculture and its eventual reabsorption elsewhere in the economy was at the heart of the farm problem that endured for several decades. This agricultural labor pool was an important source of aggregate growth in the nonfarm economy as the labor with low value in agriculture was shifted to uses of higher value.

The population characteristics examined above provide a clear notion of the extreme magnitude of the problem that has beset American agriculture and of the out-migration that has occurred over time. Another perspective on this resource displacement is provided by reviewing the use of labor and other resources and the measures of productivity change in the farm sector. The data in table 5 reveal that the total inputs committed to agricultural production have increased only slightly (5.1 percent) since 1920. Yet the composition (and undoubtedly the quality) of those inputs has changed markedly. The amount of land has declined only slightly (3.9 percent), but the substitution of capital (in the form of machinery and equipment) for labor has been dramatic, making agriculture today one of the most capital-intensive sectors of the economy.

The total output obtained with this nearly constant total input bundle has, of course, increased significantly (137.3 percent) since 1920. Total factor productivity (changes in output obtained from all inputs) has risen 125 percent since 1920, an average annual growth rate of 1.41 percent. For the almost sixty years considered here, the increase by decade in total factor productivity was

1920–1929	0.0 percent
1930–1939	15.7 percent
1940–1949	18.3 percent
1950–1959	22.5 percent
1960–1969	14.4 percent
1970–1978	14.7 percent

suggesting that the rate of increase in the 1940s and 1950s was somewhat faster than in the last two decades.

The rate of productivity growth for two of the major inputs, land and labor, presents an interesting picture. The productivity of land,

14

TABLE 5

Index Measures of Resource Use, Output, and Farm Productivity, 1920–1978

(1967 = 100)

Year	All Inputs	Selected Inputs			Output			Productivity (output/input)		
		Labor	Real estate	Mechanical power and machinery	Livestock	Crops	Total	All inputs	Land[a]	Labor
1920	98	341	102	31	44	65	51	52	61	14
1930	101	326	101	39	54	59	52	51	53	16
1940	100	293	103	42	60	67	60	60	62	20
1950	104	217	105	84	75	76	74	71	69	34
1960	101	145	100	97	87	93	91	90	89	65
1970	100	89	101	100	105	100	101	102	104	115
1971	100	86	99	102	106	112	110	110	112	128
1972	100	82	98	101	107	113	110	110	115	136
1973	101	80	97	105	105	119	112	111	116	130
1974	100	78	95	109	106	110	106	106	104	136
1975	100	76	96	113	101	121	114	115	112	152
1976	103	73	97	117	105	121	117	115	111	162
1977	104	71	99	118	106	130	121	117	117	173
1978	103	67	98	120	106	131	121	117	121	183

[a] Measured as crop production per acre.

SOURCE: Department of Agriculture, Economics, Statistics, and Cooperatives Service, *Changes in Farm Production and Efficiency, 1978.*

15

FIGURE 2

LABOR PRODUCTIVITY

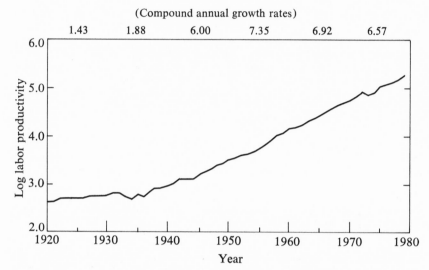

(Compound annual growth rates)

SOURCE: U.S. Department of Agriculture, Economics, Statistics, and Cooperatives Service, *Changes in Farm Production Efficiency, 1978,* Stat. Bul. No. 628, January 1980 and *Changes in Farm Production and Efficiency* (Special issue featuring historical series), Stat. Bul. No. 561, September 1976.

measured as crop production per acre, almost doubled (rising 98.4 percent over the almost six decades from 1920 to 1978), increasing most rapidly in the 1950s and slowing in the 1960s and 1970s.

Labor productivity over this period rose a phenomenal 1,207 percent, at an average rate of 4.53 percent per year. This rapid rate of growth would be expected in a labor-surplus sector where the surplus was migrating out, especially if that sector also experienced extensive technological innovation, as agriculture did; the influx of large amounts of capital and the out-migration of labor—the capital-labor substitution —made the remaining labor more productive. Labor productivity grew somewhat in accordance with the out-migration of people and generally rose most rapidly when the out-migration was most rapid (figure 2 and table 6). Likewise, as the labor out-migration slows and ends, the rate of productivity increase could be expected to slow, just as the index seems to suggest is occurring.

Whether there is perceptible slowing in the rate of total productivity growth in agriculture is a subject of some controversy. The inability to delineate weather effects and the crudeness of the produc-

TABLE 6

AVERAGE ANNUAL PRODUCTIVITY GROWTH IN AGRICULTURE, 1920–1978

(percent)

Period	All Factors	Land	Labor
1920–29	0.00	−0.82	1.43
1930–39	1.57	1.32	1.88
1940–49	1.83	1.29	6.00
1950–59	2.25	2.32	7.35
1960–69	1.44	1.91	6.92
1970–78	1.63	1.82	6.57

SOURCE: U.S. Department of Agriculture, Economics, Statistics, and Cooperatives Service, *Changes in Farm Production Efficiency, 1978*, and *Changes in Farm Production and Efficiency* (special issue featuring historical series), Statistical Bulletin no. 561, September 1976.

tivity measures, owing to definitional, procedural, and data limitations, preclude definitive judgments.[6] If, however, the rate of productivity growth is indeed slowing and given that the readily available land resource (the other source of increased output) is fully committed, the prospects for output expansion are not bright, absent a major breakthrough in production technology. Yet increasing global demands for food and for U.S. exports are quite likely.

Growth in Foreign Markets. Another major development in the 1970s, related to the emerging relative resource equilibrium, was the rapid growth in importance of foreign markets for U.S. farm products. The abrupt shift in demand that occurred in 1972 proved to be a continuing phenomenon and promises to remain so. The significance of foreign

[6] At the July 1980 annual meetings of the American Agricultural Economics Association, John E. Lee, Jr., discussing a paper by D. Gale Johnson, most succinctly, and a bit facetiously, summarized the situation: "A year ago Vernon Ruttan stood before you and stated that productivity growth in agriculture had definitely slowed and that inflation was partially responsible. Today, D. Gale Johnson stood before you and said productivity growth in agriculture had not slowed—was in fact growing faster than in the 1960's—and that inflation had no measurable impact. Now, I stand before you and, as one with some responsibility for the data used by both these distinguished gentlemen, suggest that the limitations in the productivity data series are probably sufficient to accommodate both views."

markets to U.S. agriculture is rapidly apparent from the following comparisons:

	Value of Exports (Bil. $)	Volume of Exports (MMT)	Proportion of Area Harvested (percent)	Proportion of Cash Receipts (percent)
1970	6.9	61.8	21.0	13.0
1980	40.0	162.0	32.3	29.0

In 1970 the production from approximately one of every five harvested acres was destined for foreign markets. Today, the production from one of every three acres goes abroad. Twenty-nine cents of each dollar of gross receipts today are derived from foreign sales; foreign sales accounted for only thirteen cents of each dollar of receipts in 1970. For individual commodities, the importance of export markets varies:

Commodity	Proportion of Production Exported (percent)
Wheat	65
Cotton	65
Soybeans	45
Rice	45
Tobacco	40
Feed grains	30

· The growth in value of exports averaged 19.2 percent annually over the decade of the 1970s. The increases in export unit values and volume were roughly equal. Concessional sales declined in importance, both absolutely and as a proportion of total exports.

A Profile of the Farm Sector

Perhaps the best known characteristic of the farm sector is the decline in the total number of farms over time and the concomitant increase in average size (figure 3). This has been the most visible manifestation of all the forces affecting the farm sector—the technological innovations presenting economic efficiencies that could be attained only by larger farms, the resulting excess labor and its out-migration, and so on. The decline in total farm numbers is also the most likely statistic to be used in discussions of general policy issues such as the demise of the family farm. Yet this statistic, though making a point about what

FIGURE 3

NUMBER AND AVERAGE SIZE OF FARMS

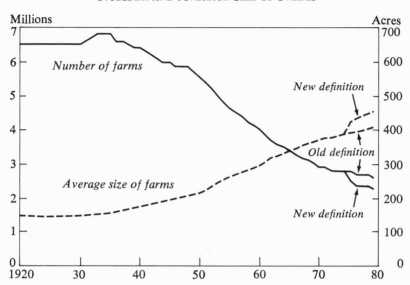

SOURCES: Average size of farms 1920–1950 from U.S. Bureau of the Census, *Census of Agriculture,* 1964; all other data from U.S. Department of Agriculture, Crop Reporting Board.

has occurred, conceals much more than it reveals about the farm sector today. This section attempts to look behind the total numbers to the sizes, types, locations, and income and wealth characteristics of the farms remaining today.

Farm Numbers and Sizes. Any discussion of farm numbers and sizes today is conditioned by definitions, perhaps much more so than when there were several millions of farms regardless of how they were defined. The most widely used source of farm numbers is the quinquennial agricultural census of the Department of Commerce. Census estimates are reported for two definitions of a farm, the official one adopted in 1978 and the old one, which is continued in use for continuity of the data series. (The old definition is used in the remainder of the paper because it is more consistent with other data that will be used.) The most recently available comprehensive estimates are from the 1974 census; data from the 1978 census have not yet been released.

The other source of farm numbers is the Department of Agriculture. These estimates are derived using the census counts as benchmarks for extrapolation with modifications as suggested by other information.[7] The department's estimates for 1978 are shown in table 7.

The new definition of a farm is more restrictive, counting a place as a farm only if it has product sales of $1,000 or more regardless of acreage. This definitional change affects only the number of farms in the smallest size category (with sales less than $2,500); the number in this category is reduced by about 302 thousand (to 609 thousand), and the estimates of the total number of farms in 1978 is reduced to 2,370,000. Thus the total number of farms in the United States is 2.672 or 2.370 million, depending on the definition used.

The size distribution of these farms reveals additional insight into their characteristics. There are, of course, alternative ways to classify farms by size—acreage, amount of hired labor, and value of product sales are common ones. None is entirely satisfactory or without limitations, but the value of sales (economic class) is frequently used and widely understood. If that distribution were "normal," an equal proportion of farms of varying sizes would fall both above and below the mean size. The distribution is, in fact, highly skewed toward the smaller sizes; there are many more farms below the mean size than above it.

The skewness is obvious and the profile becomes much clearer when we add the contribution of farms in each size category to the total value of all food and fiber production. These data (table 7) reveal that the relatively numerous smaller farms contribute proportionally much less to total output. For example, farms with less than $10,000 in sales constitute 54.9 percent of all farms, but they contribute only 4.2 percent of the total sales; farms with less than $40,000 of gross sales are 78.0 percent of all farms but account for only 18.7 percent of total sales. Conversely, farms with $40,000 or more in gross sales are only 22.0 percent of all farms but account for 81.3 percent of gross sales. Further, the very largest farms, those with gross sales of $200,000 or more, constitute only 2.4 percent of the total but have 39.3 percent of the total sales.

It is obvious from these data that production is heavily con-

---

[7] The enumeration procedures used in the 1974 census of agriculture did not completely count all farms. Primarily, they tended to miss small farms. To account for any discrepancies, a census survey on the completeness of the enumeration was made along with the actual census. Some time after the census data are released, adjustment percentages are made available to account for any differences between the reported census numbers and what are believed to be the "actual" numbers. The Department of Agriculture then uses the adjustment percentages to recalculate the census numbers for such publications as *Farm Income Statistics* and the *Balance Sheet of Agriculture*. (However, not all USDA publications use the adjusted estimates.)

TABLE 7

NUMBER OF FARMS, SALES, AND OFF-FARM INCOME BY VALUE OF SALES, 1978

Sales Class (dollars)	Number of Farms (thousands)	Percentage of Farms	Sales (million $)	Percentage of Sales	Off-Farm Income (million $)	Percentage of Off-Farm Income
Less than 2,500	911	34.1	1,056	0.9	15,760	46.0
2,500–4,999	275	10.3	1,289	1.1	4,506	13.1
5,000–9,999	281	10.5	2,580	2.2	3,814	11.1
10,000–19,999	294	11.0	5,259	4.6	2,980	8.7
20,000–39,999	323	12.1	11,406	9.9	2,520	7.4
40,000–99,999	398	14.9	28,962	25.0	2,670	7.8
100,000–199,999	126	4.7	19,708	17.0 }	2,029[a]	5.9[a]
200,000 and over	64	2.4	45,513	39.3 }		
Total	2,672	100.0	115,773	100.0	34,279	100.0

[a] Off-farm income is calculated for farms of $100,000 in sales and over; separate data are not available for farms with sales of $200,000 and over.

SOURCE: U.S. Department of Agriculture, Economics, Statistics, and Cooperatives Service, *Farm Income Statistics*, 1979.

centrated among the larger-size farms. These data also suggest that if farming were the sole or even the primary source of income, there would be many economically disadvantaged farm families (and many below the poverty standard) on the smaller farms. Even with the best of management, a farm that grosses only $40,000 is unlikely to provide a net income to the operator and family that would be considered adequate today by almost any standard. The income from farming on many of the smaller farms is supplemented, however, by a larger amount of income from nonfarm sources.

Since a consideration central to farm policy has traditionally been the level of incomes in the farm sector, that question merits further examination from two views: the economic well-being of farm people and the sustained economic viability of farm businesses. Are total incomes of farm people below a socially acceptable norm? Are the rates of return on investments in farm businesses sufficient for continued viability or survival?

The Economic Well-Being of Farm People. When viewing the well-being of the farm population, it is now widely recognized that examining only the average income of farm operator families from farm sources gives a misleading indication of the well-being of farm families.[8] The significant incidence of off-farm income earned by farm families is a relatively new phenomenon, having grown rapidly in the last two decades (table 8). Off-farm income is of greater importance to the smaller farms, being several times farm income for farms with sales under $20,000.

Off-farm income declines as a proportion of farm income as the size of farms increases, declining from ten times greater than farm income for the smallest size class to only one-fifth of farm income for the largest farms during 1975–1978. Today, in the aggregate, nonfarm income earned by farm families exceeds the income these families earn from farming; during 1975–1978 it exceeded farm income by over 40 percent. Including income from all sources, the average income per farm operator family in 1978 was almost $23,000, 30 percent more than the national median family income.

The growth in nonfarm income has contributed to a much more equal distribution of total income among farm families (figure 4), narrowing the income disparity considerably. This also emphasizes the close linkage of the economic well-being of a majority of farm families to the nonfarm economy, a linkage growing stronger over time. When

[8] Donald K. Larson, "Economic Class as a Measure of Farmers' Welfare," *American Journal of Agricultural Economics*, vol. 57, no. 4 (November 1975), pp. 658–64.

TABLE 8

OFF-FARM INCOME PER FARM OPERATOR FAMILY
AS A PERCENTAGE OF
NET FARM INCOME, 1960–1978

Sales Class (dollars)	1960–64	1965–69	1970–74	1975–78
Less than 2,500	408	646	857	1,006
2,500–4,999	128	261	472	902
5,000–9,999	68	130	217	423
10,000–19,999	31	54	91	174
20,000–39,999	24	30	38	66
40,000 and over	17	22	17	25
40,000–99,999	n.a.	23	21	30
100,000 and over	n.a.	20	14	21
All farms	89	115	104	141

NOTE: n.a. = not available.

SOURCE: Adapted from U.S. Department of Agriculture, Economics, Statistics, and Cooperatives Service, *Farm Income Statistics*, Statistical Bulletin no. 627, October 1979.

total income is compared to the median income of the total population, only two size categories of farms are seen to be slightly below the median. These size categories are somewhat in between, neither primarily reliant on off-farm income nor large enough to achieve comparable farm incomes.

The sources of the nonfarm income for the smaller farms could be especially revealing for policy purposes, if they suggested something more of the motivation of people living in these places. Are many of these smaller places really rural residences only? Is this income from wages or salaries earned by the household head who claims an occupation other than farming? Or is this income earned by the spouse or other family members in supplementary employment? Unfortunately, little definitive information on such questions is now available.[9] Some insights can be gained, however, from the results of disparate studies with data from varying time periods.

One recently completed study by Crecink, using data from a 1973 national farm family living expenditure survey, examined character-

[9] Surveys are currently being conducted for the U.S. Department of Agriculture to provide data on the occupational status and income composition of farm families.

FIGURE 4

INCOME PER FARM OPERATOR FAMILY, BY FARM SIZE, 1978

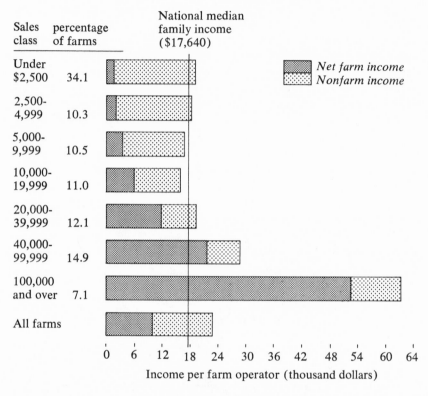

SOURCE: U.S. Department of Agriculture, Economics, Statistics, and Cooperatives Service, *Farm Income Statistics,* Statistics Bulletin no. 627, October 1979.

istics of farm households associated with their economic well-being.[10] He specifically focused on the level, sources, and distribution of income for four groups of rural people: low-income farm operator households; households associated with small farms; households dependent solely on farming; and households dependent primarily on off-farm income. His findings revealed:

• Only one in twelve farm families depended entirely on farming as their source of income in 1973. Of the others, almost eight in ten had

[10] John C. Crecink, *Families with Farm Income, Their Income, Income Distribution, and Income Sources,* U.S. Department of Agriculture, Economics, Statistics, and Cooperatives Service, Economic Development Division, November 1979.

income from wages and salaries, the most important source of non-farm income. Generally, as total family income rose, the portion from wages and salaries rose, except at the highest incomes.

• Farm families reporting farm profits had a significantly higher average total income than those families reporting farm losses. The farm losses reported were generally small and frequently reported by younger operators who had higher wage and salary earnings and less total income from nonwork sources (for example, dividends, rents, and royalties). The most frequently reported sources of off-farm income were wages and salaries, nonfarm business returns, pensions including social security payments, unemployment compensation, private pensions, welfare payments, and investment income (interest, rents, royalties).

• Regional disparities in incomes were associated with nonfarm job opportunities and farm household characteristics. Most low-income farm families were in the South and associated with the older farm households. The absence of a full-time wage earner in the household contributed to the low-income problem. Households with farm income only had a much higher probability of being in the low-income category than households reporting income from both farm and nonfarm sources.

• Small farms and low-income households are not synonymous. Low farm income may contribute to low household income, but except for households with farm income only, it is not the sole cause of poverty.

• Families with only farm income had average farm product sales almost four times as great as families who had farm and nonfarm income. The operator whose sole income came from farming was younger and had a slightly larger family than operators with both farm and nonfarm income.

• Surprisingly, 10.6 percent of the farm families (301,000) fell below the poverty threshold, the greatest concentration occurring in the South.

The data and study results presented in this section clearly reveal that total income for all farm size categories, and notably the smaller sizes, compares favorably to income elsewhere in the economy. From examining average total annual (current) income per farm for the sector as a whole, one must conclude that incomes of farm people are no longer low by any reasonable standard. This does not mean, according to Crecink, that there are no farm families with low incomes or no considerable remaining poverty problems. Incidences of poverty, however, are now associated with particular circumstances and geographic regions, not pervasive across the entire farm sector, as was once the case.

These data further illustrate rather clearly that while policies designed to improve farm income would benefit all farm operators to varying extents, the benefits and the effects on household income will vary directly with the reliance of the household on farm income and with the size of the farm operation. It is clear that policies that affect commodity prices to enhance farm incomes will be of little benefit to the 65.9 percent of farms (1.8 million) with sales of less than $20,000. This is borne out by studies of the distribution of farm program benefits, which show that the greatest proportion of the benefits accrue to the larger farmers, those with the greatest volume of production and hence greater farm income.[11]

The Economic Viability of Farm Businesses. The previous discussion examined income in the sense of well-being of farm people. What about the well-being of the farm business in an economic sense? That is, what are the earnings of resources productively employed by farm businesses?

A business firm is viable over the long run if it generates enough income to pay all of the factors of production employed (land, labor, capital, and management) a rate of return sufficient to hold them in the particular business endeavor. Alternatively stated, the rate of return must be comparable to rates the resources could earn elsewhere, or (under certain specific assumptions, such as complete factor mobility) the resources will move to another endeavor where the return is greater. This is precisely what happened in agriculture: for several decades the annual income generated by the sector was insufficient, when distributed among all resources, to provide returns comparable to those earned elsewhere. A low rate of return resulted, and the excess

[11] A study by William Lin, James Johnson, and Linda Calvin, "Farm Commodity Programs: Who Participates and Who Gets the Benefits," U.S. Department of Agriculture, Economics, Statistics, and Cooperatives Service, National Economics Division, mimeographed, February 1980, of the 1978 commodity programs revealed the following distribution of direct payments as a percentage of total payments received by farmers of each of these commodities:

Commodity	Smallest 50% of Farmers	Largest 50% of Farmers	Largest 10% of Farmers	Number of Farmers
Wheat	10.9	89.1	50.5	38,734
Cotton	6.2	93.8	53.3	5,045
Rice	7.0	93.0	39.8	1,658
Feed grain	13.3	86.7	39.5	62,037
Total	9.7	90.3	46.0	73,635

Producers were arrayed by the size of their normal cropland acreage. The "smallest 50 percent of farmers" thus means the 50 percent of farmers with the smallest normal cropland acreage.

resources gradually shifted to other sectors of the economy where the earnings were greater. With the assertions that the farm sector is in relative resource equilibrium today, how do earnings now compare with those in the nonfarm sector?

Empirically, rates of return can be computed in several different ways, combining information from the balance sheet and from the income statement. First, income can be measured in different ways, all using legitimate accounting concepts. Assets can be measured at cost (book value) or at current market value. Further, the type of earnings, such as annual income or capital gains arising from appreciation of the value of the asset itself, for different investments must be considered. Finally, when comparing rates of return among assets, the variability and riskiness of the return must also be considered.

The Department of Agriculture has collected data sufficient to permit computation of returns to the farm sector back to 1940. These estimates of the rate of return to equity (current market value of assets less the outstanding debt) in agricultural production assets from current income (gross receipts less production expenses including interest paid and operator and family labor) are shown in table 9.[12] Several inferences may be drawn from these estimates:

• The higher returns in the form of current incomes during the 1940s reflect the high commodity prices resulting from wartime conditions. The total returns were relatively stable through the 1950s and 1960s. The boom time of the early 1970s is reflected in both current income and capital returns.

• The return in the form of capital gains primarily reflects increases in the value of the largest production asset, land. These returns were

[12] When discussing rates of return to the farm sector and including increases in asset values (capital gains), objections are always certain to arise. The objections, in essence, are that the capital gains are an unrealized or illiquid form of wealth: the increase cannot be captured without selling the asset, an unreasonable action, of course, for one wishing to continue operating a farm business. The point neglected by the dissenters is that capital gains can be monetized by borrowing against them for farm expansion.

The inappropriateness of adding the rate of return from current income to the rate of return from nominal capital gains has been pointed out by Melichar and others. They have also overcome this objection, however, by calculating the real return from asset appreciation (capital gains), which is comparable with net income. Real capital gains (the increase in wealth after adjusting for inflation) represent the amount of increase in the wealth of the farm business that could be taken out without reducing the real wealth position, the viability (proportion of equity) of the business. Thus real increases in asset values are not less a return to farming than current income.

For further discussion of this subject, see Emanuel Melichar, "Capital Gains versus Current Income in the Farming Sector" (Paper presented at the American Agricultural Economics Association Annual Meeting, Washington State University, August 1, 1979).

TABLE 9

RETURNS TO INVESTMENT EQUITY IN
FARM PRODUCTION ASSETS, 1940–1979

Period	Equity in Assets	Residual Income to Equity	Real Capital Gains	Rate of Return to Equity Investment from		
		(billions of 1967 $)		Current income	Capital gains	Total
1940–44	81.3	6.3	6.2	7.8	7.4	15.2
1945–49	115.8	8.3	1.1	7.2	1.0	8.2
1950–54	133.1	6.4	0.8	4.9	0.8	5.7
1955–59	144.5	4.1	6.9	2.8	4.8	7.7
1960–64	161.8	5.3	5.0	3.3	3.1	6.4
1965–69	178.3	7.3	5.4	4.1	3.1	7.2
1970–74	192.0	11.8	13.2	6.1	7.0	13.1
1975–79	241.4	8.8	19.6	3.7	8.2	11.8

NOTE: Farm production assets are valued at current market prices deflated to a constant dollar basis. Residual income to equity equals income to production assets minus interest on real estate and non–real estate debt.
SOURCE: U.S. Department of Agriculture, *Balance Sheet of the Farming Sector*, 1979 supplement.

relatively stable through the immediate post–World War II decade and the 1960s but then increased rapidly, reflecting the sharp escalation in land prices that began after 1972.

• The average total return to equity is appreciably higher for the decade of the 1970s than for the previous three decades (excluding the war years of the early 1940s).

While we find that the total returns to agriculture have increased appreciably in the 1970s, this provides little information on the relative resource equilibrium question without comparison to earnings elsewhere in the economy. Such comparisons are fraught with limitations, to be sure, impairing their strict validity. Even so, some useful insights can be gained if the limitations are recognized.

The current income and capital gains returns to common stock and long-term government bonds are frequently viewed as representative earnings in the nonfarm economy. Lins has developed estimates for stocks and bonds for comparison with farm sector earnings. His estimates are shown with the Department of Agriculture estimates of farm sector earnings in table 10 (again recognizing that they are not strictly

TABLE 10

RATES OF RETURN TO STOCKS, BONDS, AND FARM ASSETS, 1950–1979

(percent)

Period	Current Income			Real Capital Gains			Total		
	Common stock	Long-term bonds	Farm assets	Common stock	Long-term bonds	Farm assets	Common stock	Long-term bonds	Farm assets
1950–54	5.85	2.61	4.95	11.95	−1.69	3.28	17.53	0.92	8.23
1955–59	3.94	3.38	3.18	13.12	−4.65	4.02	17.06	−1.27	7.19
1960–64	3.20	4.00	3.61	7.45	−1.49	2.42	10.65	2.51	6.02
1965–69	3.18	5.01	4.46	1.61	−9.09	2.48	4.79	−4.08	6.94
1970–74	3.47	6.25	6.26	−8.66	−8.65	6.15	−5.19	−2.40	12.41
1975–79	4.68	7.49	4.50	−4.09	−12.06	5.10	0.59	−4.57	9.60
Coefficient of variation[a]	22	26	34	281	192	106	152	185	60

[a] The coefficient of variation is the standard deviation of the data series divided by the mean and expressed as a percentage.

SOURCE: Stock and bond returns are adapted from David A. Lins, "Financial Performance and Economic Well-Being of the Farm Sector and Rural People," mimeographed, U.S. Department of Agriculture, Economics, Statistics, and Cooperatives Service, National Economics Division. Farm asset returns are calculated from data in annual issues of U.S. Department of Agriculture, *Farm Income Statistics*.

comparable). These estimates also permit some interesting observations:

• The rates of return to current income among the three investments are not greatly different in magnitude over the entire thirty-year period, especially in the past fifteen years, with long-term bonds consistently but not greatly outperforming the other two. Judged by the coefficient of variation, farm income is the most volatile of the three.

• The capital gains returns to equity are greater for stocks and farm assets than for long-term bonds. Stocks outperformed farm assets in the 1950s and 1960s, but the reverse occurred in the 1970s. Interestingly, farm capital gains returns are much more stable than returns to the other two.

• During the past fifteen years, the rates of total returns to farm investment equity have substantially exceeded investments in common stocks and bonds. Even though annual farm income is most variable, that variability is more than offset by the more stable capital gains returns; thus the variability (risk) in the farm investment has been substantially lower than investment in the other two.

Overall, these data suggest that, to the extent stocks and bonds are good proxies for both current income and capital gains returns in the nonfarm economy, the agricultural sector as a whole lagged until the late 1960s but today enjoys comparable or superior rates of earnings.

The preceding discussion focused on the economic rates of return to agriculture, and viewed the sector as a whole. Estimates of rates of return by size of farm would augment the profile. Unfortunately, the only such data available, from a special 1970 survey by the census of agriculture, are now over a decade old. A similar survey was conducted for 1979 as a follow-on to the 1978 census, but the data are not yet available. It is unlikely, however, that the general pattern of earnings would have changed significantly.

The 1970 data are summarized in table 11. These data show the smaller size farms to have negative returns to investment equity. This occurs because net income becomes negative after substracting from the gross income an imputed return for operator and family labor and management. The return increases as farm size increases. Beginning with farms of at least $20,000 of gross sales, the total return is generally comparable to that in the nonfarm sector. One could reasonably expect that the patterns would be reconfirmed by the 1979 data but that, because of inflation and farm size adjustments, achieving comparable rates of returns to those in the nonfarm sector would begin with farms of gross sales greater than $40,000.

TABLE 11

RETURNS TO INVESTMENT EQUITY IN
FARM PRODUCTION ASSETS BY SIZE OF FARM, 1970

Sales Class (dollars)	Average Investment Equity (dollars)	Rate of Return to		
		Current income	Capital gains	Total
Less than 2,500	22,208	−6.1	3.7	−2.4
2,500–4,999	38,898	−6.5	3.9	−2.6
5,000–9,999	55,058	−0.1	4.2	4.1
10,000–19,999	84,489	2.9	4.4	7.3
20,000–39,999	128,345	4.4	4.5	8.9
40,000–99,999	201,493	5.9	4.7	10.6
100,000 and over	522,027	6.9	4.3	11.2
All farms	69,736	2.1	4.3	6.4
All but the smallest class	100,294	3.3	4.4	7.7

NOTE: The capital gains estimates are nominal, unlike the estimates in the previous tables, which are in real terms.

SOURCE: Adapted from Bruce J. Hottel and Robert D. Reinsel, "Returns to Equity Capital by Economic Class of Farm," U.S. Department of Agriculture, Economics Research Service, August 1976.

Variability of Income and Returns. A second important facet of rates of return from annual income and asset appreciation is their *variability*. The previous discussion examined the amount of income (farm and nonfarm) by farm size and the amount of return relative to the size of the investment. Generally, the data showed the amount of total income to farm families in recent years to compare favorably with the national median family income. Similarly, the total rate of return to investment in farm businesses since about 1970 compares favorably with rates that could be earned in the nonfarm economy. What about the variability or stability of current income and investment earnings?

First, the stability for the sector as a whole is examined by measuring the variability in commodity group prices and incomes for three periods (table 12). These data suggest:

• The periods 1955–1963 and 1964–1971 were stable relative to 1972–1978: variability in prices received for all products in that period increased sixfold; over sixfold for crop prices and over twofold for livestock prices. The variability in cash receipts from crops doubled.

• The variability in farm income was over three times as great in

TABLE 12

COEFFICIENT OF VARIATION IN FARM INCOME
AND PRODUCT PRICES, 1955–1978

	1955–63	1964–71	1972–78
Index of prices received			
All farm products	2.6	5.9	14.6
Crops	2.9	3.8	18.9
Livestock	5.5	11.3	13.7
Cash receipts			
Crops	10.4	9.1	20.6
Livestock	8.3	14.6	15.7
Personal income received by the farm population			
Farm income less government payments	9.4	18.6	24.3
Farm income	5.1	9.8	21.7
Nonfarm income	12.5	16.0	15.7
From all sources	5.5	12.1	13.9

NOTE: The coefficient of variation is the standard deviation of the data series divided by the mean and expressed as a percentage.

SOURCE: Calculated from Department of Agriculture, *Farm Income Statistics*, various issues, and *Agricultural Prices, Annual Summary*, various issues.

the 1970s as it was from 1955 to 1963. Income variability in all periods is reduced by government payments and declines even further when income from nonfarm sources is included in total income to the farm sector.

• Nonfarm income received by the farm population was relatively stable in all three periods, primarily reflecting economic conditions in the nonfarm rather than the farm economy.

Overall, these estimates confirm that farm income variability has increased for the sector as a whole in recent years.

To look beyond sector aggregates, farm operator family income by source and size of farm is examined. The stability of farm income and total (farm plus nonfarm) income is examined for two periods, the 1960s and the 1970s (table 13). Some observations from those estimates:

• The variability in farm income increased substantially for farms of all sizes in the 1970s over the 1960s.

TABLE 13

Coefficient of Variability in Farm Income per Farm Operator Family by Size of Farm, 1960–1978

Sales Class (dollars)	Net Farm Income		Total Income	
	1960–72	1973–78	1960–72	1973–78
Less than 2,500	8.5	10.8	33.2	15.6
2,500–4,999	6.9	16.2	30.6	14.6
5,000–9,999	4.4	16.0	23.9	12.2
10,000–19,999	6.8	15.7	18.9	7.3
20,000–39,999	11.9	13.7	15.0	7.7
40,000–99,999	12.9	15.2	8.6[a]	10.7
100,000 and over	19.6	32.0	16.3[a]	26.5

[a] For the time period 1965–1972.

SOURCE: Calculated from Department of Agriculture, *Farm Income Statistics*, various issues.

• The variability in farm income is more than twice as great for the farms with more than $100,000 in gross sales as for those with less gross sales.

• In the 1970s total income was less variable than farm income alone because the addition of nonfarm income reduces the variability for all sales class sizes except the very smallest.

Overall, these data also indicate that variability of income was greater in the 1970s than in the 1960s. Further, since farm income is a smaller proportion of total income on small farms than on large farms, small farms are less affected by fluctuations in farm earnings.

The implications of this increased economic instability in the farm sector are perhaps more significant today than formerly because of the changed financial structure of farms today. In previous times, farm families were thought to be very resilient: during periods of adverse economic conditions, they simply "tightened their belts," reducing personal consumption expenditures and weathering the period until conditions improved. They were much less dependent on purchased inputs from the nonfarm sector, and their fixed annual cash obligations were relatively small. But that is no longer true; modern agriculture purchases a high proportion of annual production inputs, and many farmers have substantial annual debt-repayment obligations for fixed assets such as machinery and land.

This situation is depicted to some extent by the ratio of cash

33

TABLE 14

CASH PRODUCTION EXPENSES AS A PERCENTAGE
OF CASH RECEIPTS, 1935–1978

| | | Farms with Gross Sales of | | |
Period	All Farms	Less than $40,000	$40,000 to $100,000	More than $100,000
1935–39	59.8	n.a.	n.a.	n.a.
1940–45	56.3	n.a.	n.a.	n.a.
1946–49	53.4	n.a.	n.a.	n.a.
1950–54	58.7	n.a.	n.a.	n.a.
1955–59	63.2	n.a.	n.a.	n.a.
1960–64	67.1	60.2	71.8	85.6
1965–69	68.5	59.6	69.4	84.8
1970–74	67.4	55.9	63.9	80.6
1975–78	72.1	57.4	63.5	81.3

NOTE: n.a. = not available. Cash receipts include marketings from livestock and crops, government payments, and income from recreation, machinery hire, and custom work. Cash expenses include operating expenses, taxes, interest on farm mortgage debt, and rent to nonoperator landlords.
SOURCE: Department of Agriculture, *Farm Income Statistics*, October 1979.

production expenses to gross farm income (table 14). The ratio for all farms has trended upward since World War II, reflecting the increased reliance on purchased inputs and the changing financial structure of farming. The reliance on purchased inputs varies by farm size, the ratio of cash expenses to receipts being much higher for the larger farms. Likewise, the extent of borrowed capital varies by farm size, the debt-to-asset ratio being much higher for the larger farms, indicating the added cash requirement for annual debt service (table 15). These data suggest a reason for the increasing discussion of farmers' cash flow situations.

The implications of an increasing ratio of cash production expenses to gross receipts are illustrated by the effects on variation in net income (table 16). A given reduction in cash receipts is much more severe when there is greater dependence on purchased inputs (the higher the ratio). The import of this is that more and more farms are vulnerable at a time when increased dependence on foreign markets means greater potential variability in market prices and hence variability in cash receipts.

TABLE 15

DEBT-TO-ASSET RATIO BY FARM SIZE, 1960–1978

(percent)

Period	All Farms		Farm Size by Sales Class					
		Less than $2,500	$2,500 to 4,999	$5,000 to 9,999	$10,000 to 19,999	$20,000 to 39,999	$40,000 to 99,999	$100,000 and over
1960–64	13.5	8.1	10.2	12.9	15.0	15.1	15.2	18.8
1965–69	16.3	9.2	9.4	14.4	17.8	17.8	19.2	23.4
1970–74	16.4	5.1	8.8	11.5	15.5	17.8	19.7	24.9
1975–78	16.0	4.7	6.9	7.6	12.2	14.9	18.2	24.9

SOURCE: U.S. Department of Agriculture, *Balance Sheet of the Farming Sector*, 1976, 1978, and 1979 supplements.

TABLE 16

ILLUSTRATION OF SENSITIVITY OF ANNUAL NET INCOME
TO CHANGES IN PRODUCTION EXPENSES

	Ratio of Production Expenses to Cash Receipts		
	70 percent	85 percent	90 percent
Gross receipts	$100	$200	$300
Production expenses	70	170	270
Net cash income	30	30	30
Gross receipts reduction of 10%	90	180	270
Net cash income	20	10	0
Percentage decrease in net cash income	33.3	66.7	100

SOURCE: Adapted from Lins, "Financial Performance and Economic Well-Being of the Farm Sector."

The "Primary" Farms. The profile thus far makes clear that several subsets of the total number of farms might be delineated, depending on the characteristics of interest and the purpose. The wide diversity among farms suggests that the effectiveness and efficiency of future policies will depend on more careful identification of the specific problems and subgroups of farmers that policy, such as targeting policy, is to treat. The number of such subgroups for policy purposes may vary, of course, and the delineation could be done in several ways.

The profile would suggest that at least two and perhaps three groups of farms today have common characteristics. The first is the very small farms, those places where production is small and nonfarm incomes are relatively high, suggesting that most may be only rural residences, hobby farms, and the like. This group would include, at a minimum, the smallest size category (under $2,500 of sales) and could reasonably include the next size category, between $2,500 and $5,000. This group, which might be labeled "rural farm residences," would encompass 44.4 percent of all the places counted as farms today.

A second group (which could be called "small farms") might include the next three sales class categories: $5,000 to $10,000, $10,000 to $20,000, and $20,000 to $40,000 of sales. Most of these farms produce too little to be able to rely fully or primarily on farming for a livelihood and must depend on supplemental nonfarm income, but to a lesser extent than the smallest farms. This group constitutes 33.6 percent of all farms.

Finally, a third category (called "primary farms") includes farms having over $40,000 in gross sales—22 percent of all farms.[13] These farms depend primarily on farming for income and produce the vast majority of the nation's food and fiber. It is this group, and perhaps the middle group as well, that are of major interest for commodity policy. The primary farms are now examined in greater detail.

The 1974 census counted 476,909 farms with gross sales of at least $40,000. (This number is estimated to have increased to 577,000 in 1978.) These farms accounted for 78.4 percent of the total output in 1974. Since these are the farms most likely to influence the effectiveness of the commodity programs as now structured and to be the beneficiaries of the program subsidies, their characteristics are of further interest. What do these farms produce? How viable are they?

The census classifies farms by type using the Standard Industrial Classification (SIC) codes of the Department of Commerce, placing a farm in a particular classification according to the commodity that accounts for more than 50 percent of the gross sales of that farm. Thirteen major farm types are delineated by the census (table 17). Of farms with more than $40,000 in sales, livestock farms (including dairy, poultry, animal specialty, and general livestock) constitute 45.5 percent; crop farms (grains, cotton, sugar, etc., tobacco, and general crop) are 48.8 percent; and horticultural and various other miscellaneous types constitute the remaining 5.7 percent.

Interestingly, the cash grain and cotton farms, those for which the major crop commodity programs have been operated for over half a century, are a relatively small proportion (39.7 percent).

The contribution of total sales by size of farms within each of these types is further revealing (table 18). As expected, the production is concentrated, with a relatively small number of producers accounting for a large proportion of total output. Concentration varies across farm types, from the larger poultry and egg farms producing virtually all the product, to the tobacco farms where the larger farms produce 43.6 percent of the output. For the cash grain farm type, the large farms account for 31.0 percent of cash grain farms and 74.2 percent of total sales.[14]

---

[13] The dollar boundaries on these delineations will, of course, change over time. For example, the $40,000 boundary will probably shift upward, as inflation and technology make this amount look smaller.

[14] This percentage only indicates that large cash grain farms account for 74.1 percent of the sales of all cash grain farms. We do not know what proportion of the grain they produce or how much grain is produced on other farms. It would

TABLE 17

FARMS WITH OVER $40,000 OF PRODUCT SALES, BY TYPE, 1974

Type of Farm	Number	Percent
Cash grain	179,701	37.7
Cotton	9,500	2.0
Sugar, peanuts, potatoes, etc.	22,966	4.8
Dairy	78,083	16.4
Poultry, eggs	32,537	6.8
Horticultural	6,578	1.4
Livestock	100,036	21.0
Tobacco	8,886	1.9
Vegetable and melon	6,000	1.3
Fruit and tree nut	13,769	2.9
General farms—crop	11,566	2.4
Animal specialty	1,703	0.4
General farms—livestock	4,518	0.9
Not classified	1,066	0.2
Total	476,909	100.0

SOURCE: U.S. Bureau of the Census, *Census of Agriculture*, 1974.

To delineate a set of primary grain farms for analysis of commodity policy, it is necessary to identify the specific grain crops produced. The census data do not, however, enable such an identification to be made directly. Rather, this must be done indirectly; one way is to identify the major grain-producing states by type of grain produced (from census acreage data) and then make the reasonable assumption that farms in these states produce those grains. This procedure identifies 115,394 primary grain farms in the five major wheat- and corn-producing states (the remaining 64,000 primary grain farms are spread throughout the United States). These delineations are shown below by state along with cotton farms in the five major cotton-producing states:

Wheat		Corn/Soybeans		Cotton	
Kansas	12,957	Illinois	26,328	Texas	2,250
North Dakota	10,952	Iowa	23,446	California	1,148
Washington	3,447	Nebraska	11,513	Arkansas	933
Montana	4,209	Indiana	11,271	Arizona	620
Oklahoma	3,909	Ohio	7,362	Mississippi	1,953
Total	35,474	Total	79,920	Total	6,904

appear, however, that the grain produced on the farms in this type and produced on farms of other types in this size category would be a large proportion of all grain produced.

TABLE 18

Distribution of Farms and Agricultural Product Sales, by Type of Farm, 1974

Type of Farm	Less Than $40,000 in Sales			More Than $40,000 in Sales			All Farms	
	Number	Percent	Percent of total sales	Number[a]	Percent	Percent of total sales	Number	Total sales (thousands of $)
Cash grain	400,553	69.0	25.8	179,701	31.0	74.2	580,254	23,672,963
Cotton	21,225	69.1	15.3	9,500	30.9	84.7	30,725	1,850,180
Horticulture	13,100	66.6	9.8	6,578	33.4	90.2	19,678	1,686,995
Livestock	393,780	79.7	19.8	100,036	20.3	80.2	493,816	22,124,669
Dairy	117,974	60.2	26.2	78,083	39.8	73.8	196,057	9,591,737
Poultry and eggs	10,153	23.8	3.3	32,537	76.2	96.7	42,690	6,356,830
Sugar, peanuts, potatoes, etc.	58,449	71.8	12.8	22,966	28.2	87.2	81,415	5,484,249
Tobacco	86,607	90.7	56.4	8,886	9.3	43.6	95,493	1,651,941
Vegetable and melon	13,548	69.3	8.2	6,000	30.7	91.8	19,548	2,144,368
Fruit and tree nut	37,501	73.1	17.6	13,769	26.9	82.4	51,270	2,858,110
General farms—crop	33,093	74.1	46.7	11,566	25.9	53.3	44,659	2,033,596
General farms—livestock	10,477	69.9	30.2	4,518	30.1	69.8	14,995	576,063
Animal specialty[a]	6,464	57.9	24.7	4,703	42.1	75.3	11,167	356,320
Not classified[a]	12,214	92.0	50.0	1,066	8.0	50.0	13,280	210,283
Total	1,215,138	71.7	29.1	479,909	28.3	70.9	1,695,047	80,598,305

[a] These figures may vary somewhat from similar aggregate data; the difference is due to disclosure problems.

Source: Census Bureau, *Census of Agriculture,* 1974, vol. 11, para. 8.

TABLE 19

AVERAGE CHARACTERISTICS OF CASH GRAIN FARMS
WITH OVER $40,000 IN GROSS SALES IN PREDOMINANT WHEAT-,
CORN/SOYBEAN-, AND COTTON-PRODUCING STATES, 1974

	Wheat	Corn/ Soybeans	Cotton
Number of farms	35,474	79,920	6,934
Land inventory (acres)			
Land operated	1,728	565	1,254
Cropland	1,199	475	982
Cropland harvested	802	431	801
Cropland not harvested	397	44	181
Pasture, range, and woodland	490	74	221
Other land	39	16	51
Tenure (acres)			
Owned and operated	940	240	635
Rented in	839	337	696
Rented out	51	12	77
Crop enterprises (acres)			
Wheat	650	40	38
Corn	40	213	4
Soybeans	15	148	109
Other grains	51	11	72
Hay and fieldseeds	52	16	34
Other crops	2	3	10
Cotton	—	—	509
Value of sales ($)			
Grain	77,414	49,895	16,741
Fieldseeds and hay	1,770	445	8,492
Other field crops	1,629	25,037	16,603
Vegetables	16	224	2,808
Fruit	3	8	900
Other crops	820	619	134,078
Livestock	10,090	11,865	3,488
Total	91,742	88,093	183,110

SOURCE: Census Bureau, *Census of Agriculture*, 1974.

Having identified the farms in these states, some notion of the
nature of these farming operations can be obtained by looking at
averages of these farms (again, recognizing the limitations of averages
in the diverse agriculture of today). The average characteristics of
these farms are shown in table 19.

TABLE 20

AVERAGE FINANCIAL CHARACTERISTICS OF CASH GRAIN FARMS
WITH OVER $40,000 IN GROSS SALES IN PREDOMINANT WHEAT-,
CORN/SOYBEAN-, AND COTTON-PRODUCING STATES, 1974

	Wheat	Corn/ Soybeans	Cotton
Balance sheet			
Assets ($)	318,310	255,158	433,180
Debt ($)	37,609	30,555	71,907
Equity ($)	280,701	224,603	361,273
Equity (%)	88.2	88.0	83.4
Current income ($)			
Gross receipts	91,661	88,095	183,111
Total expenses	56,329	53,038	147,899
Net income to equity	35,332	35,057	35,212
Other income ($)			
Net farm related	1,278	2,759	3,289
Nonfarm	2,708	2,761	4,178
Total	3,986	5,520	7,467
Total income ($, all sources)	39,318	40,577	42,679
Total income ($, farm sources)	36,610	37,816	38,501
Real estate asset appreciation ($)	16,582	9,244	−14,967
Returns to equity from:			
Annual farm income (%)	13.04	16.84	10.66
Real capital gains (%)	5.91	4.12	−4.14
Total (%)	18.95	20.96	6.52

NOTE: The financial characteristics were determined in the following manner: Gross receipts are equal to total market value of agricultural products sold. Total expenses were calculated weighting the average variable costs for farms with gross sales of more than $100,000 with those of farms having gross sales of $40,000 to $100,000. Wheat farms were those classified by the census of agriculture as cash grain farms in the predominant wheat-growing states of Kansas, North Dakota, Washington, Montana, and Oklahoma; corn/soybean farms were cash grain farms in the predominant soybean and corn states of Illinois, Iowa, Nebraska, Indiana, and Ohio; and cotton farms were listed as cotton farms in Texas, California, Arkansas, Arizona, and Mississippi. Total variable costs include cash rent, taxes, interest, and depreciation as well as the cutomary cash items. In addition, a management charge of 5 percent of total sales and a labor charge calculated from crop production budgets were included. Returns to equity were calculated by taking the ratio of total income from farm sources to equity and the ratio of real estate asset appreciation to equity.

SOURCE: Calculated from Census Bureau, *Census of Agriculture*, 1974 data.

The average financial situations of these farms are shown in table 20. Using the census data, current income and capital gains returns have been computed and compared with the operator's average equity in the farm business. These data reveal that the returns are variable from state to state but that the total rates of return are comparable to returns in the nonfarm economy for this year (see table 10). Likewise, the total income (farm and nonfarm) accruing to the farm operator families is comparable to the median family income for 1974.

Again, it should be emphasized that these are average situations. The average amount of operator equity in these farm businesses is quite large, and cash flow requirements in such cases are much less stringent than would be the case for a renter or beginning farmer more likely to have a much smaller equity.[15]

Economies of Size. An additional topic that merits discussion here relates to production efficiency and farm size. The farm size–efficiency trade-off has long been one of the major considerations in farm policy. The conventional wisdom held that technological advancements over time created efficiencies that could more effectively be captured by increasing the size of farms (for example, substituting machines for labor, with the investment cost of the machine per acre or per unit of output being reduced by increasing the farm size up to some point). Further, the argument goes, the cumulative effect has been the consolidation of farms and the reduction of unit costs of production and food costs; thus consumers were the ultimate beneficiaries of technology innovation and farm consolidation.[16] The most frequently cited evidence of societal benefits is the declining proportion of real disposable income spent by the consuming public for food.

There is no doubt that consumers have benefited significantly from past gains in efficiency in the farm sector: that the trade-off between farm numbers and food costs has been decidedly advantageous to consumers. But the question now arises (especially with arguments that the sector is in relative resource equilibrium, if for no other reason) whether, given existing technology and relative prices, there are further significant gains in efficiency to be realized from continued consolida-

---

[15] For additional analyses of the effect of the amount of equity on cash flow for several typical farming situations, see U.S. Department of Agriculture, *Status of the Family Farm*, third annual report to the Congress, September 1980.

[16] The argument is illustrated below. In the short run, some factors of production are fixed (cannot be immediately varied). Thus firm (plant) size, for example, is fixed. If a firm is of the size represented by SAC_1, the optimum operating point would be C_1, where unit cost is lowest. Over time, however, all factors can be varied, and the firm could move to the optimum size; in this case it would attempt to reach the size represented by SAC_3, the optimum long-run firm size with unit cost (C_3) at a minimum. In a competitive economy, product prices would reflect the lower costs and ultimately be reflected in food prices. There would exist no further *cost reduction* incentive for a firm to grow beyond the

tion of farms.[17] Is this farm size–food price trade-off still valid? Have the primary farms realized most of the attainable size economies (for example, are they now operating at or to the right of the minimum on their long-run average cost curves)?

As with most other questions pertaining to the heterogeneous farm sector, any generalizations are severely limited. Moreover, there are conceptual and empirical difficulties in determining size economies. These involve the appropriate treatment of operator labor, land, and management costs, difficulties peculiar to agriculture. (The specific nature of these difficulties is elaborated and their implications are drawn elsewhere.)[18] Current studies are reexamining technical economies of size, however,[19] and preliminary estimates of least-cost farm sizes for seven farming situations have been developed (table 21).

least-cost size. Any size growth beyond (to SAC_4) would also yield no benefits to consumers in lower food costs.

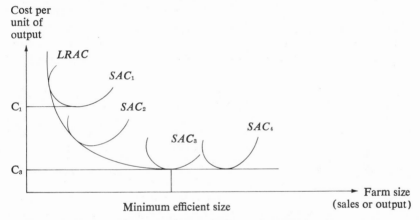

Cost per unit of output

LRAC

SAC_1

SAC_2

SAC_4

C_1

SAC_3

C_3

Minimum efficient size

Farm size (sales or output)

[17] If it is assumed that the sector is in long-run equilibrium and technology is unchanged, there can be no efficiency gains from increasing farm size. If the long-run average cost curve is flat, however, the individual firm can increase total profit by expanding in size even though there are no efficiency gains and no gains to society. It is important to note that changes in size in the past have not occurred with given technology but with rapidly changing technology. The important question is whether future technical change will exhibit a size bias.

New technology will obviously keep changing the cost curves. One issue may be whether a new technology (for example, a larger tractor) actually lowers costs for a large farm or simply raises costs for smaller farms. Such a technology might provide only incentives for growth but not lower food costs.

[18] Thomas A. Miller, "Economies of Size, Structural Change, and the Impact of a Family Farm Policy" (Paper presented at the Western Agricultural Economics Association Annual Meetings, Las Cruces, New Mexico, July 21–22, 1980).

[19] *Technical* economies of size refer to those savings or efficiencies gained by using resources more efficiently within the firm. They contrast with *market* economies resulting from obtaining higher prices for products sold and lower prices for inputs purchased.

TABLE 21

LEAST-COST FARM SIZES FOR
VARIOUS FARMING SITUATIONS, 1979

Region/Farming Situation	Size at Which 90% of Economies Attained		Size at Which 100% of Economies Attained	
	$ sales	Acres	$ sales	Acres
Northern plains/wheat-barley farm	13,000	177	105,000	1,475
Pacific Northwest/wheat-barley farm	54,000	449	156,000	1,887
Corn Belt/corn-soybean farm	60,000	299	145,000	639
Southern plains/wheat-sorghum farm	28,000	399	100,000	1,488
Delta/cotton-soybean farm	47,000	335	122,000	1,237
Southern high plains/ cotton-sorghum farm	58,000	395	175,000	974
Southeast/peanut-soybean-corn farm	55,000	143	130,000	399
Average (arithmetic) of seven farms	45,000	314	133,000	1,157

SOURCE: U.S. Department of Agriculture, Economics and Statistics Service, National Economics Division, unpublished studies.

These estimates of the long-run average cost curve for agriculture correspond to previous studies that show unit costs declining very rapidly as farms grow from a very small size. The curve then becomes relatively flat over a wide range in size, that is, most of the economies are attained at relatively modest sizes. Capturing the remaining relatively small economies involves further growth beyond the size at which most economies can be attained.[20]

There may, however, be significant market economies in the purchase of inputs and sale of outputs that can be achieved by further

[20] Miller explores some of the fundamental questions of what causes structural changes in farming, specifically focusing on the role of economies of size. He cites studies that would suggest that (1) increasing average sizes of farms do not necessarily imply the existence of attainable economies of size but only the absence of significant diseconomies of size; (2) growth in farm sizes may be due to increasing income per capita in the nonfarm sector nationwide and the farm size needed to obtain comparable incomes; (3) given the observed heterogeneity of farm size, there are no significant economies of size in agricultural production and any enterprise that exhibits significant economies of size breaks away from agricultural production to become a separate industry (e.g., broilers). It could also be suggested that, historically, economies of size have more commonly caused functions or operations (such as marketing and processing of products) rather than production to break away from farming.

growth of the firms. To the extent that these market economies result from real savings in the cost of providing these farm services, they contribute to lower food costs for consumers. (Studies are under way to identify and evaluate such market economies.) Further, even though farm firms have achieved a size that captures most efficiencies, there may be other incentives for continued growth, including simply increasing total income to keep pace with nonfarm increases.

How do the major commodity farms in the principal producing states on average compare with the least-cost sizes noted above? Again, the comparison is limited: the census data are for 1974, and the eight farming situations are for 1979. If the 1974 data are adjusted to 1979 dollars, some notion of relative magnitudes can be gained. The relevant comparisons, shown in table 22, suggest that most primary farms have attained a size at which most of the technical economies can be attained.

Some Implications

The evidence suggests that some of the most fundamental developments in agriculture in the last fifty to sixty years occurred in the 1970s. In combination, these developments have enormous implications for agriculture in the 1980s and beyond—for problems of the farm sector, the appropriate public policies, the agricultural institutions, and on and on. If the interpretation of the developments proves to be even reasonably correct, then the problems of the farm economy could be almost precisely the opposite of those of the past, which have conditioned our mind-sets about agriculture and our views about public policy.

• It appears that the long concern with chronic excess capacity, burdensome surpluses, low commodity prices, and low farm incomes may be largely behind us.

• The farm sector now has little slack; the readily available cropland is largely committed to production; there is a growing concern about productivity growth; and we face growing demands from abroad (and new demands—liquid fuel from agricultural products—at home).

• The incomes of farm people compare favorably with those of nonfarm people. As a group, the many small farms no longer appear chronically poor, owing largely to the increased importance of off-farm income.

• The total rates of return to investment in farming have increased significantly in the last decade and apparently compare favorably with nonfarm investment earnings.

• A relatively small number of farmers account for most of the food and fiber production. Their incomes and earnings, as a group, are no

TABLE 22: AVERAGE SIZES OF FARMS COMPARED WITH EFFICIENT SIZES

Primary Farms	Acres, Average Cropland 1974 Census	Acre Size Where Specified Percentage of Economies Is Realized		Average Gross Sales, 1974	1974 Gross Sales in 1979 Dollars[a]	Gross Sales to Attain Specified Percentage of Economies	
		100%	90%			100%	90%
Wheat farms							
Kansas	1,003	1,488	399	93,432	137,649	100,000	28,000
North Dakota	1,214	1,475	177	82,292	121,237	105,000	13,000
Washington	1,470	1,887	449	131,930	194,367	156,000	54,000
Montana	1,853	1,475	177	88,248	130,012	156,000	13,000
Oklahoma	868	1,488	399	80,945	119,253	100,000	28,000
Corn/soybean farms							
Illinois	472	639	299	90,904	133,925	145,000	60,000
Iowa	401	639	299	83,349	122,794	145,000	60,000
Nebraska	638	n.a.	n.a.	90,229	132,930	n.a.	n.a.
Indiana	478	639	299	91,796	135,239	145,000	60,000
Ohio	464	639	299	84,162	123,992	145,000	80,000
Cotton farms							
Texas	1,019	974	395	93,510	137,764	175,000	58,000
California	925	n.a.	n.a.	360,065	530,468	n.a.	n.a.
Arizona	890	n.a.	n.a.	306,015	450,839	n.a.	n.a.
Arkansas	823	1,237	335	124,310	183,141	122,000	47,000
Mississippi	1,078	1,237	335	172,771	254,536	122,000	47,000

NOTE: n.a. = not available.
[a] The 1974 dollar sales estimates were inflated to 1979 dollars by the changes in the Consumer Price Index from 1974 (CPI, all items, 1974 = 147.7; 1979 = 217.6).
SOURCE: Census Bureau, *Census of Agriculture*, 1974, and table 21.

longer chronically low. But their annual cash requirements for production inputs have increased, and many are highly leveraged financially, further increasing cash flow requirements. As a result, these farms are very vulnerable to instability in prices and incomes.

• There are prospects for continued growth in demand in foreign markets for our products. In fact, we could see a reversal in the trend of declining real commodity prices over most of the postwar period—we could have increasing real commodity prices in the 1980s. As our role in the international markets becomes even more dominant, this means potentially much more instability. Production and consumption changes virtually anywhere in the world are transmitted as amplified fluctuations in demands for U.S. exports. Hence, the instability that increased greatly in the 1970s compared with the 1950s and 1960s could become even greater in the 1980s.

• This might suggest a greater future concern with shortages rather than surpluses, unstable rather than low commodity prices, rising food prices, and, as economic incentives encourage more intensive production of acres now cropped and cultivation of marginal lands, a more urgent concern over conservation of land and water resources and the environment.

• This further suggests a reexamination of the adequacy of commodity (and all other) policies and programs to cope with the new conditions and, especially, their distributive effects (the benefits, to whom they are accruing, and their costs). Further, the "chemistry" of these programs operating in conjunction with tax, credit, regulation, and other programs and their direct and indirect effects on the structure of the farm sector seem to merit renewed attention.

Consequences of Farm Policies during the 1970s

Bruce Gardner

In its management of the commodity programs that have dominated farm policy since the 1930s, the U.S. government made significant moves toward market orientation in the 1970s. Consequently, the importance of government in determining farm incomes, asset prices, and labor returns declined. These developments are discussed in the first section of this paper. In other respects, however, governmental involvement in U.S. agriculture increased in the 1970s. Two broad areas of expanded activity may be distinguished, responding to two areas of longstanding concern: (1) instability in farm commodity prices and farm incomes and (2) protection of farmers and consumers against natural hazards and middlemen. The second section of this paper considers the results of recent attempts by the United States Department of Agriculture (USDA) to manage the grain markets in pursuit of price stability. The third section considers protection regulation. The concluding remarks on farm policy issues of the 1970s complete the paper's descent from facts and analysis to opinion and speculation.

Developments in Traditional Farm Programs

The structure of the main commodity programs continued an evolutionary development in the 1970s but continued to be composed of four main instruments of intervention: (1) market price supports by means of government offers to purchase commodities, (2) control of production, (3) direct payments to farmers based on the difference between market prices and target prices, and (4) restraints on imports.

The Republican and Democratic administrations of the 1970s were both pleased to describe their farm policies as market oriented. This label is justified principally by reductions in real market price supports and in relaxation of efforts to control production. Let us consider a few

48

indicators of market orientation. The first is the difference between the average price received by farmers for a commodity and the support price. The greater the difference, the greater the market orientation. Figure 1 shows farm prices and support prices for each of the major commodities that have had continuing price-support programs. There are three categories of results: commodities that show a clear increase in market orientation, commodities that show no apparent increase in market orientation, and commodities that have an ambiguous record.

Only two commodities show a clear and sustained increase in market orientation, upland cotton and soybeans. They both show a much wider difference between the support price and the farm price throughout the 1970s than in previous decades. The long-term trend toward reduction in real support prices, however, had been reversed for both commodities by the late 1970s. The measurement of prices in real (deflated) terms means that reductions in support prices do not require explicit policy decisions under inflation. Thus the nominal support price was essentially constant between 1966 and 1973, as was the soybean support price between 1969 and 1974. Yet real support prices declined substantially. The real policy moves toward market orientation were made in 1966 for cotton and in 1969 for soybeans.

Soybeans show the clearest apparent evidence of an effect due to party dominance of the executive branch. In the crop years 1961–1968, when loan rates were established by the Democratic administration, there was an obvious upward shift in the real support price, as there was in the years 1977–1979, compared with the surrounding Republican years. Cotton, however, does not reveal this pattern.

The commodities that show no apparent move toward market orientation are milk, flue-cured tobacco, and peanuts. Milk is the only major commodity that has a definite rising trend in real price throughout the past twenty years. It seems likely that this is in part attributable to the dairy programs. No clear partisan pattern to the real support price emerges, although there were especially sharp increases during the later Nixon and Ford years. Peanuts are different in that farm and support prices for peanuts were as close together as ever in the late 1970s, even though the real support price was declining substantially. Because legislation for peanuts, like that for tobacco, involves production control, the difference between farm price and support price does not tell the whole story about market orientation. Production controls can hold prices well above the unregulated market level without an explicit support price as high as the observed market price. This is the case with flue-cured tobacco, where government purchases work primarily to support particular grades of tobacco leaf and to provide price stabilization pending adjustments in marketing quotas. From this

FIGURE 1

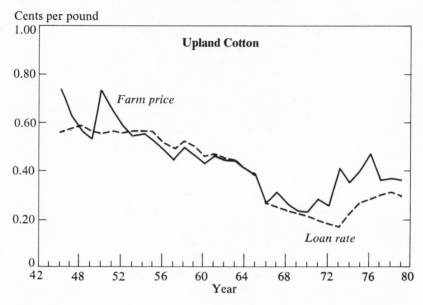

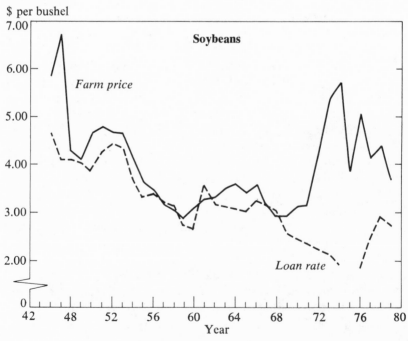

FIGURE 1 (continued)

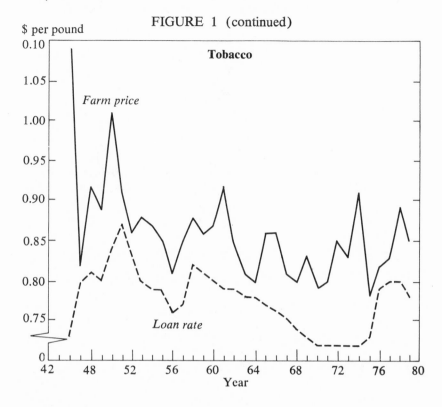

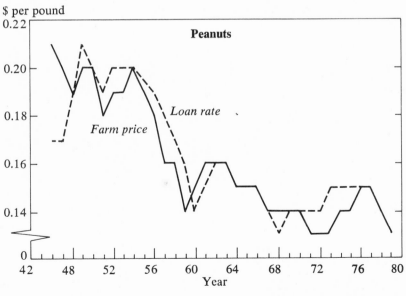

FIGURE 1 (continued)

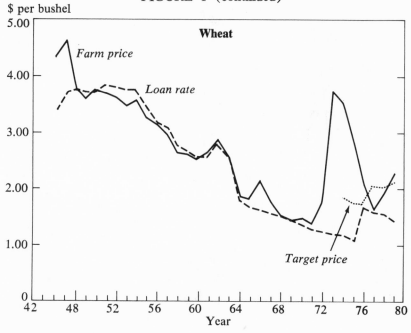

$ per bushel

Wheat

Farm price

Loan rate

Target price

Year

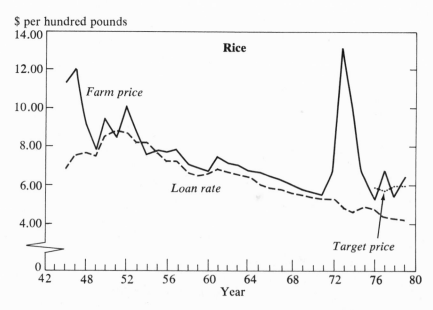

$ per hundred pounds

Rice

Farm price

Loan rate

Target price

Year

52

FIGURE 1 (continued)

$ per hundred pounds

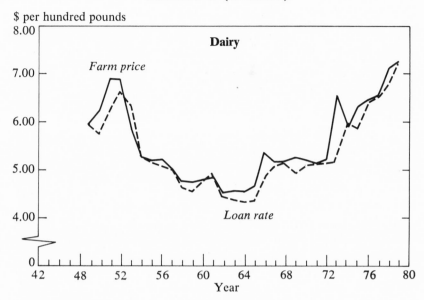

$ per bushel

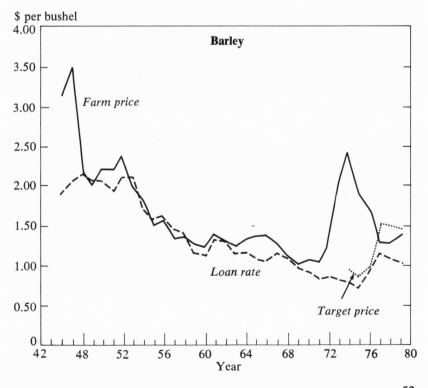

FIGURE 1 (continued)

$ per bushel

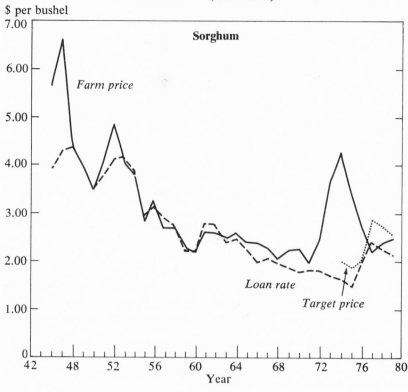

Sorghum

Farm price

Loan rate

Target price

Year

$ per bushel

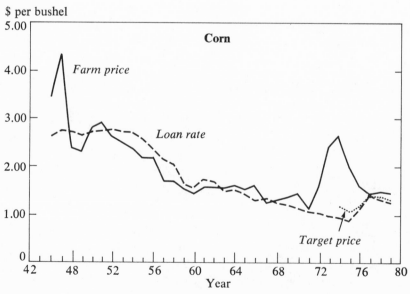

Corn

Farm price

Loan rate

Target price

Year

FIGURE 1 (concluded)

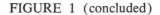

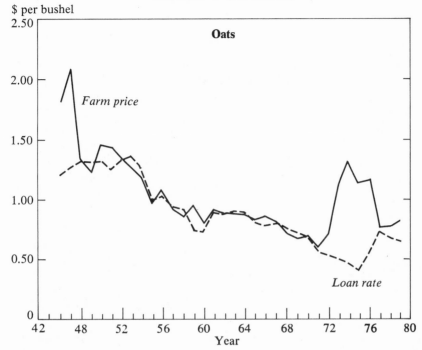

$ per bushel

Oats

Farm price

Loan rate

Year

NOTE: Prices are deflated.
SOURCE: United States Department of Agriculture, Agricultural Stabilization and Conservation Service, *Commodity Fact Sheets.*

point of view, the notable fact about peanut policy is that it allowed real market prices to fall substantially in the late 1970s. In this sense, peanut policy is more market oriented despite the small difference between the market price and the support price. Moreover, beginning with the 1978 crop, a support price for production of peanuts above the quota level was introduced at about 60 percent of the support price for quota peanuts. Because this low marginal price is associated with production controls, however, it should not be considered a move toward market orientation, any more than should the penalties for exceeding the tobacco marketing quota.

The ambiguous category consists of the grains, including rice. They have been subject to dramatic market events as well as substantial policy changes in the Agriculture and Consumer Protection Act of 1973, the Rice Production Act of 1975, and the Food and Agriculture Act of 1977. The combination of world grain-market events and policy change no doubt resulted in much more market orientation during the 1970s than in the preceding four decades. It is not so clear, however,

55

that by the end of the decade a foundation had been established for greater future market orientation than had existed previously.

Rice shows the strongest move toward market orientation. The extremly high prices of the early 1970s and geographical shifts in production gave impetus to scrapping the old program based on production controls. In 1976 the concept of target price was applied to rice, and payments of $1.12 per hundred pounds produced (16 percent of the average farm price) were made on that year's crop. The average market price again fell below the target price, by 10 percent, for the 1978 crop. Nonetheless, the market support price remained well below the market price. The sharp drop in the support price between 1975 and 1976 (figure 1) lends credence to the idea that direct payments based on target prices are a political substitute for intervention to support market prices. In this sense, the two legislated prices placed in effect for the grains in the mid-1970s were a move toward market orientation.

The market support price as established by loans made by the Commodity Credit Corporation (CCC) is a put option on grain for delivery. It is a combination marketing aid and price insurance for farmers. The target price is price insurance, which also has characteristics of a put option (an option to sell at a prespecified price). But the loan price is like a put option on actuals, in the grain trade's terminology, while the target price is a put option on a nondeliverable futures contract. The move toward market orientation in grains policy is to reduce the role of the CCC loan option by introducing the pure price insurance option.

Wheat and the feed grains do not reveal this substitution as clearly as rice. Increases in the wheat loan rate in the election years 1976 and 1980 have put real market support levels higher at the end of the 1970s than at the beginning. Problems have been avoided so far because real market prices have also been higher. If we compare market prices and loan rates, we see that barley and oats seem to be in about the same position as wheat in the later 1970s. The more important feed grains, corn and grain sorghum, are more problematic. Real loan rates in the late 1970s were raised almost as near market prices as in the 1960s. For sorghum and barley, the sharp increases in target prices were not accompanied by a move toward lower real loan prices.

Further questions about the extent of market orientation in the grains are engendered by the imposition of production controls on the 1978 and 1979 crops of wheat and feed grains. It appears that the budget costs of deficiency payments are as onerous to the government as the costly buildup of stocks under market price supports. As a result, the two-support-price scheme has not delivered the benefits hoped for in resource allocation. In 1978, the Agricultural Stabilization and Conservation Service (ASCS) estimated that 9.6 million acres of wheat and 8.3 million acres of feed grains were idled by programs.[1] The relative impact was greater for wheat in that wheat acreage harvested is only about 60 percent of feed grain acreage. The percentages of wheat acreage idled or grazed under the special grazing and hay program was 14.5 percent of planted acreage in 1978 and 11.4 percent in 1979. Even if, as seems likely in view of production outcomes in these years, the acreage reductions were only about half as effective in reducing output, the programs reduced U.S. wheat production by 6 to 7 percent in these two years. An elasticity of demand of -0.5 to -1.0 implies a range of possible price effects of 6 to 14 percent in raising the price of wheat. Thus set-asides are capable of explaining a substantial fraction of the roughly 15 percent increase in the real price of wheat that occurred in the 1978 and 1979 crop years, although the Soviet production shortfall was probably more important in 1979. These estimates are conjectural and await more precise econometric investigation. My point is simply that set-asides are evidence that the traditional elements of market intervention did not disappear in the grain policies of the 1970s.

Although the future direction of grain policy is uncertain, the effect of traditional government programs on the markets was undeniably less important in the 1970s than earlier in the post–World War II period. It should be recalled, too, that the markets for hog and poultry products were essentially unregulated in the 1970s. Beef, however, provides a counterindication in that new import-restraining legislation was in operation. Although the Meat Import Act became law in the mid-1960s, its main market effects occurred in the 1970s; but it is doubtful it ever caused more than a 1 or 2 percent increase in U.S. prices of cattle or beef.[2] A more dramatic change in the 1970s in the international area was the expiration of the Sugar Act of 1948. It had kept U.S. sugar prices as much as several hundred percent above world prices by means of quantitative import quotas and fees. The new sugar legislation is certainly not a model of market orientation. Though still in flux, it has involved CCC support prices at levels that resulted in substantial government acquisition of sugar, deficiency payments, and import fees that in 1978 placed the U.S. price at almost double the world price. Since mid-1980, however, the sugar market has changed

[1] U.S. Department of Agriculture, Agricultural Stabilization and Conservation Service, *Commodity Fact Sheets*, various dates.

[2] See J. W. Freebairn and G. C. Rausser, "Effects of Changes in the Level of U.S. Beef Imports," *American Journal of Agricultural Economics* (November 1975), pp. 676–88.

so drastically that world prices are about double the U.S. support prices. At this stage both the market and U.S. programs are too volatile to draw any firm conclusions about fundamental policy effects.

Overall, the extent to which farm policy influenced the markets was reduced substantially in the 1970s. To give a full assessment of this influence is beyond my present capabilities. To assess the effects of farm policies in the 1970s is to estimate what events would have occurred if these policies had not been in effect. The assessment depends on the hypothetical, "would have been" situation. This situation depends on the operation of economic forces, which are not well specified quantitatively, under unknown circumstances. Part of these circumstances consists of the policy regime we would have had in the 1970s if we did not have the programs we did have. The preceding discussion has contrasted the behavior of some key variables, mainly prices, in the 1970s and in earlier years.

To conclude this section, let us consider several broader indicators of the extent of market intervention. First, one can estimate an overall degree of protection for U.S. commodities as a weighted average of ratios of prices determined by policy to estimated prices not determined by policy. I have estimated that this ratio varied from 1.88 for sugar to 1.02 for rice and cotton (and 1.0 for hogs, poultry, and soybeans) in 1978–1979, for an overall degree of protection of 1.05 to 1.06;[3] that is, farm programs in this period created prices 5 to 6 percent higher than they would otherwise have been. I do not have a directly comparable measure for the 1950s or 1960s. Some work done earlier suggests a degree of protection in the neighborhood of 1.15 to 1.20 in the early 1960s.[4]

A second rough indicator considers quantities rather than prices: the stocks of commodities held by the Commodity Credit Corporation. Table 1 shows that for all commodities together, and for the major individual commodities except for dairy products, the 1970s were marked by substantially reduced CCC inventories. The main reduction in total value occurred not in the 1970s but in the 1960s, from a peak of $6 billion in 1960 to a $1 billion value at the end of 1967.

Another quantitative indicator of intervention is acreage idled under programs. This amounted to 18 million acres for grains in 1978 but was zero for most years in the 1970s. In contrast, typical grain acreage idled in the 1960s was in the 30- to 40-million-acre range.

[3] Bruce Gardner, *The Governing of U.S. Agriculture* (Lawrence, Kansas: Regents Press, forthcoming).

[4] See G. E. Brandow, "Policy for Commercial Agriculture, 1945–1971," in L. Martin, ed., *A Survey of Agricultural Economics Literature*, vol. 1 (Minneapolis: University of Minnesota Press, 1977), esp. pp. 249–50.

TABLE 1

PRICE-SUPPORTED COMMODITIES OWNED BY
CCC AT FISCAL YEAREND, 1964–1979

Year	Corn (millions of bushels)	Cotton (thousands of bales)	Dairy Products (millions of pounds)	Wheat (millions of bushels)	Value of All Commodities[a] (millions of dollars)
1964	835	7,793	245	712	4,611
1965	530	10,155	163	572	4,110
1966	156	8,389	—	216	2,340
1967	138	1,247	424	109	1,005
1968	261	135	457	100	1,064
1969	296	2,221	284	168	1,784
1970	215	2,077	231	283	1,594
1971	144	—	191	372	1,118
1972	140	—	134	267	830
1973	70	—	20	139	394
1974	6	—	191	15	188
1975	—	—	450	—	402
1976	—	—	479	—	634
1977	1	—	1,001	34	1,104
1978	77	—	900	50	1,186
1979	100	—	805	50	1,162

NOTE: Dashes indicate a negligible amount.

[a] Includes, in addition to commodities itemized, barley, dry beans, flaxseed, sorghum grain, oats, peanuts, rice, rye, soybeans, and tung oil. Values determined by support prices.

SOURCES: U.S. Department of Agriculture, *Agricultural Statistics*, 1979; and Commodity Credit Corporation, *Report of Financial Conditions and Operations*, September 30, 1979.

Thus, the quantity indicators, like the price data, show that although traditional farm programs were not totally inactive in the 1970s, their effects on the markets overall were much smaller than in the 1960s.

Finally, consider the aggregate government payments made to farmers. The picture here changed dramatically in the mid-1970s, particularly in 1974. In the period 1961 through 1973, government payments averaged $3.5 billion (in 1972 dollars) per year. They were quite stable from year to year, never falling below $2.2 billion or rising above $4.3 billion. Payments averaged 20 percent of net farm income (11 percent of farm household income from all sources). In contrast, in the post-1973 period, payments averaged $0.8 billion, 5 percent of net farm income and 2½ percent of farm household income from all sources.[5] The distribution of these benefits among resource owners is discussed below.

Market Management by the U.S. Department of Agriculture

The data on CCC stocks of grains are a somewhat misleading indicator of the extent of governmental intervention in the later 1970s. They exclude substantial quantities of grain owned by farmers but to some extent under the control of the Department of Agriculture. The farmer-owned reserve (FOR) program, introduced in 1977, is the most striking example of governmental intervention going beyond the traditional policy instruments.

Although the USDA has long conducted stabilization policy through its CCC commodity stocks, such policy was a byproduct of farm price and income support. Support objectives tended to take precedence over stabilization objectives. Indeed, farm interests to this day express ambivalence about price stabilization per se as a policy goal. Recent work by economists has seriously questioned whether producers gain from price stabilization.[6]

The stabilization programs introduced in the 1970s seem to be one of the rare instances of economic policy whose primary impetus came from economists rather than from the political power of interested parties. The commodity price increases of the mid-1970s were widely seen as a social problem that required national, and even international, policy remedies. This view was reflected in the World Food Conference of 1974 and supported by the Nixon-Ford administration, especially within the State Department. Independent observers tended to agree but emphasized governmental responsibility for past policy failures in arguing for new policies. John Schnittker, for example, gave five reasons

[5] Data from U.S. Department of Agriculture, *Farm Income Statistics*, October 1979.

[6] See the survey of recent work in S. J. Turnovsky, "The Distribution of Welfare Gains from Stabilization: A Survey of Some Theoretical Issues," in F. G. Adams and S. A. Klein, eds., *Stabilizing World Commodity Markets* (Lexington, Mass.: Lexington Books, 1978), pp. 119–48. Willard W. Cochrane, in "Some Nonconformist Thoughts on Welfare Economics and Commodity Stabilization Policy," *American Journal of Agricultural Economics* (August 1980), pp. 508–11, argues that the results obtained depend on a uselessly complicated and even frivolous view of how people think and behave. Actually, the question from the producers' side is simply whether they can expect to receive greater or lesser returns, on average, under stabilized or unstabilized prices. This indeed turns out to be a complicated issue, but the literature is valuable, if for no other reason, in demonstrating the relevance of the statement to which this footnote refers.

for the price increases of 1972–1973, three of which were policy moves by the U.S. government and two of which he regarded as mistakes in agricultural stabilization policy.[7]

Though somewhat skeptical about the outcome, the Ford and Carter administrations participated in international negotiations for coordinated grain reserves. The negotiations eventually proved fruitless. The Department of Agriculture under Bob Bergland, however, was substantially more favorably disposed to introducing some sort of domestic stabilization program than under Earl Butz. Within three months of coming to power, the Carter administration introduced the farmer-owned reserve program. Congress included the program in the Food and Agriculture Act of 1977.

The FOR program has become quite complex, but its essential features are simple. It is an attempt to establish federally managed, subsidized holding of grain stocks by farmers. The subsidy in itself should lead to increased mean stocks and hence increased price stability. The federal management was introduced, as I understand it, because it was felt that farmers could not be relied upon to add to and sell from stocks in such a way as to stabilize prices optimally.

The main instrument for federal management of FOR stocks, and hence of the grain markets, is the requirement that producers not sell FOR grain within a three-year period unless market prices reach specified levels, or else the storage subsidies will be forfeited. When market prices exceed certain levels, steps are taken to encourage farmers no longer to hold grain. The Department of Agriculture has never, to my knowledge, given a clear rationale that these trigger prices should be at any particular level or that there should be any trigger prices at all. If a farmer wishes to hold wheat at $5.50 per bushel, why discourage him from doing so? Presumably because the department knows that this is an abnormally high price and should be brought down. If the department is wrong, however, it will make the same mistake that was made in 1972—unloading stocks before the real shortage appears. If a farmer has a hunch about this eventuality, why not permit or even encourage him to hold stocks against the prospect?

The number of changes in trigger prices, the interpretation of when a given trigger price has been reached, and the various steps taken when it has been triggered, all indicate uncertainty within the Department of Agriculture on just how the grain markets ought to be

---

[7] John Schnittker, "The 1972–73 Food Price Spiral," *Brookings Papers on Economic Activity*, vol. 2 (1973), pp. 498–507. Perhaps the most glaring error was the announcement of wheat set-asides for the 1973 crop in July 1972 and the maintenance of this policy throughout the planting season for winter wheat. See also Fred Sanderson, "The Great Food Fumble," *Science* (May 1975), pp. 503–9.

managed. Generally, more emphasis is put on very short term stabilization than is implicit in the basic idea of the FOR. The reserves concept seems most readily applicable to carry-over stocks in pursuit of price stability on a year-to-year basis, so that prices will not vary as widely between years of plenty and years of scarcity. This approach would call for only annual determinations (or perhaps semiannual, based on Southern Hemisphere crop outcome) of storage subsidies or release triggers. Prices would have to remain on average above trigger levels for a period of several months at least before policy changes would be made. Instead, the Department of Agriculture announces program changes almost weekly. For this sort of short-term market management, the government really should have its own stocks out of which to buy and sell. With its bids to buy and sell in the first half of 1980, the department became in fact more of a direct short-term market manager. It seems to desire to perform something like the market-making functions of a specialist on the floor of the New York Stock Exchange. Why the department wants to undertake short-term market management, or believes that it can do the job well, I do not know. My point here is that this is an important area of commodity policy as we enter the 1980s and, contrary to trends in the traditional programs, it is moving away from market orientation.

While the evidence is fragmentary, let us consider the likely effects of the FOR program to date. By the end of the 1978–1979 marketing year (ending on May 31 for wheat and September 30 for corn), reserve stocks of these two commodities were 34.4 million metric tons, 42 percent of the total of 57.9 million tons of carry-over wheat and corn.[8] This quantity of stock could have a substantial stabilizing effect. It is not clear, however, that the program added as much to total stocks because farmers and others would probably have held larger speculative stocks if FOR stocks did not exist to limit the potential for future price increases. Some relevant data are shown in figure 2. In these diagrams, ending stocks of corn and wheat are plotted against the deflated price, averaged over the season, received by farmers. The downward slope of any function fitted to these points indicates that lower prices are associated with larger carry-over stocks. This behavior is sensible when prices fluctuate randomly with a relatively fixed mean because low prices increase the opportunity for profitable speculative storage. The functional relationship between price and stocks is labeled the reservation demand for grain stocks. The question is whether the FOR program has increased the stocks held at a given price (or, alternatively,

---

[8] U.S. Department of Agriculture, *Agricultural Supply and Demand Estimates*, July 17, 1980.

FIGURE 2

RESERVATION DEMAND FOR ENDING STOCKS

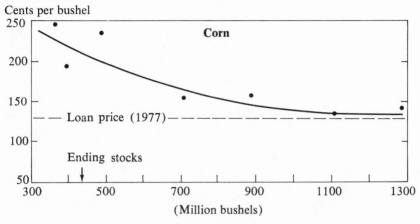

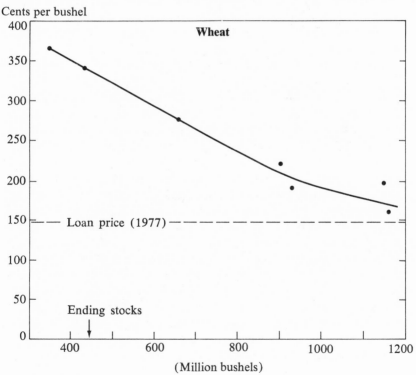

NOTE: Cents per bushel are measured in 1972 dollars.
SOURCE: Author.

increased the price associated with given stocks). If the program had no effects, the same function would fit all the points. Positive effects would be indicated by points for the 1977, 1978, and 1979 crop years to the right of the pre-FOR demand function. For wheat, there is no immediately apparent effect. For corn, a strong effect of the program would be indicated by a linear function fitted through the 1973 to 1976 points, but a nonlinear function is clearly appropriate for corn and probably for wheat, too. The reason, apart from any behavioral characteristics of stockholders, is the existence of the market support price at a level just below the point labeled 77 in figure 2 for both corn and wheat. It is not clear that the FOR program has added significantly more to either corn or wheat stocks than would have been achieved by the CCC loan program without it.

The preceding analysis is admittedly a crude attempt to measure the effects of the program. More detailed econometric analyses have indicated larger effects, perhaps one bushel of added total stocks for every three to five bushels placed in the reserve. I have estimated net price stabilization benefits of about $75 million from a reserve program of this order of effectiveness and of the size achieved in 1978–1979, at a cost to the government of about $250 million. Much of this cost, however, is a transfer to farmers, paying them to store grain they would have stored anyway, and so does not constitute a net social cost. The real resource costs of the program appear to be of the same order of magnitude as the social benefits, as expected from a reasonably conducted price stabilization program.

The social benefits referred to are hypothetical, based on expected year-to-year price stabilization caused by increased carry-over stocks. Directly observable market management under the FOR pertains to short-term price movements. The Council of Economic Advisers analyzed the record of the program as follows:

> The first test of how well the managed reserve concept could weather a period of tight supplies occurred in the spring of 1979. . . . Even with the prospect that world carryover stocks might decline more severely than in 1972, a rapid rise in grain prices was avoided. The price increases in the late spring brought the wheat and the feed grain reserves into release status. . . . As this grain came into the market the price increase slowed. . . . The concept of a farmer-owned grain reserve has been tested, at least to a point, and has proved capable of moderating volatility in grain prices.[9]

[9] Council of Economic Advisers, *Economic Report of the President* (January 1980), pp. 151–52, 154.

The analytical basis for this judgment has not been made public, and there is some question whether any such basis exists, apart from observation of the raw data. The data clearly show that grain went into the FOR in 1978 and came out in 1979. But, as the preceding discussion indicates, it is not clear that there was a large effect on total stocks.

To look a little more systematically at short-term effects on price stability of grain market management under the FOR, I compared the variability of daily wheat and corn prices for two twenty-seven-month periods. The first is pre-FOR, from January 1975 through March 1977. The second is under the FOR, from January 1978 to March 1980. Both periods contain unexpected Soviet purchases in the summer of the first year, with resulting sudden price increases, and both periods contain embargoes of grain sales to the Soviets lasting about three months. The coefficient of variation of the daily cash wheat price at Chicago was 13.8 (standard deviation of 46 cents divided by mean of 334 cents per bushel) in the pre-FOR period. It was 14.3 under the FOR. Similarly, the coefficient of variation of the daily cash corn price at Chicago increased from 8.3 before the FOR to 10.1 under the FOR. Moreover, the short-term price increases associated with news of Soviet production shortfalls were about the same in June and July 1979 as in July and August 1975.

The question immediately arises whether the two periods differed in other significant respects besides the FOR that could have caused increased instability. Perhaps the exogenous shocks were greater in 1977–1980? The most notable shock, the Soviet grain production shortfall, was a little larger in 1975. The main difference I could find is that mean stocks were substantially larger in the FOR period for both corn and wheat. This, however, should have promoted stability under the FOR and so could not have biased downward the raw data's indication of FOR short-term ineffectiveness. As a rough control variable, consider soybeans, for which there was no FOR. The coefficient of variation of the daily soybean price at Chicago declined from 16.7 in the pre-FOR period to 8.1 under the FOR. Therefore, it provides no indication of a generally more volatile economic environment that FOR management had to deal with than in the pre-FOR period.

My provisional conclusion is that if short-term market management under the FOR has had any effects at all on price variability, they have been perverse. My hypothesis on the reason is that the release and call trigger prices increase the volatility of prices in the range between the CCC loan price and the release price, even though the FOR may well reduce the probability of prices above the release price.

Further work is needed to accept or reject either the conclusion or the hypothesis with confidence.

Regulation of Resource and Product Markets

Protection against Natural Hazards. The 1973 and 1977 acts expanded the governmental role in insuring farmers against economic losses due to crop failure. This Disaster Payments Program, especially under the 1973 act, is far from insurance of the type a profit-seeking commercial enterprise would provide. Since 1974 disaster payments have been in the range of $300 to $600 million per year for grains and cotton. Other commodities are not covered. No premiums are charged for this insurance, but benefits have been conditioned on participation in set-asides in some cases. While the modifications of the 1977 act should have reduced the demand for disasters somewhat, the availability of disaster payments still serves to encourage the expansion of farming into marginal producing areas where the risk of crop loss would ordinarily make production uneconomic. In the 1976–1978 period, the humid eastern Corn Belt states of Iowa, Indiana, and Ohio received only 3 percent of the feed grains payments although they normally produce about 30 percent of U.S. feed grains. The overall resource-allocation effects of disaster payments have not been assessed system-atically, but Miller and Walter's localized study suggests that the effects may be substantial.[10]

Other production insurance programs of the 1970s include emergency feed programs, hay and cattle transportation payments, and bee-keepers' indemnity payments. They totaled $110 million in 1977 and $169 million in 1978. The beekeeper indemnity program, a small but particularly striking example of distorted incentives that compensates beekeepers for bees killed by pesticides, appears to be on its way out of existence. But the general thrust is toward expanded intervention in this area.

The Carter administration sought from the beginning to develop and enact a comprehensive, all-risk, subsidized production insurance program. The subsidies would inevitably continue the resource-allocation problem of encouraging production practices more risky than warranted from the social-welfare point of view. The ready availability of special loan and loan-guarantee programs in officially declared disaster areas has a similar effect.

[10] T. A. Miller and A. S. Walter, "An Assessment of Governmental Programs That Protect Agricultural Producers from Natural Risks," *Agricultural-Food Policy Review* (January 1977), pp. 93–103.

Beneficiaries of 1970s Farm Programs. The disaster payments beneficiaries are expected to be the owners of assets intensive in high-risk farm production. These are predominantly the owners of land in drought-prone but not irrigated areas or of land subject to flooding or other natural hazards.

The concentration of program benefits on landowners is consistent with the pattern found by earlier investigators for traditional farm programs. The lower degree of protection of farm commodity prices in the 1970s than in previous periods means, however, that capitalized program benefits must have been substantially smaller. Even in tobacco and peanuts, the maintenance of previously existing programs probably resulted primarily in the avoidance of capital losses by landowners.

It might be thought that a substantial potential for creation of new rents and asset values was created by the wheat program of the 1977 act. I argued above that set-asides in 1978 and 1979 increased the price of wheat by perhaps 10 percent. In addition, deficiency payments on the 1977 and 1978 crops amounted to about 15 percent of the price. The consequences of these gains for income distribution, however, are not necessarily favorable to land because of the tying of program benefits to set-asides.

The analysis of gains and losses under this policy regime is somewhat complicated. It can best be explained with the aid of figure 3. The top panel of figure 3 shows a constrained product-market equilibrium under deficiency payments sufficient to guarantee target price PT, but with payments contingent on set-asides that shift the supply of land and output from S to S'. Price in the absence of any program would be PE, with corresponding input prices RE and WE. The offer of the PT guarantee induces output expansion, but it must take place along the constrained supply curve S'. The resulting production equilibrium is at point w, with output QC. This quantity clears the market at price PC, which is the price paid by users of the product. The positions of PT, PC, and PE are chosen to be consistent with the effects of the 1978 wheat program—market price about 10 percent above the no-program price, with deficiency payments resulting in a producer price about 15 percent above the market price ($PT = \$3.40$, $PC = \$2.94$, $PE = \$2.65$ per bushel).

The losers from this program are taxpayers, who pay an amount equal to $(PT - PC) \times QC$ to farmers (amounting to about \$1 billion), and consumers, who lose consumers' surplus equal to the difference $(PC - PE)$ between the vertical axis and the demand function. The gains to farmers are equal to area $A - B - N$. A is new producers' surplus (aggregate of rents to agricultural factor owners) between points PT, PE, w, and x. B is loss of previously received pro-

FIGURE 3

GAINERS AND LOSERS FROM DEFICIENCY PAYMENTS CONTINGENT ON SET-ASIDES

Product Market

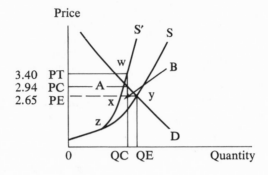

Land Market   **Nonland Input Market**

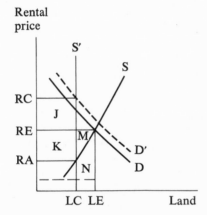
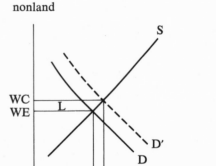

SOURCE: Author.

ducers' surplus within points x, y, and z. N (in the land market) is loss of revenue from set-aside land. If set-aside land were allowed to go into its best alternative use, such as a substitute crop, area N would not be lost. The requirement that this land be placed in low-return uses means, however, that the opportunity returns are not given by land's supply function S but have some lower value, shown as RA in the figure.

Subtracting consumers' and taxpayers' losses from producers' gains gives the net social cost of this program, which is the shaded area in the upper diagram plus area N. The social cost for this program relative to the market value of the commodity tends to be substantially higher than for simple subsidies without set-asides.

It is possible that area $A - B - N$ could be negative, in which case producers would not participate in set-asides, would forfeit deficiency payments, and we would end up at PE, QE. That the program drew participation indicates that producers expected to profit; that about half the producers chose not to participate may be taken as evidence that the producer benefits were in fact small. There is, however, a free-rider problem in that, given participation by everyone else, a nonparticipating producer will receive PC, not PE, since others' set-asides suffice to boost the market price. Therefore, that many producers chose not to participate does not imply that aggregate net benefits were small. If the schema of figure 3 is roughly correct, net producer benefits of the wheat program may have amounted to something like half the consumer and taxpayer costs, perhaps $600–900 million per year.

With respect to income distribution issues, first consider the representation of the land market in figure 3. The derived demand for land is increased to D' by the target price, but acreage is held to S' by set-asides. New rents gained are area J. Old rents lost are area $M + N$. Thus net gains to landowners are $J - M - N$. A sufficient but not necessary condition for landowners to be gainers is that the derived demand curve for land be inelastic. Landowners could be losers if demand was elastic, the shift from D to D' was small, and RA was low. It is quite unlikely, however, that the demand for wheat land, or any agricultural land, is elastic enough. Using the derived demand elasticity formula of Hicks,[11] the largest elasticity is attained when other (nonland) inputs are perfectly elastic in supply, in which case the elasticity of demand for land is a weighted average of the elasticity of substitution between land and nonland inputs in production and the elasticity of final product demand. These are unlikely to average more than 1 in absolute value. Using what seem to me plausible values (elasticity of substitution, 0.5; elasticity of wheat demand, -0.7; nonland input supply elasticity, 2.0; land's relative share of costs, 0.3), the resulting elasticity of derived demand for land is -0.56.

With respect to nonland inputs, the target price will tend to increase the demand for them. This effect will be reinforced by set-asides if the elasticity of substitution between land and nonland inputs exceeds the elasticity of product demand but will tend to be offset if the product demand elasticity is greater (in absolute value), as my "plausible" parameters have it. Given the demand shift, the change in rents

[11] J. R. Hicks, *The Theory of Wages* (New York: Macmillan, 1932).

to nonland inputs, area L in figure 3, is determined by the elasticity of supply of these inputs. Floyd's finding, however, that income redistribution relatively favorable to land results from price supports whenever land is less elastic in supply than nonland inputs does not hold for a program of this type.[12]

The lack of clear income redistribution effects from the wheat program and the reduced importance of traditional programs in the 1970s suggest that income redistribution and asset-value effects may have been quite minor in recent years. The new emphasis on stabilization and insurance programs suggests that more significant effects may have been in the risk-taking and managerial areas. The increased importance of subsidized-credit programs probably works in the same direction. This leads to the question of the structural consequences of agricultural policy in the 1970s. I do not have any evidence or good ideas to offer on this subject, however, and leave it as a possibly fruitful area for future research.

Regulation of Middlemen. While the consequences cannot be assessed with confidence, a treatment of agricultural policies in the 1970s would be seriously incomplete without some discussion of product-market regulation. The 1970s experienced a substantial amount of institutional innovation in marketing, with proliferating schemes of forward contracting, risk sharing, pricing, development of futures and options strategies, vertical integration, promotional activities, and information services. Governmental efforts concentrated on attempts variously to socialize, regulate, or prohibit these activities.

New efforts to regulate marketing activities were initiated by the grain inspection titles in the 1977 act, by various product-promotion laws, by legislation to promote direct marketing of farm products to consumers, and by increasing involvement in international marketing (such as bilateral agreements to guarantee access to U.S. markets). These efforts have not received detailed analysis. Their effects have probably not been great. Though motivated to some extent by mistrust of middlemen, these moves have apparently not affected the private marketing sector significantly. More important may have been continued attempts to support activities of cooperatives in commodity storage, handling, and trade as against other profit-seeking private businesses. But there are no apparent major trends in this area either, and large dairy cooperatives especially are engaged in defensive action against consumer-protection regulation.

[12] J. E. Floyd, "The Effects of Farm Price Supports on the Returns to Land and Labor in Agriculture," *Journal of Political Economy* (April 1965), pp. 148–58.

To me the most significant, and potentially socially harmful, new regulatory actions of the 1970s were the attempts to stifle innovation and change in contracting, pricing, and risk sharing. It is easier to license a nuclear power plant in the wake of Three Mile Island than to win permission from the Commodity Futures Trading Commission to trade in commodity options. The government seems to desire a more active role as referee in all manner of pricing and contracting arrangements. The goal of influencing farm structure may lead to further steps in this direction.

The 1970s also witnessed expanding regulatory interest in food safety, labeling of product weight and ingredients, nutrition, the safety and economic benefits of farm workers, environmental regulation, and control of land use and sales. An assessment of the consequences of these interventions is beyond the scope of this paper, and indeed the economic literature on these topics, though expanding, is still quite sketchy.

The chief problematical element of the emerging agenda of market management and regulation is the tremendous amount of general and specific knowledge, both positive and normative, necessary for socially beneficial government action in these areas. The Department of Agriculture is being called upon by Congress to undertake, and is taking upon itself, impossible managerial tasks. Department officials, for example, declare their intention of establishing support prices necessary to bring long-term capital into agriculture without causing surpluses or of establishing the most suitable floor and ceiling prices for grain price stability. In all the department publications on commodity economics, however, one searches in vain for a scientific basis for determining such prices or price ranges. We see only extremely ad hoc rationales and assurances in congressional testimony or in speeches by department officials. We do not see detailed analytical bases for these policy decisions because they do not exist. The problems are simply too difficult. In these circumstances, failure to attain optimality seems assured. Agricultural economists will probably find as much gainful employment assessing and attempting to correct government failure in the future as they have done with market failure in the past.

Concluding Remarks

Although this paper has discussed consequences of agricultural policies in the 1970s, I believe it is fair to say that the primary movers of events in the farm sector were not matters of agricultural policy. As argued in the first section, the traditional farm programs had much less impact in the 1970s than in earlier years. Ironically, liberal opinion leaders who had traditionally been somewhat sympathetic to New Deal–type farm programs are now taking in some cases an exaggerated antiprogram stance. For example: "The farmer is protected against every contingency by a dizzying array of federal assistance programs that make the Chrysler bailout look like small change."[13] This statement accurately senses a new comprehensiveness in governmental attempts to manage markets, regulate behavior, and cushion random hazards, but these efforts have not yet generated anything like the impact on the farm sector that the traditional programs had in the 1950s and 1960s.

I hypothesize that governmental action in nonagricultural areas—monetary policy, international trade policy, tax policy—made more difference to the farm sector in the 1970s than explicitly agricultural policy. Perhaps the most fundamental service that government can provide is stability in the socioeconomic environment, a task at which the record of the U.S. government in the 1970s is not good. To go one step further, however, I believe that the main movers of farm prices and incomes in the 1970s were not matters of policy at all. I say this not so much to pay homage to the weather, the corn blights, or Soviet grain shortfalls, but in recognition of the widespread and still increasing integration of the farm and nonfarm economies. One simply cannot greatly influence the returns to labor in agriculture for any sustained period because of the opportunity wages available in the nonfarm sector. The same is even true to some extent of the land market. But, most important, it is true of the capital market, where investment in farm enterprises must meet the test of promising returns comparable to returns available in nonfarm enterprises. This applies not only to the banker and the off-farm investor but increasingly to the farm operator.[14] These developments suggest not only that input prices and returns to resources in the farm sector are highly susceptible to nonfarm events but also that these prices and returns are not so susceptible to specifically agricultural policy as was once the case.[15]

---

[13] "Farming for Dollars," *New Republic* (July 19, 1980), p. 12.

[14] For an interesting discussion of the importance of off-farm investment by farmers, see D. W. Hughes, "Measuring Farm Operators' Nonfarm Wealth" (Paper presented at American Agricultural Economics Association meetings, Pullman, Washington, August 1977).

[15] I have discussed evidence on this proposition further in "Seasonal Farm Labor and U.S. Farm Policy," U.S. Department of Labor, forthcoming, and in "The Impact of Recession on the Rural/Farm Economy," *Southern Journal of Agricultural Economics*, vol. 8 (July 1976), pp. 13–22. See also literature cited in these papers.

Commentary

Phillip F. Sisson

The facts presented by Dr. Penn are not disputable, since they are generally part of the record. My remarks will be oriented toward concerns generated by developments in agriculture during the 1970s.

U.S. farm income during the 1970s rose to new peaks, over $33 billion in 1973 and in 1979, but the ravages of inflation resulted in average net income for the decade in 1967 dollars virtually the same as in the 1960s. In addition, the vagaries of weather, both in the United States and in foreign areas, have contributed to a range in real net farm income between $10.9 and $25.1 billion over the past decade. In 1980 net farm income will be less than $10 billion.

The rapidly rising and extremely volatile prices for commodities create major problems for U.S. farmers, food processors, and consumers, as well as for foreign buyers. The years when farm incomes have risen rapidly are also the years with large increases in expenditures by U.S. consumers for food. These same years have coincided either with shortfalls in U.S. agricultural production or with major increases of demand from foreign buyers as a result of weather-related reductions in production or growth in demand that could most easily and inexpensively be met by purchases from the United States.

One major problem with world food and agricultural policy during the 1970s is that the shortfalls in production, whether of U.S. or of foreign origin, have been absorbed by U.S. consumers, most other users around the world feeling little or no impact of the higher world prices. The European Economic Community, with its high protective tariffs, felt none of the impact of the sharp commodity price adjustments that occurred in 1973 and 1974 and the volatility since then. Certain products may not have been available to the Soviet and East European consumer, but prices for available products were unchanged as these governments continued to subsidize food prices. These are only examples. Many other nations have similar policies.

One of the most devastating impacts on U.S. agriculture as well as U.S. consumers and the economy in general is the inflation experienced during the latter half of the 1970s. One of the hidden costs of inflation is that U.S. resources must be exported. A ton of corn or soybean meal costs the foreign buyer the same today in foreign currencies such as the deutsche mark or yen as it did five years ago. The U.S. user's costs are up 30–45 percent. If the foreign buyer's exchange is based on gold, the same ton of corn or soybean meal today costs 75–80 percent less than five years ago. Under those conditions foreign demand for U.S. production should expand greatly as incomes in foreign nations continue to rise. In addition, the cost of energy, an extremely important input to U.S. agricultural production, has risen 160 percent in the United States over the past five years and less than 100 percent in West Germany and Japan, while the gold-oriented country has had a drop of over 50 percent in the cost in gold of a barrel of oil.

The marketing bill for U.S. farm foods has increased significantly during the 1970s. The changes have been fairly well in line with changes in farm value. This occurred even while some important changes were taking place in the food distribution channels:

• An increasing percentage of food dollars is being expended in away-from-home eating. (This is a labor-intensive area that has historically paid very low wages now increasing rapidly with the rises in the minimum wage.)
• There has been a significant expansion in the availability and variety of convenience foods and foods in general. The increased demand is attributable to the rise in the number of women in the labor force and to inflation.

The data suggest that returns on equity to food processors and retailers during the last half of the 1970s do not compare favorably with returns to the farm sector. Returns in the first quarter of 1980 imply that investors' returns on average would have been higher for investments in certificates of deposit or money market funds.

Past U.S. agricultural policy has generally been oriented to income supports for cash grain, cotton, peanuts, tobacco, and dairy products. No consideration has historically been given to livestock and poultry. In fact, the supports have generally had an adverse impact on these enterprises. Even price controls were placed on livestock, or at least on meat, while dairy prices continued to be supported. It is time for an appraisal of the policy tools for supporting certain enterprises, especially when they spell very high costs to American consumers and to U.S. taxpayers. Too often the value of these supports is incorporated into land values.

As we look at the past decade and consider the decade of the 1980s, there are some very important areas of concern:

- inflation
- the need for major importers of agricultural commodities to have consumer economies that are reflective of world commodity market changes
- the possibility that the major increases in agricultural productivity have already occurred (Penn suggests that no new technologies are just around the corner, the transition to larger production units has been made, and no major economies of scale are possible through future size increases)
- that increases in cropland will come only at high investment cost or increased risks from bringing fragile land areas into cultivation
- that dollar expenditures for agricultural research in the United States are not keeping pace with inflationary increases (within the private sector, the real dollar expenditures are down significantly from their peak)
- the indications that weather is becoming increasingly more variable from year to year as well as throughout the year (many climatologists suggest that this variablity will increase, not decrease, over the next decade, adding to more uncertainty for agricultural production and volatility in commodity prices)

Agricultural policy in the 1980s is facing a considerably different set of uncertainties that will require new policy tools different from those of the 1970s, when the transition from surpluses to an agricultural economy oriented to world markets began to occur.

W. E. Hamilton

Professor Gardner has presented an interesting and provocative paper. Since I have not been engaged in econometric research, I assume that my role is to supplement his observations, to present a different perspective where possible, and to raise questions. Insofar as possible, I shall try to follow his outline.

Developments in Traditional Programs

I do not think we should find it surprising that "the Republican and Democratic administrations of the 1970s were both pleased to describe their farm policies as market oriented." Popular support for the idea of a "market-oriented agriculture" grew out of frustrations engendered by earlier programs that discouraged consumption, limited access to foreign markets, piled up huge government-owned surpluses, and subjected producers of some commodities to mandatory production controls based on outmoded historical records. As many observers have noted, agricultural policy develops in an evolutionary fashion; so it is only natural that recent administrations of both parties have used the term "market-oriented" to indicate that their policies have been different from those of the 1950s and 1960s.

Again, I do not find it surprising that the record with regard to the relative dedication of Republican and Democratic administrations to market-oriented policies is somewhat ambiguous. Regardless of party, an administration must work within the framework of laws written by the Congress. The Congress has been overwhelmingly Democratic, and Republicans from farm areas often tend to favor a considerable amount of governmental intervention in agriculture. Finally, both legislative and administrative decisions are strongly influenced by current conditions, the specifics of individual commodity situations, and the attitudes of producer groups toward governmental programs.

The "difference between the average price received by farmers for a commodity and the support price" is an important indicator of market orientation, but it has limitations due to significant differences in key features of the various commodity programs.

The task of measuring changes in market orientation is easiest for soybeans, since the only program authorized for soybeans is a commodity loan. Loan rates are at the discretion of the secretary of agriculture, and producers generally have been restrained in their requests for higher rates. Thus changes in the difference between the loan level and the price of soybeans may be one of the best available indications of the influence of party dominance of the executive branch on market orientation.

Cotton presents a different situation because recent laws have virtually eliminated administrative discretion by tying the cotton loan rate to market prices. This action was taken to prevent the loan rate from being set at a level that would price cotton out of the market and pile up government-owned surpluses. It thus represented a definite shift by the Congress toward market orientation.

The record of the dairy price support program during the 1970s seems to me to reflect opportunism on the part of the advocates of higher supports and a little understood aspect of the parity formula. Price supports were raised during a period of relative shortage in the early 1970s, and the Congress was persuaded to raise the minimum support to 80 percent of parity. One of the arguments used for higher supports in this period was that they would not cost anything because market prices were above the proposed support levels.

The establishment of a higher minimum support level for dairy products was a definite step away from market orientation, which has continued to affect operation of the dairy program. Because of the nature of the modernized parity formula, the 80-percent-of-parity minimum support level has exerted an upward pressure on the parity price of milk. As a result, support prices for dairy products have tended to rise faster than the parity index. (Actual prices enter into the computation of parity prices, because base prices are recalculated annually by dividing the most recent ten-year average of the prices received for a commodity by the ten-year average index of prices received for all farm commodities. As a result, anything, including a price support program, that causes the price of a commodity to rise faster than the average of all farm commodity prices increases the base price of that commodity for the determination of future parity prices.)

Although the peanut and tobacco programs are similar in many respects, there are important differences. Market prices have been closer to support prices for peanuts than for tobacco because production controls have been used more effectively for tobacco. Generally speaking, tobacco producers have had a strong commitment to the idea that they have a responsibility to keep supplies in line with demand in return for price support, and they have supported a number of legislative and administrative changes designed to make the control program more effective. There is, however, some reason to believe that tobacco growers are becoming more concerned about the effect of price supports on their ability to compete for markets. Peanut producers have supported production controls, but they have also supported a minimum national allotment, which has limited the effectiveness of efforts to control peanut production.

Rice is somewhat different from other grains in that it has been more dependent on governmental assistance in the form of Public Law 480 exports. I am not sure that rice would show "the strongest move toward market orientation" if Public Law 480 exports were taken into consideration. In comparing recent trends in the loan rates for rice and other grains, it should be noted that the maximum loan rates for rice are established by statutory formula but that it has been possible to increase the rates for other grains by administrative action.

The establishment of set-aside provisions for the 1978 and 1979 crops of wheat and feed grains must be classed as a move away from market orientation. I would not, however, refer to these programs as "production controls." The set-aside and acreage diversion programs authorized by current laws are voluntary, and participation has been relatively low, particularly for feed grains. In comparison with the marketing quota programs, which were promulgated for wheat and rice in earlier years, the voluntary nature of recent acreage adjustment programs represents definite progress toward market orientation.

The rice program appears more market oriented than the wheat and feed grain programs, at least in part, because of a quirk in the law that operates against the establishment of a set-aside for rice. Statutory authority for the establishment of an acreage set-aside for rice was imposed on top of an old law that requires the establishment of acreage allotments. Since price support and target price protection are available only for rice grown on allotted acres, a set-aside would impose a new requirement for price support on growers who have allotments and, if anything, encourage farmers who do not hold allotments to expand production. This makes it very difficult for the secretary of agriculture to use his set-aside authority for rice.

Market Management by the U.S. Department of Agriculture

Introduction of the farmer-owned reserve (FOR) program clearly must be classed as an example of increased governmental intervention. On the other hand, it seems to me that the original concept of farmer-owned reserves is more market oriented than the government-owned stocks of earlier years. This judgment is based on the following considerations:

• The legislative authority for the FOR indicates that it was designed specifically to help farmers practice orderly marketing rather than to raise domestic prices above world prices.
• The rules under which reserves are to be operated are announced in advance and are made a part of formal contracts with participating producers.
• Although farmer-owned reserves are designed to encourage participating producers to take certain actions at various times, final decisions are left to the judgment of the individual producers.

The basic rationale of the FOR, as I understand it, is that it would be desirable to reduce the destabilizing effects of variations in domestic production and foreign demand for U.S. grain. The rationale for the trigger points presumably is that there ought to be some limit on how far the government will go in encouraging farmers to withhold grain from the market in a period of rising prices. I find more justification for the release level, which is primarily designed to limit government subsidization of the program, than for the call level, which is more definitely designed to encourage the marketing of reserve grain. I agree that there does not seem to be any rationale for establishing the trigger points at any particular level.

Although I see some merits in the farmer-owned reserve in comparison with government-owned stocks, I also see some dangers. The temptation to use the FOR primarily to limit declines in farm prices and increases in consumer prices—rather than primarily to promote the orderly marketing of large crops—may be too great for administrators to resist. One of the vulnerable aspects of the FOR is that the trigger points are tied to commodity loan rates. The loan rates for wheat and feed grains are subject to administrative discretion. Administrative increases in the loan rates for these commodities, which seem to be characteristic of presidential election years, can lead to higher trigger points and a further reduction in market orientation.

The frequent changes made by the Carter administration in programs that affect prices support the idea that farmer-owned reserves are being used primarily for short-term stabilization. A number of these changes have resulted from the tendency of market prices to fluctuate around the trigger points. This suggests that the role and operation of the trigger points should be reconsidered. It probably should also be noted that at least some of the numerous program changes announced by Department of Agriculture in the first half of 1980 reflected efforts to reduce the shock caused by the president's partial embargo of grain shipments to the Soviet Union.

Regulation of Resource and Product Markets

I share Professor Gardner's misgivings with regard to disaster programs and subsidized crop insurance. These programs are popular with politicians and farmers in disaster-prone areas, but they undoubtedly encourage the misallocation of resources.

While I consider voluntary acreage programs more market oriented than mandatory programs, I agree that the voluntary approach encourages free riders. It has often seemed to me that some of the strongest supporters of voluntary acreage reduction programs are producers who do not expect to participate but expect to benefit from the participation of others. If the income redistribution and asset-value effects of governmental farm programs have, as Professor Gardner suggests, been "quite minor in recent years," I would consider this a positive indication that these programs have become more market oriented.

The new emphasis on stabilization, insurance, and subsidized credit programs noted by Professor Gardner may have been stimulated, at least to some degree, by the higher inflation rates of recent years.

Concluding Remarks

While Professor Gardner has presented a considerable amount of analytical evidence on the effects of governmental farm policies, his paper also illustrates both the complexity of these programs and the difficulty of producing clear-cut, conclusive evidence of what their effects have been. This consideration probably helps to explain why we have some of the programs we now have. There is, however, another reason. It is difficult—and often impossible—to keep politically determined decisions in line with good economics, as revealed by aggregated analyses of costs and effects. The individual farmer who is in an uncomfortable economic situation is likely to be more concerned with his perceived need for assistance than with the aggregate effects of governmental policies; he probably is also more likely to participate in efforts to generate political pressure than the producer who is in a stronger position.

In conclusion, I share Professor Gardner's belief that the primary movers of events in the farm sector in the 1970s were not matters of agricultural or other policy. I also agree that "widespread and still increasing integration of the farm and nonfarm economies" has made prices and returns in the farm sector less susceptible to manipulation by agricultural policy than they once were.

Part
Two

World Food Production, Consumption, and International Trade: Implications for U.S. Agriculture

Timothy Josling

Developments in world agriculture are of vital importance to the U.S. economy and to the farm sector. Sales of American agricultural goods rose from about $15 billion in 1973 to about $40 billion in 1980. Helped at first by high prices, this export boom is now firmly based on rising volume. The U.S. capacity to provide these exports is equally crucial to the world at large. No other major exporting country appears to have the ability to meet growing world food requirements and the need for animal feeds and oilseeds. Despite uncertainties created by the embargo on 17 million tons of grain destined for the Soviet Union, the future demand for U.S. farm products abroad looks strong. This paper discusses some of the developments in world agriculture and in the policies of countries that influence such developments.

The topic of world agricultural development is, of course, too large to be treated in detail in this paper. To keep the task manageable the focus is limited to those aspects of world agriculture that appear to be of direct importance to U.S. agricultural exports. This necessitates the omission of a number of significant subjects, including world hunger, income generation and distribution in poor countries, developments in nonagricultural markets (which will have major bearing on the ability of countries to purchase U.S. farm products), the ability of the United States to continue to supply increasing quantities of farm products, and the detailed policy decisions taken by countries that will influence their actions in agricultural and other markets.

The pattern of U.S. agricultural exports in the 1970s is a convenient starting point for discussing the most significant aspects of world agriculture from the point of view of the U.S. farm industry. After a brief review of this pattern, I will turn to consumption and production trends, policies in other countries, exchange earnings, and

83

TABLE 1

U.S. AGRICULTURAL EXPORTS BY REGION, 1970 AND 1978

Region	1970		1978		Annual Growth 1970–1978[a]
	Millions of $	Percent	Millions of $	Percent	
Western Europe	2,528	34.8	9,451	32.2	17.9
Eastern Europe and U.S.S.R.	185	2.5	2,874	9.8	40.9
Asia	2,717	37.4	10,448	35.5	18.3
Latin America	688	9.5	3,157	10.7	21.0
Canada[b]	826	11.4	1,671	5.7	9.2
Africa	259	3.6	1,644	5.6	26.0
Oceania	54	0.7	150	0.5	13.6
Total	7,259	100.0	29,395	100.0	19.1

NOTE: Columns may not add to totals because of rounding.
[a] Compound rate of growth.
[b] Excluding transshipments.
SOURCE: U.S. Department of Agriculture, *Foreign Agricultural Trade of the United States*, various issues.

other aspects of the relationship between world developments and U.S. agriculture. I will then provide a brief account of some of the international policy options that relate to agricultural trade, followed by a summary indicating the choices for U.S. policy.

U.S. Agricultural Exports during the 1970s

The regional pattern of U.S. exports is shown in table 1. Western Europe and Asia share the lead as regional markets, each taking about one-third of the value of U.S. exports. Both show a slight decline in share since 1970, but this represents a gradual diversification in favor of Africa, Latin America, and Eastern Europe. It is notable that these two major regional markets have both grown at roughly the same rate (18 percent per year) over the decade. For those countries within Western Europe but outside the European Economic Community (EEC), the growth rate has been higher (22.6 percent). Even in the EEC, with a highly protective agricultural policy, however, the value of exports has increased by 16.5 percent per year.

The Asian region (defined to exclude the Soviet Union) includes subregions with rather different characteristics. The newly rich countries of West Asia have increased purchases at a rate of 25 percent per year—an important offset to U.S. oil purchases from that region. South Asia, by contrast, has increased inputs from the United States of farm products by less than 9 percent—the slowest growth of any subregion. The more dynamic economies of East and Southeast Asia, including Japan, have had market growth rates of 17 to 18 percent, representing both increased food purchases and greater specialization in processed agricultural products.

The region with the most dramatic increase in growth rate of export markets is the Soviet bloc (41 percent annually), heavily weighted by the increase in exports to the Soviet Union (80 percent). This figure, however, reflects a low base, and sales to this area in 1978 constituted less than 10 percent of U.S. agricultural exports, about the same proportion as to Latin America. In contrast to sales to Western Europe, which have risen in every year over the period, sales to Eastern Europe and the Soviet Union declined steeply in 1974 and 1977— reflecting the uncertain nature of much of this trade.

Trade with Africa and with Latin America has also been growing steadily, at rates of 26 and 21 percent respectively. The chronic inability of agriculture in Africa to keep up with demand pressures has necessitated a steady increase in imports of basic foodstuffs. Latin American production has also been sluggish, but much of the increase in trade has resulted from specialization in production—somewhat along the lines of U.S. trade developments with Europe. Increased trade with Brazil and Mexico exemplifies this development, although the share of total U.S. agricultural exports going to these countries is small.

The broadly competitive regions of Canada and Oceania have proved less dynamic as markets for U.S. exports, and the share of trade going to them has fallen. In the context of future developments in demand for U.S. products, those regions are important largely in relation to their own export capacity.

U.S. Agricultural Export Trade by Commodity. The commodity composition of U.S. exports gives another view of these developments. Table 2 shows the value of commodity sales over the 1970s. Like the country composition, the pattern has not changed dramatically, although the shifts are significant. The relative importance of grain (from 36 to 39 percent) and oilseed products (from 27 to 28 percent) has risen at the expense of animal products (down from 12 to 10 percent). The share held by cotton is up (from 5 to 6 percent) and by tobacco is down (7 to 5 percent) over the period. Although eight years is a relatively short period in which to look for major shifts in

85

TABLE 2

U.S. Agricultural Exports by Commodity, 1970 and 1978

Commodity	1970		1978		Annual Growth 1970– 1978[a]
	Millions of $	Per-cent	Millions of $	Per-cent	
Animal products and meat	850	11.7	2,975	10.1	17.0
Cotton, raw	372	5.1	1,740	5.9	21.3
Fruits and preparations	334	4.6	1,014	3.4	14.9
Nuts and preparations	69	1.0	324	1.1	21.3
Grains and preparations	2,596	35.8	11,534	39.2	20.5
Oilseeds and products	1,921	26.5	8,355	28.4	20.2
Tobacco, unmanufactured	517	7.1	1,358	4.6	12.8
Vegetables and preparations	206	2.8	676	2.3	16.0
Feeds and fodders (excluding grain)	138	1.9	603	2.1	20.2
Other	256	3.5	816	2.8	15.6
Total	7,259	100.0	29,395	100.0	19.1

[a] Compound rate of growth.

Source: U.S. Department of Agriculture, *FATUS*, various issues.

export patterns, the stability is still notable: the growth in exports has been widely shared among commodities.

In spite of this stability, certain highfliers among the export commodities stand out. Corn exports have increased at 26 percent per year, now accounting for 18 percent of exports—up from 11 percent in 1970. Meat exports are climbing at a rate of over 20 percent per year, though from a low base. Cotton, nuts, wheat, and soybeans have all expanded their markets faster than the average (19 percent), although hides and skins, fruits, rice, and tobacco are among those with a slower growth rate than the total. In terms of absolute size, six of the major product groups (grains, oilseeds, animal products, cotton, tobacco, and fruits) contributed over $1 billion each to U.S. export earnings from agriculture in 1978.

Although changes in the value of commodity trade are an appropriate indication of the earning power of U.S. agriculture, trade volume can be used to confirm that these changes reflect more than just price increases. Table 3 shows the general expansion of the volume of commodity exports over the decade. Poultry (14.5 percent), feed grains (13.8), and meats (12.4) led the pack; vegetable oils (9.7), cotton

TABLE 3

VOLUME OF SELECTED AGRICULTURAL EXPORTS, 1970 AND 1978

(in thousands of metric tons)

Commodity	1970	1978	Annual Growth 1970–1978[a]
Poultry meats	63	186	14.5
Meats and products[b]	159	406	12.4
Wheat and products	19,377	35,469	7.9
Feed grains and products	19,990	56,153	13.8
Rice	1,788	2,171	2.5
Soybeans	11,954	20,705	7.1
Protein meal	3,800	6,424	6.8
Vegetable oils	984	2,063	9.7
Tobacco	242	318	3.5
Cotton	648	1,347	9.6
Feeds (excluding grains)	1,379	2,588	8.2

[a] Compound rate of growth.
[b] Excluding poultry.
SOURCE: U.S. Department of Agriculture, *FATUS*, various issues.

(9.6), and wheat (7.9) also achieved very strong growth. The market for rice (2.5 percent) has not exhibited the same dynamic growth as that for other cereals, and tobacco (3.5 percent) has also had a rate of growth in export volume that is below average.

The volume, or rather the weight, of agricultural trade has a further significance. Transportation and marketing systems will generally have to respond to the quantity rather than the value of commodity movements, as will processing capacity. The dominance of wheat, feed grain, soybeans, and oilseed products in this regard is notable, and the doubling of the quantity handled over this period has necessitated a major expansion of these facilities. Projected quantities have similar implications for the adequacy of the marketing system to handle the products in the future.

U.S. Export Trade with Major Countries. The regional and commodity export patterns give an overview of the development of trade. A discussion of the future market for agricultural exports cannot, however, avoid identifying specific national markets. To complete this brief re-

TABLE 4

U.S. AGRICULTURAL EXPORTS TO
MAJOR COUNTRIES OF DESTINATION, 1970–1978

(in millions of dollars)

Rank in 1978	Country	1970 Value	1970 Per-cent	1978 Value	1978 Per-cent	Annual Growth 1970–1978
1	Japan	1,214	16.7	4,435	15.1	17.7
2	Netherlands	527	7.3	2,327	7.9	20.4
3	U.S.S.R.	16	0.2	1,687	5.7	79.0
4	Canada	826	11.4	1,631	5.5	10.5
5	West Germany	529	7.3	1,502	5.1	13.9
6	Korea	224	3.1	1,148	3.9	22.7
7	United Kingdom	411	5.7	1,051	3.6	12.5
8	Italy	210	2.9	1,001	3.4	21.6
9	Mexico	156	2.1	903	3.1	24.6
10	Taiwan	134	1.8	825	2.8	25.5
11	Spain	143	2.0	821	2.8	24.4
12	People's Rep. of China	0	—	573	1.9	—
13	France	164	2.3	568	1.9	16.8
14	Egypt	26	0.4	554	1.9	46.6
15	Brazil	69	1.0	534	1.8	29.1
16	Poland	51	0.7	503	1.7	33.1
17	Iran	30	0.4	493	1.7	41.9
18	Belgium-Luxembourg	157	2.2	462	1.6	14.4
19	Venezuela	98	1.4	387	1.3	18.7
20	Portugal	35	0.5	371	1.3	34.3
21	Hong Kong	57	0.8	359	1.2	25.9
22	Indonesia	133	1.8	317	1.1	11.5
23	Saudi Arabia	28	0.4	315	1.1	35.3
24	Nigeria	30	0.4	300	1.0.	33.4
25	Israel	97	1.3	298	1.0	15.1
26	India	256	3.5	282	1.0	1.2
	Total, countries above	5,621	77.4	23,647	80.4	19.7
	Total, all countries	7,259	100.0	29,395	100.0	19.1

NOTE: Dashes mean none.
SOURCE: U.S. Department of Agriculture, *FATUS*, various issues.

view of trade patterns over the 1970s, the data for sales to individual countries are shown in tables 4 and 5. The twenty-six countries included in the tables were those that took at least 1 percent of total

TABLE 5

U.S. Agricultural Exports, Principal Commodities, 1978

(in millions of dollars)

Country	Corn	Soy- beans	Soy- bean Oil	Meal	Wheat	Cotton	Rice
Japan	911	1,031	—	58	432	348	—
Netherlands	280	1,135	—	126	141	—	7
U.S.S.R.	1,053	222	—	—	356	—	—
Canada	—	100	16	84	—	65	—
West Germany	217	393	—	221	35	—	26
Korea	209	77	—	—	215	378	—
United Kingdom	185	179	—	—	30	—	—
Italy	241	235	—	149	88	—	—
Mexico	160	179	20	22	89	—	—
Taiwan	196	255	—	—	78	141	—
Spain	155	445	—	60	27	—	—
People's Rep. of China	112	15	26	—	291	157	—
France	—	174	—	44	—	—	—
Egypt	—	—	—	—	155	20	—
Brazil	132	—	—	—	349	—	—
Poland	161	40	—	109	68	—	—
Iran	—	—	73	—	155	—	119
Belgium-Luxembourg	—	—	—	—	—	—	—
Venezuela	—	—	—	—	102	—	—
Portugal	141	39	—	28	81	23	13
Hong Kong	—	—	—	—	—	152	—
Indonesia	—	27	—	—	71	75	117
Saudi Arabia	—	—	—	—	13	—	151
Nigeria	—	—	—	—	106	—	138
Israel	—	99	—	—	68	—	—
India	—	—	163	—	8	—	—
Total, countries above	4,153	4,645	298	901	2,958	1,359	571
Total, all countries	5,237	5,208	569	1,242	4,335	1,740	693

NOTE: Dashes mean none.

SOURCE: U.S. Department of Agriculture, *FATUS*, various issues.

U.S. agricultural exports. Together they account for 84 percent of U.S. exports and contain 71 percent of the world population outside the United States.

Table 4 demonstrates the impressive size of the Japanese market, which absorbed 15 percent of U.S. agricultural exports in 1978. The

Soviet Union stood in third place among individual markets in 1978, ranked behind the Netherlands and ahead of Canada as a trade partner, with West Germany the fifth largest market.[1] Korea, a rapidly industrializing country, was in sixth place, followed by the United Kingdom, Italy, Mexico, and Taiwan. These ten countries maintained their dominance in the market in 1979: preliminary estimates show each country importing products worth at least $1 billion in that year, with the Soviet Union ($2.9 billion) displacing the Netherlands ($2.56 billion) as the second largest market. Taiwan ($1.07 billion) and Mexico ($1.02 billion) caught up with the United Kingdom ($1.06 billion) and Italy ($1.00 billion) in the race to import. Japan, at $5.26 billion, still leads the pack by a wide margin.[2]

The commodity composition of the trade flows in 1978 is presented in table 5. Japan's imports are predominantly in corn and soybeans, although they include sizable cotton and wheat purchases. The Netherlands and West Germany buy corn, soybeans, and meal for their large feed-processing sectors, and the Soviet Union is the largest single market for corn. Feed grains and oilseeds are somewhat less dominant in British and Italian markets and in sales to Korea and Taiwan. Exports to Canada are even more diversified, with considerable sales of fruits, vegetables, live cattle, and other products.

Closing fast on the leading markets are Spain and the People's Republic of China. China promises soon to join the $1 billion club, with estimated purchases of $990 million in 1979, an impressive growth since agricultural sales to China began again in 1972. Wheat and cotton have been the major products exported to China, and Spain has offered a rapidly growing market for soybeans. Other markets that developed quickly during the 1970s include Egypt, perennially in need of wheat; Brazil, importing wheat and corn; Iran, a market for wheat and rice until the change in regime; Saudi Arabia, Indonesia, and Nigeria, buying rice and wheat with oil revenues; and Poland, with substantial imports of feed grains and soybean meal.

To put another perspective on the nature of these twenty-six markets, table 6 gives some comparative data on income, growth, and population. U.S. exports have clearly found a place in the affluent markets of the world. However valid the proposition may be that

[1] The countries of the European Economic Community together account for about 24 percent of U.S. farm exports, a figure that would be increased to 28 percent by including the countries (Spain and Portugal) that are presently negotiating membership in the Common Market.

[2] Detailed trade data by country and commodity for 1979 were not available at the time of writing. These estimates are taken from U.S. Department of Agriculture, *Foreign Agriculture*, May 1980.

American exports go to feed the poor and the hungry in other nations, it is also clear that they help to enrich the diets of the relatively well-to-do. Most of the developed Western nations have both high incomes and significant purchases of farm products from the United States, as do a number of the faster growing developing countries. The larger and the poorer developing countries, such as India, Indonesia, and Nigeria, have a much lower ranking among export destinations for farm products.

Growth in Consumption and Production

The demand for foods and other agricultural products grows in a reasonably predictable way with increases in population and with aggregate income; it responds in a more complex but still measurable way to changes in the age structure, location, and employment of the population and in the distribution of income among households. The demand for particular foods is also influenced by price changes, in particular when the prices of alternative products diverge. More elusive as a determinant of demand is taste, a concept usually employed as a catchall for behavior not measurable by economic and demographic means.

The response of demand to increases in income itself varies in a reasonably regular way. People in subsistence and preindustrial economies tend to spend any additional income on food. This income elasticity of demand falls fairly steadily as an economy develops, so that inhabitants of mature and reasonably affluent societies have little propensity to spend additional income on food. The same pattern can be seen in households of different incomes within a society. The range of such income elasticities (for food products) probably extends from about 0.9 at one extreme to not much above 0.1 at the other.[3] Income growth therefore has very different implications for the food sector in different countries. A household or country that spends 70 percent of its present income on food will, if the income elasticity of demand is 0.9, spend 63 percent of its extra income on food; if the proportion of food expenditure is 25 percent and the income elasticity 0.1, the extra spending on food will be 2.5 percent of the additional income. These can be assumed to be the two extremes, with most households or countries falling in between.

Population increases and income growth also seem to be related to the stage of development, though more indirectly. There appears to

[3] There are a number of agricultural products with higher income elasticities than that for food as a whole, but these are found mainly in high-income countries.

TABLE 6

Characteristics of Major Markets for U.S. Agricultural Exports

Rank[a]	Country	1976 Population (in millions)	1976 Income per Capita (in dollars)	Annual Income Growth 1960–1976 (percent)	U.S. Agricultural Sales, 1978 (in million $)	U.S. Agricultural Sales per Capita, 1978[b] Value ($)	Rank[c]
1	Japan	112.8	4,910	7.9	4,435	39.3	(7)
2	Netherlands	13.8	6,200	3.7	2,327	168.6	(1)
3	U.S.S.R.	256.7	2,760	3.8	1,687	6.6	(21)
4	Canada	23.2	7,510	3.5	1,631	70.3	(4)
5	West Germany	62.0	7,380	3.4	1,502	24.2	(12)
6	Korea (Rep.)	36.0	670	7.3	1,148	31.9	(10)
7	United Kingdom	56.1	4,020	2.2	1,051	18.7	(14)
8	Italy	56.2	3,050	3.8	1,001	17.8	(15)
9	Mexico	62.0	1,090	3.0	903	14.6	(17)
10	Taiwan	16.3	1,070	6.3	825	50.6	(5)
11	Spain	35.7	2,920	5.5	821	23.0	(13)
12	People's Rep. of China	835.8	410	5.2	573	0.7	(25)
13	France	52.9	6,550	4.2	568	10.7	(20)
14	Egypt	38.1	280	1.9	554	14.5	(18)
15	Brazil	110.0	1,140	4.8	534	4.9	(22)
16	Poland	34.3	2,860	4.1	503	14.7	(16)

17	Iran	34.3	1,930	8.2	493	14.4 (19)
18	Belgium-Luxembourg	9.8	6,780	4.2	462	47.1 (6)
19	Venezuela	12.4	2,570	2.6	387	31.2 (11)
20	Portugal	9.7	1,690	6.5	371	38.2 (8)
21	Hong Kong	4.5	2,110	6.5	359	79.8 (3)
22	Indonesia	135.2	240	3.4	317	2.3 (24)
23	Saudi Arabia	8.6	4,480	7.0	315	36.6 (9)
24	Nigeria	77.1	380	3.5	300	3.9 (23)
25	Israel	3.6	3,920	4.3	298	82.8 (2)
26	India	620.4	150	1.3	282	0.5 (26)

[a] Rank indicates size of total 1978 market for U.S. agricultural products.
[b] Calculated as the ratio of 1978 sales to 1976 population.
[c] Rank indicates descending order of per capita imports of U.S. agricultural products in 1978.

SOURCES: World Bank, *World Development Report 1978*; and U.S. Department of Agriculture, *FATUS*.

TABLE 7

RANGE OF POSSIBLE VALUES FOR GROWTH IN
DEMAND FOR FOODSTUFFS, BY STAGES OF DEVELOPMENT

	Preindustrial Stage	Rapid-Growth Stage	Mature Stage
Income per capita, annual growth rate (percent)	0.9	2.8	3.4
Income elasticity	0.7–0.9	0.4–0.7	0.1–0.4
Population growth (percent)	2.4	2.7	0.9
Total demand growth (percent)	3.0–3.2	3.8–4.7	1.2–2.3

SOURCE: Per capita incomes and population trends are for 1960–1976 for low-income, middle-income, and industrialized countries as classified by the World Bank. Income elasticities are from Theodor Heidhues, *World Food: Interdependence of Farm and Trade Policies*, Trade Policy Research Centre, International Issues No. 3 (London, 1977).

be a tendency for population to increase somewhat faster in the initial stages of transition from a preindustrial society, together with the increase in the growth in incomes. As the nation matures economically, these population growth rates drop significantly, as does total income growth, although per capita incomes often continue to rise. The effect of the combination of such factors on the demand for agricultural products, particularly food commodities, is illustrated in table 7. One would expect to see demand growing at about 3 percent in low-income countries, rising to perhaps 5 percent when income growth outstrips that of population, and falling back to around 2 percent as consumption switches in affluent societies to other goods.

The implication for future demand is that the relative performance of the world economy will have a considerable impact upon demand for food and other agricultural products. As more developing countries enter the phase of rapid growth, demand for food products will increase. The demand in some of the industrializing countries will slow as incomes approach those typical of developed countries. Any transfers of income from rich to poor countries or households have a significant potential impact on food demand: the net increase in spending on foodstuffs could conceivably be as much as one-half of the total value of the transfer. Using the two households mentioned above, $100 transferred from the rich one to the poor one increases net spending on food by $60.50. Clearly the circumstances surrounding the transfer will influence the impact on food consumption. Conversely, transfers in the other direction retard the growth of demand for food.

In terms of differential income growth, as opposed to uniform expansion of incomes, several recent studies have shown the potential impact on demand for food. One illustration will make the point. It has been estimated that for a typical country with an income of about $500 per capita, an income increase of 4 percent each year enjoyed solely by the poorest 60 percent of the population might raise food consumption by about 3.2 percent annually; if the extra income were distributed proportionately, the increase would be perhaps 1.4 percent; and if it went only to the top 20 percent, the increase in food consumption would be only 0.26 percent.[4] Potential expansion in food demand from progressive income redistribution is clearly substantial if these figures are a guide, although the problems of achieving such major redistribution are such that it may not seem realistic to inject an effect of this size into projections of demand.

The picture of global food demand seems, therefore, to have several slowly moving elements and one more volatile factor. Population increases, though subject to much debate by demographers, are fairly easily predicted within a tolerable margin of error in the short run. Populations of developing countries have increased at about 2.5 percent per year for the last twenty-five years, and even the decrease in fertility recently observed will not make much of an impression over the next decade or so.[5] Any impact of population stability on growth rates in agricultural demand will not be felt within the time scale discussed here. Similarly, income distribution is unlikely to disrupt projections based on past trends, and consumer behavior with respect to food can reasonably be taken as stable. The volatile element is income growth itself. Since this has much to do with the overall development of international economic relationships, the topic is taken up in the section on foreign exchange constraints on trade.

The supply picture is less easy to characterize. There are clearly constraints on land area in the long run, and the availability of technology and resources will be a limiting factor for many countries. But the performance of the world's agricultural sectors varies so greatly from region to region and over time that a uniform pattern is elusive.

[4] These figures are quoted in Albert Simantov, "Outlook for World Agricultural Markets: A General View," in Michael Tracy and Ivan Hodac, eds., *Prospects for Agriculture in the European Economic Community* (Bruges: De Tempel, 1979).

[5] A provocative paper on this subject is Donald J. Bogue, "Policy Implications of the Changing Relationship between Population and Economic Growth," in D. Gale Johnson, ed., *The Politics of Food* (Chicago: Council on Foreign Relations, 1980). It suggests that the world population might stabilize by the first half of the next century. But even their lowest projections give a world population of 5.8 billion in the year 2000, compared with "official" estimates of 5.9 billion (World Bank), 6.2 billion (United Nations), and 6.4 billion (U.S. Census Bureau), and an actual 4.0 billion in 1976.

TABLE 8

INDEX OF TOTAL PRODUCTION OF CROPS AND LIVESTOCK, 1974–1978, AND ANNUAL RATES OF CHANGE IN RECENT PERIODS

	Index (1969–1971 = 100)					Annual Rate of Change		
	1974	1975	1976	1977	1978[a]	1976–1978[b]	1974–1978[b]	1970–1978[c]
Developing countries	110	116	119	122	125	2.7	3.2	2.9
Developing market economies	109	115	117	121	125	3.0	3.5	2.9
Africa	106	106	110	108	113	1.1	1.6	1.5
Far East	106	115	115	123	126	4.3	4.3	3.0
Latin America	113	117	122	126	130	3.0	3.5	3.5
Near East	114	120	126	125	128	0.9	3.4	3.5
Asian centrally planned economies	113	118	121	123	126	2.2	2.6	2.9
Developed countries	110	112	113	116	121	3.1	2.2	2.3
World	110	113	115	119	123	3.0	2.6	2.6

[a] Preliminary.
[b] Compound annual rates of growth from first to last year in period.
[c] Exponential trend over period as a whole.
SOURCE: United Nations Food and Agriculture Organization, *Production Yearbook*, vol. 32.

The trend in agricultural production for the recent past is given in table 8. This shows food production in developing countries increasing at 2.7 percent per year over the period 1976–1978. The last column shows that production since the beginning of the decade, pulled down by the generally slow growth from 1971 to 1973, has increased at a rate of only 2.9 percent each year, about the same as that achieved in the previous decade. This can be compared with the figure of 3.4 percent often used as an estimate of the growth in demand for foodstuffs in developing countries, although, as I have already indicated, this will depend on income trends.[6]

This overall rate of growth hides substantially different experiences among the developing regions. In the period from 1974 to 1978, production in Asia and the Far East rose by 4.3 percent annually while African production increased at only 1.6 percent. Regional growth rates over short periods of time are, of course, heavily influenced by variations in weather, but it is clear that the very low increases in food production in Africa are the result of much more fundamental problems. Per capita food in that continent has declined steadily in recent years to the consternation of agricultural decision makers.

It might be thought that the traumatic experience of developing countries in the food crisis years of 1973–1975 would have caused a noticeable shift in development priorities toward food production and hence an increase in the rate of growth of output. This does not appear to show up either in planned growth rates of agriculture (or cereals) or in the planned proportion of investment going to agriculture. A survey of the national development plans, conducted by the United Nations Food and Agriculture Organization, illustrates this point.[7] The proportion of countries with high agricultural growth targets shows little increase since the food crisis: the corresponding proportions relating to investment plans also show no dramatic shift after 1973. The conclusion based on these plans seems to indicate that little has happened in recent years at the national level to suggest any major swing of resources toward agriculture in developing countries.[8]

If capital investment does not seem to be flowing to agriculture

---

[6] The target rate of growth agreed for the UN second development decade (the 1970s) was 4 percent for developing countries; it is not clear whether anyone seriously expected this target to be achieved.

[7] For more detail on this study, see Food and Agriculture Organization, *International Agricultural Adjustment: Second Progress Report*, FAO conference document C 79/20 (Rome, August 1979).

[8] Data on actual investment in agriculture are scarce for developing countries. United Nations figures on agriculture's share of gross capital formation for about twenty countries where such information is available show it well below the share of agriculture in GDP and possibly declining since the turn of the decade.

in developing countries, the current growth rate in agriculture must be supplied by the use of more land, labor, and such current inputs as fertilizer and by the increased productivity of those inputs. Happily the news is brighter on this front. Land area devoted to arable crops is still expanding at a rate of about 0.7 percent in developing countries, and irrigated land area is increasing by about 2.0 percent. Fertilizer use continues to expand at about 10 percent per year and tractor use by 8 percent.[9] A sampling of countries in Asia where high-yield varieties of wheat and rice have been introduced suggests that the area under these improved varieties is also rising steadily, at a rate of 11 percent for wheat and 14 percent for rice. In the Near East, adoption of these new varieties has progressed even faster, although the proportion of land area being used for these crops is still low. It is premature to dismiss the effect of this "green revolution" on future supply possibilities: the new varieties are presently being harvested on less than 20 percent of cropland, and their impact on food supplies could match that of their dramatic entry into the scene in the late 1960s.

One issue that underlies the question of future supply response is that of climatic change in the world, and especially in the major food-growing areas. There is now considerable evidence of the influence of climatic variables on crop production, and a twenty- to twenty-two-year double sunspot cycle has been linked with cereal yields in the United States. Droughts in the 1930s, the 1950s, and the 1970s have stimulated concern about climatic changes and brought forth a mixture of serious and sensational predictions. Climatologists disagree as often as demographers on questions of long-term trends and turning points. But recent work has tended to confirm the intuitive notion that various cooling and warming trends over time have as many positive as negative effects on food production. Whereas most crops are reasonably well suited to the area in which they grow, they can still benefit from slightly more or less rainfall or warmth. Thus a recent Department of Agriculture study of potential grain production in the year 2000 concluded that, whether we assume a trend of "normal" weather on the one hand or a pronounced warming or cooling trend on the other, there is a difference of less than 1 percent in the outcome, although the regional distribution of grain production could vary considerably.[10]

[9] These figures relate to developing market economies, and are taken from FAO, *International Agricultural Adjustment: Second Progress Report.*

[10] For a fuller discussion of this study and a review of the controversy on climatic change, see Louis M. Thompson, "Climate Change and World Grain Production," in Johnson, *The Politics of Food.*

Domestic Farm and Food Policies. Imports of food products run up against entrenched policy attitudes in both developed and developing countries. Most developing countries seek a high degree of self-sufficiency in basic food products. Among the many reasons is the need to save scarce foreign exchange. The presumed political vulnerability of dependence on imports and the dangers of instability arising from fluctuating import prices are also often cited. In addition, the absence in many cases of adequate internal transportation, the existence of large peasantries unable or unwilling to work in nonfarm employment, and the absolute lack of opportunities for such employment are often as important in persuading governments to emphasize domestic production of basic foods. Stimulating indigenous agriculture is widely seen as an aspect of general economic development.

There are, however, forces that act in the other direction. Large-scale subsidization of agriculture is an expensive business for countries with perhaps three-quarters of their labor force on farms. Indeed, agriculture is often seen as a source of tax revenue rather than as a sector requiring support. Investment plans typically call for expansion in modern industrial sectors rather than in traditional agriculture. Producer prices necessary for expansion often require either higher consumer prices or costly subsidy schemes, neither attractive to governments of developing countries. Moreover, imports of the production requisites and investment goods necessary for expansion of domestic agriculture can put almost as much strain on the payments position as importing the foodstuffs. A continued expansion in food imports by developing countries may be forced on countries by economic circumstances.

The phenomenon of the taxation of agriculture in developed countries is widespread. Theodore Schultz has commented that if one classifies countries into those that overvalue domestic farm production and those that undervalue such output, the developing countries would with few exceptions fall into the second category.[11] This can be seen by comparing the general level of product prices across countries or by comparing output prices with the cost of purchased imports, such as fertilizer. Willis Peterson has calculated the number of kilograms of fertilizer that could be purchased by a farmer with the revenue from 100 kilograms of wheat, or the equivalent value of other products, in a

[11] For a detailed description of the price disincentives in the developing countries, see the article by Theodore W. Schultz in Schultz, ed., *Distortions of Agricultural Incentives* (Bloomington: Indiana University Press, 1978), and articles in the same book by Gilbert Brown, Martin Abel, and D. Gale Johnson.

number of countries.[12] Although his calculations refer to the 1968–1970 period, the relative position of countries will have changed little since then. The range is from 53 kilograms in Japan to 7.1 in Niger. Most developed countries fall, by this measure, between Canada (28 kilograms) and the United States (44 kilograms). By contrast, all of the twenty-seven developing countries for which Peterson collected data fall below 28 kilograms, sixteen countries exhibiting prices that would enable their farmers to buy between 10 and 20 kilograms of fertilizer. Since inorganic fertilizers are widely traded and quite uniform in quality, the main reason for the generally lower input-purchasing power in developing countries is the domestic prices for the product: on average these appear to have been about one-half those found in developed nations.

The desire for self-sufficiency is less a realistic objective than a reflection of the frustrations of domestic policy making. Developing countries find it difficult to raise consumer prices because of the significant impact on the urban electorate. Substantial direct payments to the farm sector are precluded by the small nonrural tax base. Self-sufficiency in this interpretation is not an immediate goal of policy (for any country can be self-sufficient just by banning imports) but an expression of the conditions under which this difficulty would apparently be resolved. The search for technology that will increase production and for an inflow of funds into agricultural investment is an attempt to escape the trap of undervalued agriculture; the reality is that such investment may not, in many cases, be profitable for either the individual producer or the government.

Developed countries have demonstrated a similar ambivalence toward the expansion of trade. Government support has often been generous toward uncompetitive sectors of agriculture in developed countries. Support prices themselves have grown out of line with world market conditions when fixed in relation to domestic inflation rates and income trends. In the period up to 1972, when world market prices for many commodities were low relative even to production costs in exporting countries, protection of domestic agriculture from the impact of these low prices was considerable throughout the industrial world. As world prices rose over the period from 1973 to 1975, domestic policy prices lagged behind, and protection levels fell, in some cases resulting in the effective taxation of farmers through export barriers. The response to subsequent inflation continued, however, and

[12] Willis L. Peterson, "International Farm Prices and the Social Cost of Cheap Food Policies," *American Journal of Agricultural Economics* (February 1979), pp. 12–20.

left agricultural policy prices in many countries on a higher plane when world prices receded again after 1975. Protection levels are once again significant, in particular where internal pricing decisions have taken scant account of market realities.

It is of course possible to recite convincing political factors that appear to compel such countries to maintain protection for less-than-efficient domestic farm production. At the same time, certain pressures contain such action and may modify its long-run impact. Taxpayers are taking a greater interest in the distribution of transfer payments to agriculture as part of a general trend toward greater accountability of government programs. Consumer groups are becoming more aware of the impact of farm policy decisions on food prices. Perhaps as significant, conflicts among domestic fiscal, foreign commercial, and agricultural policies are intensifying, with a weakening of the historical tendency for agricultural interests to prevail. Such factors operate in all industrial countries, whether food exporters or importers, but the credibility of traditional farm support programs is most vulnerable in importing countries.

A third, more subtle factor in both developed and developing countries has tended to act against trade expansion. This is the uncertainty generated largely by variability in production due to weather. In such circumstances the underlying situation on world markets is difficult to distinguish from short-run occurrences. In addition, world prices for the major farm products have been heavily influenced by the marketing policies of governments, not least the storage and export subsidy programs pursued by the exporting countries. These two factors have a cumulative impact on price stability. When supplies are adequate, as they were in the 1960s, world prices are depressed by the actions of developed country governments. Developing countries, whose imports of cereals began to rise rapidly in this period, understood that the attractive terms of such purchases were made possible by considerable subsidies in the form of farm programs and overseas aid.

The price explosion of 1973–1975 illustrates this problem. Countries previously concerned with surpluses began to squeeze world supplies so as to soften the impact of harvest shortfalls on the rate of inflation at home.[13]

---

[13] For evidence of the impact of these policies on world food supplies, see Timothy E. Josling, *Developed-Country Agricultural Policies and Developing-Country Food Supplies: The Case of Wheat*, International Food Policy Research Institute, Research Report no. 14 (Washington, D.C., March 1980). The policy effect appears to have been of about the same magnitude as the original shocks to the food system from poor harvests.

The dramatic rise in cereal prices during 1973 had an effect on attitudes toward agriculture. It led to the holding of the World Food Conference in 1974 and the increased international priorities accorded to agricultural production and trade problems. In food-importing industrial countries, agricultural support was paraded as a necessary insurance against shortages, and in exporting countries the presumption grew that the higher price levels ushered in a period of economic prosperity and sellers' markets. Scientists began to look for evidence of climatic shifts and technical production limits, which might combine with resource scarcity to cause a shortage of basic foods. In such an atmosphere, rational decisions on long-run resource deployment, both by governments and by individual farmers, were difficult to make. This period clearly generated a confusion about the interpretation of world market prices.

At the risk of oversimplifying a complex situation, one can therefore conclude:

• Developing countries, despite their self-sufficiency goals, in fact tend to tax their agriculture, keeping production lower than would otherwise be the case.

• The governments of developed countries support their agricultural producers in such a way as to weaken world markets and distort trade patterns, at the expense of their own taxpayers and consumers.

• Price uncertainty in world markets generates policy reactions as countries try to divorce their own national prices from world market conditions at the cost of intensifying market instability.

These realities are unlikely to change rapidly. Developing countries may well try to increase the incentives given to their own producers, but neither the urban consumer nor the taxpayer in these countries is likely to allow a rapid shift toward higher farm prices. In industrial countries the reverse is true: farm protection will decrease slowly, but the government is unlikely to leave the health of the farm sector to the test of international competitiveness. Instability will continue to be a problem for as long as nations persist in placing domestic price stability ahead of responsibilities to the international community.

The Degree and Nature of Competition

The last general category of influences on trade prospects has to do with the nature of competition in agricultural markets. This is in turn influenced by (1) the capacity of other suppliers to capture and develop present or prospective markets and (2) the extent to which competitors coordinate behavior to avoid low or unstable prices. With respect to the competition from other suppliers, U.S. agriculture is in a more favorable position than many other export sectors of the economy. Only a few other countries have the excess capacity to move significant amounts of products into world markets. The potential threat to the U.S. market position comes as much from the subsidized exports of countries with high levels of agricultural protection as from the more regular and more soundly based production of commercial exporters. These disruptive surpluses are also a major stimulus to exporters to try to regulate trade to avoid their price-depressing effects.

The countries that compete directly with the United States in the major export markets include Canada, Australia, the European Economic Community (EEC), and Argentina for wheat; Argentina, Thailand, and South Africa for corn; Brazil and Argentina for soybeans; Thailand for rice; Canada for tobacco; and Egypt for cotton. Many of these "traditional" exporters seem unlikely to raise their overall market share, although they may expand in particular markets as trade patterns adjust. Domestic constraints in these countries would appear to preclude dramatic increases in export sales. Expansion of the land area in Canada would necessitate that farmers move into less hospitable regions, and that does not seem to be a likely prospect. South Africa and Australia also have spare land resources that would only come into full production with very different price incentives. The growth of exports from Thailand, though impressive in recent years, is again constrained by resource endowments, as is the capacity of Egypt to produce export crops on what many consider to be land that could be transferred to food production. The EEC bears a heavy cost for its excursions into the export market and shows no sign of becoming competitive without subsidies.

The two countries that stand out as having considerable export potential are Brazil and Argentina. Both have adequate land reserves, especially Brazil, and a long tradition of export-oriented agriculture. Argentinian exports for many years were hampered by heavy taxation, in part for revenue and in part to keep domestic food costs down. Domestic agriculture grew rather slowly, and overseas markets were lost. The more aggressive export stance in recent years has raised the possibility of significantly increased foreign sales. Sales of soybeans from Argentina have overtaken those from Brazil and are second only to U.S. exports, although, as is clear from table 9, Brazil leads both Argentina and the United States in exports of soybean meal.[14] Brazil

---

[14] There is a growing trade in soybean oil, in addition to meal and the uncrushed soybeans. The United States and the EEC have the major part of this market, with Brazil, Argentina, and Spain also important. Exports of Brazilian and

TABLE 9

EXPORTS OF MAJOR AGRICULTURAL PRODUCTS FROM
SELECTED COUNTRIES, 1976/1977 TO 1979/1980

(in thousands of tons)

	1976/1977	1977/1978	1978/1979	1979/1980
Wheat				
Canada	12.9	15.9	13.5	15.0
Australia	8.5	11.1	6.7	14.9
Argentina	5.6	2.6	3.3	4.7
Western Europe	6.3	6.3	9.5	10.4
United States	26.1	31.5	32.3	37.2
Coarse grains				
Canada	4.6	3.7	3.9	4.8
Australia	3.3	1.9	2.5	3.5
Argentina	9.5	11.0	11.5	6.6
South Africa	1.4	2.9	2.9	2.7
Thailand	2.3	1.3	2.2	2.1
Western Europe	4.6	6.0	6.2	5.1
United States	50.6	52.1	56.9	71.6
Soybeans				
Brazil	2.6	0.7	0.6	1.5
Argentina	0.6	2.0	2.8	2.4
United States	15.4	19.1	20.5	23.1
Soybean meal				
Brazil	5.3	5.4	4.8	7.3
Argentina	0.3	0.3	0.2	0.3
United States	4.1	5.5	6.0	7.0

SOURCE: U.S. Department of Agriculture, *Foreign Agricultural Circular*, various issues.

is also stimulating export sales of a number of commodities and diversifying away from the more traditional exports, such as coffee. Because of the massive burden of petroleum imports on the Brazilian economy, the search for export markets has a sense of urgency and purpose.

When looking for potential competitors, it is wise to consider the large economies in which relatively minor production increases can

---

Argentinian soybean oil clearly cut into the market for U.S. products, but Spanish and EEC oil exports are largely derived from soybeans imported from the United States.

have a marked effect on exports. The Soviet Union and India are two such countries. India has in fact entered grain markets as an exporter on occasions, but the massive problem of upgrading the diets of its people will undoubtedly absorb most of the output increases from Indian agriculture. It is argued in the next section that the Soviet Union is likely to remain an importer of basic foodstuffs, with exports limited to sales to its political allies. It would take major changes in the organization of Soviet agriculture to generate a steady export surplus, and there is no indication that this will be possible within the next decade.

Considerable attention has been given in importing countries to the question of how to diversify the sources of imports. This comes in part from the feeling of vulnerability to supply fluctuations and in part from the perceived political costs of dependence on one or a few countries for food supplies. The use of trade embargoes by exporters undoubtedly weakens confidence in the world's trading system. But the actions of countries do not always reflect these political concerns. Japan, for example, is reputed to have invested heavily in soybean production in Brazil following the interruption of supplies from the United States in 1973—but still purchases the bulk of its soybean imports from this country.

U.S. Policy toward Farm Exports

International Action to Reinforce Trade Expansion. The continued expansion of agricultural trade seems to require two developments, both of which the United States can stimulate by international action. First, individual countries should be able to purchase foodstuffs on world markets when their own production is deficient. Whether a country can afford to buy extra imports is largely a function of its wealth and economic strength, but ready access to credit facilities would materially help many countries at times when their import requirements are high. Balance-of-payments facilities exist through the International Monetary Fund (IMF), both to help developing countries offset fluctuations in commodity export earnings and in general to assist in periods of crisis. A specific facility related to food imports could well supplement these schemes and give particular impetus to the development of freer trade policies in developing countries.[15]

[15] A variation on this theme is to set up a system whereby developing countries may insure against variation in their import requirements with either one or a group of the developed countries. Payments from this insurance policy, either in kind or in cash tied to import purchases, would follow shortfalls from domestic production trends. This device would ensure that such food aid would be granted

Second, market performance can be improved by increasing the stability of world market prices. This too influences the willingness of developing countries to pursue trade-oriented food policies. Several approaches to this problem have been discussed over the years. One method that has an intuitive appeal has been to attempt to regulate world prices directly by means of accords among importers and exporters. Under such a scheme, fixed maximum and minimum trading prices would be agreed upon with the objective of limiting price variability. Such proposals suffer from the drawback that a more rigid international market means that national markets must become more flexible to absorb the fluctuations that cause prices to vary. Countries do not appear to accept the degree of domestic market adjustment called for by rigid price agreements.[16]

Price variations are triggered by fluctuations in market balance, usually arising from the side of supply. Such fluctuations cannot be wished away: they will show up either as variations in consumption or as changes in stock levels. The international market plays a role in determining where such stock and consumption changes take place. This function is impaired if world prices are fixed. Exporters have no incentive to mobilize additional supplies, and importers are not encouraged to reduce their call on world markets in years of shortage. On the other hand, with a sufficient level of domestic stock and consumption adjustment, world prices will tend to be more stable than at present. Stable international prices are ultimately the outcome of the appropriate use of domestic policy instruments. It is doubtful whether fixed world prices would be adequate to ensure the requisite domestic policy changes.

Among the suggestions for enhancing market stability, besides those that envisage rigid price agreements, are those that aim to improve the link between world and domestic markets, most simply achieved by liberalizing trade. The less obtrusive is government policy in the decisions relating to production, marketing, and distribution of agricultural products, the more the normal market mechanisms will

---

when and where it was most needed and improve upon such ad hoc methods of distribution of sales concessions as now exist. See the proposals by D. Gale Johnson, "Increasing the Food Security of Low Income Countries," in Johnson, *The Politics of Food*, and by Panos Konandreas, Barbara Huddleston, and Virabongsa Ramangkura, *Food Security: An Insurance Approach*, International Food Policy Research Institute, Research Report no. 4 (Washington, D.C., 1978), for details of these schemes.

[16] Indeed, those countries, such as members of the EEC, that have most explicitly proposed the negotiation of such commodity agreements are also those that appear to be least willing to countenance the requisite domestic policy adjustment.

be able to absorb unavoidable changes in supply. The fact that such a solution is consistent with an expansion of trade gives it an additional appeal to the United States, although for the same reason it raises objections by interests adversely affected by such improvements.

To be successful, trade liberalization requires a positive commitment on the part of governments to allow international price variations to impinge on domestic conditions—not just in normal times but also when such price movements are most embarrassing. It also requires that governments become sufficiently convinced of the longer-term benefits to allow them to resist the temptation to intervene for shorter-run objectives. Such a commitment is clearly not present at the moment. Indeed it could be that the degree of price instability in world markets even under the most favorable conditions of trade might exceed that which countries found tolerable in domestic terms. Under such circumstances the trade liberalization approach would not be adequate in itself to meet domestic policy objectives.

The third category of measures discussed in the context of world price stability emphasize cooperation in the management of stocks. Such reserve management can be seen either as desirable in its own right and neglected in the past through the lack of appreciation of the severe effects of sudden price movements or as a way of compensating for the effects of domestic policies that prevent adjustment to market conditions. In spite of general agreement that coordination of stocks is of some merit, international negotiations have not so far been successful.

The major problems encountered in such international arrangements have more to do with their costs and the difficulties of implementing them than with any doubts about their effectiveness. Complete price stability would certainly be costly; anything less than an agreement to defend a particular price (or price band) through stock purchases and sales requires complex management rules binding on individual governments or imposed by an international authority. A major disadvantage arises from the tendency for stocks to obscure the longer-run price trends necessary for the stimulus of production in appropriate locations.

Progress in International Discussions on Agricultural Trade. Despite the widespread view that these various actions would improve the performance of the trading system for basic foods, little progress has been made in international discussions in recent years. The period after the 1972–1974 crisis was marked by a significant upturn in diplomatic activity in this regard, and civil servants concerned with international agricultural matters have been meeting tirelessly in various institutional settings for the past five years. Yet the degree of progress remains small, and the problems loom almost as large as ever.

To date the United States has not identified itself with any scheme to maintain and increase the purchasing power of developing countries in the specific area of food imports. Such proposals have come from research personnel interested in the problem of developing country trade.[17] They reflect an approach, somewhat out of line with official thinking, that dollars are cheaper to store than grain and that financing problems are best dealt with by financial means. Public officials perhaps are more conscious of the difficulties of holding foreign exchange when all sectors of the economy are putting demands on scarce reserves and are more aware of the loss of autonomy associated with further borrowing from abroad and the increased debt burden that such borrowing would entail. Grain in the silo seems much more politically acceptable as a way of achieving food security.[18]

With respect to negotiations in trade and market stability, the political activity has been considerable. The recent round of multilateral trade negotiations held under the General Agreement on Tariffs and Trade (GATT) began in September 1973 amid hopes that agriculture would at last join most other sectors of world trade in the liberalized system of international commerce.[19] This did not materialize: the notion that agricultural trade policies are an outgrowth of domestic policies and hence to be defended rather than amended in international discourse prevailed. Finally the hope had to be abandoned that significant pressures could be put on domestic policies that would materially improve the conditions of agricultural trade.

Two developments, however, do hold out some hope for a future assault on these difficult issues of the relation between implacable domestic policy actions and desirable trade improvement aims. First, the multilateral trade negotiations drew up a code of conduct on export subsidies, which relates to agriculture as well as to other commodities. It is too early to say what impact this will have on national decision making, but the fact that certain practices will be explored and criticized within the framework of the GATT may have a restraining influence on governments. In particular, it may allow governments who use such subsidies only reluctantly in the face of domestic pressure to resist

[17] For a discussion of these proposals, see Alberto Valdés, ed., *Food Security for Developing Countries* (Boulder, Colo.: Westview Press, 1981).

[18] While this approach may be reasonable in some cases, it loses some of its appeal if developing countries have to borrow to obtain the grain to be stored.

[19] For a discussion of the agricultural questions in the multilateral trade negotiations, see Timothy E. Josling, *Agriculture in the Tokyo Round Negotiations*, Trade Policy Research Centre, Thames Essay no. 10 (London, 1977).

the blandishments of those who see the world market as a natural repository for production in excess of normal market needs. The use of export subsidies has, arguably, been of greater significance than import barriers in weakening the trading system. Governments now have a more direct way of scrutinizing such procedures and of seeking less disruptive alternatives.

The second potential advance in the multilateral trade negotiations has been to establish a body within the GATT to discuss general problems arising in the area of agricultural trade. Although judgment on this development will have to wait until this body meets and acts, a direct channel of this type offers some limited hope for progress. Again, the major requirement is to support the positive pressures existing within national administrations for responsible domestic decisions against those who resent the intrusion of the realities of economic and political interdependence.

Despite the long-running saga of the GATT negotiations, perhaps more hopes were placed in the parallel talks on a new wheat agreement. The present agreement contains no effective provisions regarding trade, although the food aid convention has remained operational.[20] The stimulus for finding a new agreement stemmed directly from the concern with the low stocks and high prices in the 1973–1974 period. It began, in other words, as a deliberate food security initiative. In the period after the 1974 World Food Conference, it was generally accepted that the major grain trading countries had to get together to coordinate their actions, in particular with respect to stocks. The improvement in food security thus generated had an important place in the more general relationships among developed and developing countries.

In the United States, by contrast, the proposals put forward in September 1975 were clearly focused on food security, with price stability as a byproduct of the attempt to avoid the macropolitical problems of another food crisis. Developing countries, as net importers of grain and as victims of the food crisis, generally supported the U.S. initiatives in the international wheat agreement. The January 1976 counterproposal by the EEC reinforced the historical tendency to view grain trade problems in terms of commercial conflicts in developed countries. Mandatory floor and ceiling prices substituted for the flex-

---

[20] The present international wheat agreement represents what remains of the more ambitious 1967 international grains agreement, which died after the collapse of market prices at the end of the 1960s. The failure of the grains agreement to stem the tide of surpluses illustrates the problems addressed earlier with respect to the fixing of trade prices. No stocks provisions were included in the 1967 agreement.

ibility of quantitative stock triggers based on market availability. The objective of maintaining "equitable and remunerative prices" had somehow supplanted that of preventing further crisis in the developing world. The good intentions of the food conference had once again given way to the traditional farm policy squabbles among industrial countries.

In the second phase of the wheat talks, the battleground was more familiar. The United States was getting back into domestic stock holding with the farmer-owned reserve, prices had dropped on world markets, and the cost of restitution payments by the EEC was once again causing concern in Europe. The new U.S. proposal of June 1977 reflected these changes. The 30-million-ton food grain stock was to be triggered by price levels that would also indicate when policy adjustments were needed. The EEC rejected the policy adjustments and argued for fixed trading prices rather than indicative triggers. A full negotiating conference—now under the wing of the United Nations Conference on Trade and Development rather than GATT—met periodically over a year until finally abandoning the search for an agreement in February 1979.

This story illustrates the problems of formulating international policy to improve the conditions of agricultural trade. The most constructive ideas in the proposals for a new wheat agreement were those that went to the heart of the problem: the constraints on domestic policy during periods of market imbalance. These were rejected as inconsistent with national sovereignty. A modest coordinated stock scheme could only be agreed upon if it was consistent with national price levels and again put no strain on existing policies. Once the food crisis had passed, the notion of managing the wheat market to assist developing countries was forgotten. Perhaps the failure to reach an agreement was not serious in the light of the weakness of the proposals themselves. But the failure let slip one element that would have been constructive. By linking domestic stock policies together, however loosely, an agreement would have institutionalized international discussion of one aspect of domestic decisions.

Summary and Conclusions

Exports of U.S. agricultural products are climbing to record levels at a time when international confidence in other aspects of U.S. trade performance is at a low ebb. This renewed importance of agricultural trade to the economy is matched by its increased significance for farm incomes. Export markets, however, bring with them uncertainty as well as opportunity. Their continued growth depends on economic conditions and governmental policies in other countries. U.S. policy instruments, limited as they are in directing market growth at home, have even less influence on foreign demand. The search for policies that will sustain the growth and profitability of international market outlets is complex. It involves national actions relating to market support, reserve management, transportation facilities, information systems, and export promotion. It includes international negotiations on trading and monetary systems, on the implications of national support policies, on attempts to improve market stability, and on the enhanced security of world food supplies. All this must be set in the context of changing international political relationships, which often seem to frustrate the apparently simple task of meeting the world's food needs from the most appropriate sources.

On the basic question of the future of agricultural trade, there is little doubt that, short of a disastrous collapse in the world economy, the growth of income and population coupled with the constraints on agricultural production abroad will lead to an increase over time in U.S. exports of foodstuffs. Variability in output both at home and abroad will continue to contribute to market uncertainty. The pressures inhibiting such trade include the desire for greater self-sufficiency in developing countries, the shortage of foreign exchange earnings in those countries, and the autarkic tendencies of the agricultural policies of industrial countries. All of these will continue to distort the flow of products from efficient suppliers to willing consumers. Demand from the needy will continue to be restricted by the widespread existence of poverty. But the imperatives of adequate nutrition and of food supplies at affordable prices will continue to overcome the reluctance of governments to see an expansion of agricultural imports.

The main task for U.S. policy makers is to press for the development of a trading system in agricultural products that will reduce those concerns of other governments that presently inhibit a more open approach to trade. This involves the conclusion of sensible international arrangements to prevent violent fluctuations in the price and availability of basic foodstuffs. Such a step would be most directly accomplished by ensuring that adjustments in both consumption and stocks are widely spread among those who can afford them, rather than being forced on a few major exporters or borne by the world's poorest consumers. A greater flexibility in the farm policies of developed countries coupled with agreed conventions on reserve holding must be a priority in international discourse. Such an approach also implies flexibility on the part of U.S. policy both to ensure the cooperation of others and to demonstrate commitment to the improvement of the trading system. Longer-term modifications in the allocation of agricultural resources in the interests of more reliable supplies of foodstuffs at reasonable prices will themselves follow more easily if the problems of year-to-year instability are overcome. Continuous scrutiny and international discussions of agricultural policies relating to price levels, investment, marketing, and trade can be constructive if basic objectives are kept in mind.

Policy developments in other areas will also have a bearing on these agricultural questions. Countries will not be able to afford food imports unless they can sell their goods abroad. In the short term, an adequate financing facility must be available for the coverage of abnormal purchases when domestic production is low. This facility might be tied to food imports directly or relate to the broader payments position. Variations on the theme of food aid that stress insurance principles should be explored. In the longer run, only an opening up of markets for foreign goods can ultimately allow other countries to take full advantage of the opportunities for trade in agricultural products.

On the domestic level, two approaches are necessary. The need to ensure that market information and marketing facilities are adequate to take timely advantage of overseas requirements is clearly an important part of policy. It is equally important that domestic market and income support policies be kept consistent with overseas trade realities. This requires difficult decisions affecting the market for imported commodities as well as the sensitive operation of price supports on export goods. Recent policy changes have given the flexibility needed to keep domestic agriculture competitive. The benefits of expanded commercial markets abroad can only be maintained if domestic policies are made consistent with these developments. The rewards are to be found in the widespread acceptance of the contribution of agriculture to the U.S. economy, the necessary degree of political and economic stability to encourage the full development of agricultural potential, and the contribution to the problem of feeding a hungry world.

Prospective Changes in U.S. Agricultural Structure

Luther Tweeten

The mushrooming volume of literature on the structure of agriculture illuminates our understanding.[1] Gaps in our knowledge remain, however, and the literature sometimes dispenses fantasy along with fact. The purpose of this paper is to close some of the gaps, solve some puzzles, dispel some fantasy, and project changes in farming structure. After briefly reviewing positive and negative elements in the changes occurring in the farming sector, the paper estimates sources of growth in farm size and uses these to project to the year 2000. In the final section, the paper addresses orthodoxy and heresy in the literature dealing with the structure of the farming industry.

Positive and Negative Elements in Farm Structure

Results of changes in the structure of the farming sector are mixed, but on balance the record is one of success. Successful elements include:

This is a professional paper of the Oklahoma Agricultural Experiment Station. Comments of Daryll Ray and Keith Scearce were much appreciated.

[1] Peter Emerson, *Public Policy and the Changing Structure of American Agriculture* (Washington, D.C.: Congressional Budget Office, September 1978); U.S. Congress, Senate, Committee on Agriculture, Nutrition, and Forestry, *Farm Structure* (Washington, D.C., April 1980); U.S. Congress, Senate, Committee on Agriculture, Nutrition, and Forestry, Print 44-916, *Status of the Family Farm* (Washington, D.C., 1979); Lyle P. Schertz et al., *Another Revolution in U.S. Farming?* Agricultural Economic Report no. 441 (Washington, D.C.: U.S. Department of Agriculture, Economics, Statistics, and Cooperatives Service, 1979); Luther Tweeten, "Public Issues and Alternatives for the 1980's," in W. Keith Scearce, ed., *Proceedings of Farmers Agricultural Policy Conference* (Stillwater: Cooperative Extension Service, Oklahoma State University, March 1980), pp. 1–15; and Thomas Miller, "Economies of Size and Other Growth Incentives," in *Structure Issues of American Agriculture*, Agriculture Economic Report no. 438 (Washington, D.C.: Department of Agriculture, Economics, Statistics, and Cooperatives Service), pp. 108–15.

113

1. Incomes of persons engaged in farming, once low when compared with earnings of those in the nonfarm sector, have gradually improved. Spectacular gains have been made by families on small farms. In recent years incomes and rates of return on investment for commercial farm families have been at least comparable to those of nonfarmers, if full accounting is made for assets and cost of living.

2. The incidence of poverty in the farming sector has fallen dramatically and is now not much above that in the nonfarm sector.

3. Millions of people have been freed from low productivity employment in farming to produce nonfarm goods (such as television sets, stereos, autos, air conditioners) and services (health care, education, entertainment) prized by a prosperous society.

4. Massive increases in farm productivity have enabled agricultural demand, growing at approximately 1.7 percent annually for decades, to be met with a nearly stable level of conventional farm production inputs. The gains in productivity are mostly the product of publicly supported agricultural research and extension. They have enabled farmers to supply over one-fifth of our nation's exports while accounting for only 3 percent of national income. Productivity advances brought environmental benefits because crop production was avoided on millions of acres of erosion-prone soils. Cropland use was less in 1978 than in 1918.

5. The real cost of food as measured by the proportion of consumer income for food, including marketing cost, has declined or held steady even as the output of farms has expanded to earn massive amounts of foreign exchange to pay for oil and other imports. Low-income consumers, because they spend a high proportion of income for food, have benefited mightily from increased farming efficiency.

6. In part because farmers save and invest 30 percent of their income, whereas the average American saves and invests only 6 percent, labor productivity of farmers has increased at 5 percent per year in recent years while labor productivity of nonfarmers has stagnated.

7. Drudgery has been largely eliminated from farm work. Labor hours per worker have been cut in farming, and the typical farm family now enjoys the conveniences and amenities found in suburban America.

Not all aspects of the farming industry are rosy. Cost-price and cash-flow problems stemming from a poorly achieving national economy continue to plague farmers.[2] Instability in farm prices and incomes is

---

[2] Luther Tweeten, "Macroeconomics in Crisis: Agriculture in an Under-Achieving Economy," *American Journal of Agricultural Economics*, vol. 62, no. 5 (December 1980), pp. 853–65.

TABLE 1

Summary Estimates of Family and Nonfamily Farm Numbers and Sales, United States, 1976

	Farms		Sales	
	Number	Percent	Value ($ million)	Percent
Family farms	584,930	21.1	53,015	55.0
Nonfamily farms				
Small farms (sales of $20,000 or less) (1)	1,996,000	71.9	9,631	10.0
Large farms				
Corporations (2)	7,500	0.3	9,640	10.0
Partnerships (3)	13,250	0.5	2,650	2.7
Vertically coordinated (other than in 1–3) (4)	9,640	0.3	4,822	5.0
Excess labor (other than in 1–4)	166,680	6.0	16,684	17.3
Total	2,778,000	100.0	96,442	100.0

Source: Luther Tweeten, "Structure of Agriculture and Policy Alternatives to Preserve the Family Farm," in Scearce, *Farmers Agricultural Policy Conference*, p. B-9.

a continuing irritation. But the issue generating the most literature is the so-called problem of structure and its centerpiece, the family farm.

The Jeffersonian ideal, which continues to be widely if not deeply held,[3] is to have as many family farms as is consistent with supplying adequate food and fiber at reasonable cost, protecting the environment, and providing a satisfactory standard of living to the operator and his family without undue subsidy. Society as well as farmers would like to see farming units operated by families that make the major part of their living from farming, own the land they operate, provide most of the labor, and make the significant decisions on the farm.

Table 1 shows estimates of numbers and sales of family and non-family farms for the United States in 1976. Of the 2.8 million farms, 2 million, or 72 percent, had sales of $20,000 or less per year and were classified as nonfamily farms because they received most of their

[3] William Flinn and Frederick Buttel, "Sociological Aspects of Farm Size," *American Journal of Agricultural Economics*, vol. 62, no. 5 (December 1980), pp. 946–53.

income from off-farm sources. Farms with sales of $9,999 to $20,000, for example, which are toward the upper end of the small category, received approximately twice as much income from off-farm as from farm sources in 1976. For smaller farms, ratios of off-farm to farm income were much higher.

Large farms accounted for 35 percent of all sales. Most of these farms were classified as large because they hired more than half their labor. The number of nonfamily corporate, partnership, and vertically coordinated (other than corporate and partnership) farms was comparatively few, but these three categories accounted for 18 percent of all farm sales.

After subtracting nonfamily farms from all farms, only 21 percent of all farms were classified as family farms, but these units accounted for 55 percent of all sales. Hence family farms accounted for a larger proportion of sales than of all farms. The proportion of family farms so defined has not changed substantially over the last several years, but the number of family farms has declined sharply.

Outlook for Farm Size and Numbers

The long-term outlook for the traditional family farm, measured either by numbers or as a proportion of all farms, is not bright. This section first analyzes past and prospective changes in average farm size; given that the area in farms is fairly stable, changes in farm size also reveal changes in the number of farms. It then turns to the position of the family farm in relation to small and large farms.

If farm resources are to earn as much as resources elsewhere in the economy, farms are required to grow in real size to keep up with (1) the real income of nonfarmers and (2) technology. In addition, farms are required to grow in nominal size to keep up with inflation. Finally, farms need to grow to eliminate any past shortfall of farm earnings. These factors requiring growth are partly offset by increasing off-farm income of people on farms. Each of these elements is quantified in table 2.

Let S be farm real sales per farm (equal to total resource cost of inputs), L_F be farm labor-management earnings, L_N be nonfarm earnings of farm people, $L = L_F + L_N$ be equal to income of nonfarmers per capita, and P be the general price level. Then nominal farm size

$$PS = \frac{S}{L_F} L \frac{L_F}{L} P$$

is a multiple of technology as measured by the reciprocal of the labor-management share of farm sales (resources) S/L_F, income per capita

TABLE 2: ACTUAL AND REQUIRED GROWTH IN SALES PER FARM BY DECADE, 1940 TO 1979, AND REQUIRED GROWTH PROJECTED, 1980 TO 1999

(annual average percent)

| Decade | Growth Required by | | | Off-farm income[c] L'_F | Sales Growth Required[d] | | Actual Sales Growth[e] |
	Technology[a] T'	National income[b] L'	Sub-total		Real S'	Inflated $(PS)'$	
Actual							
1940–49	3.4	2.6	6.0	−4.1	1.9	7.5	12.6
1950–59	3.6	1.2	4.8	−5.4	−0.6	1.5	5.3
1960–69	3.3	3.0	6.3	−6.0	0.3	3.0	7.3
1970–79	3.2	2.0	5.2	−2.9	2.3	9.4	7.8
Projected							
1980–89	3.1	1.5	4.6	−1.4	3.2	12.2	—
1990–99	3.0	1.0	4.0	−1.2	2.8	11.8	—

[a] T' measured by annual percentage change in hired plus family labor share of farm inputs, with sign reversed and assuming that inputs equal total outputs. From unpublished annual data with benchmark data published in Bruce Gardner, Donald Durost, William Lin, Yao-Chi Lu, Glenn Nelson, and Norman Whittlesey, "Measurement of U.S. Agricultural Productivity," (Report of joint AAEA-ESCS task force on agricultural productivity), Technical Bulletin no. 1614 (Washington, D.C.: Department of Agriculture, Economics, Statistics, and Cooperatives Service, 1980), p. 8.

[b] L' measured by average annual percentage increase in real U.S. disposable income per capita. Council on Economic Advisers, *Economic Report of the President* (Washington, D.C., January 1980), p. 229.

[c] L'_F measured by the annual percentage change in proportion of total farm income from farm sources. U.S. Department of Agriculture, *Farm Income Statistics*, Statistical Bulletin no. 627 (Washington, D.C.: Department of Agriculture, Economics, Statistics, and Cooperatives Service, October 1979), p. 31.

[d] Real required growth is $T' + L' + L'_F$; P', defined as the annual percentage increase in the consumer index, is added to measure nominal required growth. Council of Economic Advisers, *Economic Report of the President*, p. 259.

[e] Computed from average gross income per farm. Department of Agriculture, *Farm Income Statistics*, p. 32.

SOURCES: See footnotes for each column.

of the nation L, the share of farm income from farm sources L_F/L. and the general price level P. Real farm size is S.

If we represent the percentage change in: (1) the reciprocal of labor share by T', (2) national income by L', (3) farm income share from farm sources by L'_F and (4) general price level by inflation P', then the required percentage increase in farm size $(PS)'$ is

$$(PS)' = T' + L' + L'_F + P'$$

in nominal terms and

$$S' = T' + L' + L'_F$$

in real terms.

Required real and nominal increases in farm size by decade are shown in table 2. Changes in technology have required farm size to increase 3.2 percent to 3.6 percent annually in the three decades since 1950.[4] Gains in earnings in the economy as measured by real disposable personal income per capita called for annual increases in farm scale of 1.2 percent in the 1950s to 3.0 percent in the 1960s. The combined effect of technology and keeping up with the Joneses would have caused equilibrium farm size to grow by 6 percent annually in the 1940s and 1960s and by 5 percent annually in the 1950s and 1970s, other things being equal.

Other things were not equal, however. Off-farm income of farm people reduced requirements for income from farm sources and for larger farms. Consequently, in real terms, farms did not need to expand markedly from 1950 to 1969. Because of inflation in the 1970s, the real annual requirement for a 2.3 percent increase translated into a nominal requirement for a 9.4 percent increase per year.

The final element is growth in farm size to close the adjustment gap—the shortfall of farm below nonfarm income—treated as a residual in table 2. Actual nominal growth (right column) exceeded required growth (second from right column) from 1940 to 1969. This enabled the adjustment gap to narrow considerably. Actual sales growth exceeded required growth by 5.1 percentage points in the 1940s, by 4.3 percentage points in the 1960s, and fell short by 1.6 percentage points in the 1970s, bringing an increase in farm income relative to nonfarm income for the entire period 1940–1979. After adjustments for cost of living, data on income and rates of return on sources indicated near-equilibrium resource use between the farm and nonfarm

---

[4] The actual changes in table 2 are the net result of the supply of and demand for technology and other elements. It would be desirable but not feasible to separate these elements of supply and demand.

sectors in 1980. Consequently, a latent adjustment gap can be omitted in projections.

The need for a significant increase in farm size is projected for the 1980s and 1990s despite a slowdown in technology and income growth in the economy because the growth of off-farm sources of income of farm people will be too slow to offset effects of technology and national income growth.[5] As a consequence, farms are projected to increase in size and decrease in numbers by approximately 3 percent per year in the 1980s and 1990s. If inflation is 9 percent annually, as projected, this real increase implies a 12 percent nominal increase. Of course, the absence of a significant adjustment gap in 1980 helps to dampen the need for growth in farm size.

Outlook for Moderate-Size Family Farms. A farming unit of economic size is defined as one that provides full-time employment for the operator and the operator's family and a level of living comparable to that of nonfarmers. Such farms on the average are large enough to realize economies of size in production and marketing. The traditional moderate-size family farm extends from approximately $100,000 in sales and $1 million in assets down to farms with sales of $20,000 per year. The outlook for these farms is not favorable, not because they are inefficient but because they cannot cope with cash-flow problems as well as large and small farms. (Farms with fewer annual sales than $20,000 are here called small farms, and those with sales of more than $100,000 a year are called large farms.) Large farms may be family farms.

Large farms, particularly of the industrial corporation type, can use insurance, hedging, forward contracting, and diversification into various farm and nonfarm activities to reduce risk. Stockholders or partners who provide equity capital for such operations may be quite pleased to receive economic benefits as capital gains rather than dividends from current earnings. Large farms can spread the cost of sophisticated management and of planning apparatus over large numbers of units. Such conglomerate operations potentially can be large enough to buy and sell individual farms to turn capital gains into current income. Such operations can cope with cash-flow problems for several reasons.

---

[5] Technology, national income, off-farm income, and other variables were projected using linear and logarithmic transformation. Equations were selected for final results on the basis of proportion of variation accounted for and realism. Linear equations, for example, were not accepted when they projected negative values. Because of structural changes in the economy, including higher costs of energy and lower real response to expansionary monetary-fiscal policy, I project real income growth per capita of 1.5 percent annually in the 1980s and 1.0 percent in the 1990s.

FIGURE 1

NUMBER OF SMALL FARMS IN THE UNITED STATES BY CATEGORY, FOR
CENSUS YEARS 1959–1974

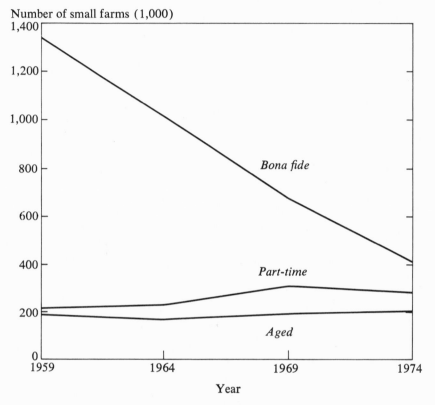

Number of small farms (1,000)

SOURCE: U.S. Bureau of the Census, *Census of Agriculture*, 1974 and earlier issues.

First, family living expenses on such farms tend to be low in relation
to total earnings. Second, large farmers have access to many potential
investors with substantial nonfarm capital if the rate of return is
favorable.

The small farmer is also in a favorable position to cope with cash
flow. Figure 1 shows that the bona fide small farm occupied by an
able-bodied full-time operator who depends on the farm for the livelihood of himself and his family is rapidly vanishing. The small farm
of the future will be dominated by the part-time operator who has
sufficient income from off-farm sources to handle interest, principal,
and other cash-flow requirements. By various means, including allocation of costs for pickup trucks and other items of general use to their

farming operations, small and large part-time farms are in a position to reap tax advantages from farming activities.

For these and other reasons listed in an earlier work,[6] I concluded that maintaining the moderate-size family farm was a major challenge. The number of farms that earn $20,000 to $100,000 in real dollars seems destined to shrink. Theory and empirical evidence predicted that farming in the future would be dominated by a few large farms producing most of the output and a large number of small farms. A recent study projects that a decline from 2.9 million farms in 1974 to 1.8 million in the year 2000 "will probably be arranged in a bimodal distribution—a large proportion of small farms, an ever-increasing proportion of large farms, and a declining proportion of medium-size farms."[7] The study projects that the 50,000 largest farms will probably produce about two-thirds of all farm output and the largest 1 million farms will produce almost all the farm output by the year 2000.[8] These largest 50,000 farms will deviate considerably from the family farm ideal.

This projected decline in the number of small farms is probably pessimistic because the authors did not account for the structural changes that are occurring in farming. Specifically, they did not recognize the demise of the full-time, able-bodied farm operator on small farms, which leaves trends to be dominated by retired and part-time operators. Nor do the projections account fully for the comparatively recent cash-flow squeeze engendered by inflation, which places especially severe hardships on expanding or entering moderate-size family farms.

Interpreting Trends in Farm Structure

Dramatic changes in the structure of the farming industry are apparent; the meaning of these changes is less clear. One view is that current trends constitute a threat to the nation's well-being and that public policy is needed to reverse or at least arrest growth in large farms and spur growth in small and moderate-size farms. This view rests in part on the proposition that conventional economic measures fail to

[6] Luther Tweeten, "Farm Commodity Prices and Income," in Bruce Gardner and James Richardson, eds., *Consensus and Conflict in Agriculture* (College Station: Texas A & M University Press, 1979), chap. 2.

[7] William Lin, George Coffman, and J. B. Penn, *U.S. Farm Numbers, Sizes, and Related Structural Dimensions: Projections to Year 2000*, Technical Bulletin no. 1625 (Washington, D.C.: Department of Agriculture, Economics, Statistics, and Cooperatives Service, July 1980), p. 12.

[8] Lin, Coffman, and Penn, *U.S. Farm Numbers*, p. iii.

account for such factors as soil erosion, the demise of the small town, the trauma experienced by farm-urban migrants, declining marginal utlility apparent in little satisfaction to large farm operators from additional income, rising energy costs that will favor small farms, and imperfect competition, which would cost society heavily if a few large producers gained control of farm output.

Another view is that public policy can continue as before because the gains in efficiency outweigh any costs of concentration of ownership and control in agriculture. Conventional economic measures do provide compelling evidence that small farms are far less efficient then large farms.[9]

In this section several widely held beliefs concerning farm structure are compared with reality and are found to be incorrect. The beliefs to be scrutinized are as follows:

- Public policy in the form of taxes and commodity programs has hastened the demise of the family farm.
- Persons operating small farms receive more personal satisfaction than persons operating moderate-size or large farms, other things being equal.
- Operators of small farms and owner-operators take better care of the environment than operators of other farms.
- The rising cost of energy will increase economic efficiency of small farms relative to large farms.
- Trauma experienced by persons freed from farming because of mechanization and consolidation of farms outweighs gains from mobility.
- The small farm is destined for extinction unless agricultural research and extension are redirected to save it.
- Appropriate adjustment for incremental utility of income, environmental factors, and noneconomic benefits of farming would make the small farm the optimal size.
- Power, wealth, and production will become concentrated in the hands of the few, who will manipulate prices and aggrandize themselves at the expense of other farmers and consumers.
- Land prices (which constitute a major barrier to owner operation of farmland) have been driven upward by speculators and urban developers to levels unjustified by prospective future earnings.
- The social and economic vitality of rural towns and small cities is drained by hinterland farm enlargement and consolidation.

[9] Luther Tweeten and Wallace Huffman, "Structural Change," in *Structure of Agriculture and Information Needs Regarding Small Farms* (Washington, D.C.: National Rural Center, 1980), pt. 1, pp. 54–59.

Have Federal Taxation and Commodity Programs Hastened the Demise of the Family Farm? Although commodity programs receive much attention in the literature on farm structure, monetary-fiscal policy probably exerts a greater effect on farm size and numbers. The cash-flow and cost-price problems related to monetary-fiscal policy are discussed elsewhere. Only the direct impact of federal income taxes is examined here. This is followed by estimates of the impact of commodity programs.

Influence of federal tax policies on typical farms. A recent Oklahoma State University study shows how growth in equity and acreage of typical farms is affected by the federal investment tax credit, depreciation alllowance, interest payment deduction, and tax rates indexed to inflation. From an initial situation for six typical commercial-size farms in 1979, farm growth is simulated for thirty years. Several observations are apparent from table 3:

1. The typical commercial farms are of family size, each requiring approximately 2,600 hours of labor and about $1–2 million of assets (see first row).

2. A farm operator who leverages equity by using debt capital to own as much land as he can service with cash flow and renting the remainder of an economic unit to use available labor fully and maintain 30 percent equity in machinery needs beginning net worth ranging from $164,799 on the Oklahoma farm to $359,139 on the Washington farm. From this baseline net worth position, the operator is able to increase real net worth to $936,724 (468 percent increase) on the Oklahoma farm and to $1,845,050 on the Washington farm (414 percent increase), provided the farm is not liquidated by a setback in early years. Acreage grows much less, in part because initial farm acreage is not allowed to expand through renting until the entire initial economic unit is owned by debt or equity financing.

3. Initial full owners expand acreage and net worth more than initial full renters. On the Illinois and Iowa farms, full renters were unable to expand acreage at all, but full owners more than doubled acreage over that of an economic farming unit. The old adage that "the second million dollars is easier to acquire than the first" applies to farmland. Data not shown in the table reveal that for any initial situation the *absolute* real growth in equity is greater in the second fifteen years of each farm's existence, although the *rate* of growth is highest in the first fifteen years.

4. The willingness of farm families to save and invest has more influence than any other growth element in table 3 on net worth ac-

TABLE 3

GROWTH IN ACREAGE AND NET WORTH ON SIX TYPICAL
COMMERCIAL FARMS IN 1979 SIMULATED OVER 30 YEARS

	Oklahoma: Cotton, Wheat, Beef		Minnesota: Corn, Fed Beef	
Scenario[a]	Acres	Net worth ($)	Acres	Net worth ($)
Full owner				
Initial value (1979)	960	1,205,964	320	925,111
Increase in 30 years	2,880	2,218,411	1,120	1,831,765
Full renter				
Initial value (1979)	960	57,439	320	68,892
Increase in 30 years	120	726,506	160	718,622
Baseline: maximum debt[b]				
Initial value (1979)	960	164,799	320	182,570
Increase in 30 years	408	936,724	308	898,238
Higher consumption	0	507,001	0	454,527
Nonindexed taxes	169	822,321	188	787,940
No interest write-off	0	582,338	108	640,260
No depreciation allowance	289	807,579	188	763,224
No investment tax credit	369	892,820	268	858,544

NOTE: Inflation is assumed to be 6 percent, but all financial amounts are in constant 1979 dollars in all scenarios. (Unless indicated, scenarios assume $12,600 annual consumption, indexed federal tax rates, and all 1979 federal tax provisions in existence.)

[a] All scenarios in this table begin with assets equal to net worth of the full equity owner.

cumulation. In the baseline case, farmers are assumed to invest all residual earnings in excess of the $12,600 required for family living. If this 100 percent marginal savings rate is reduced to 30 percent (the mean rate for the farming industry), real net worth is increased only $302,177 over thirty years rather than the $631,746 in the baseline case on the Iowa farm.

5. Of the federal tax alternatives considered in table 3, elimination of the interest deduction has the greatest single impact. On the typical Washington wheat farm, the interest deduction is worth nearly $800,000 in real terms (1979 dollars) over the thirty-year horizon.

Illinois: Corn, Soybeans		Iowa: Corn, Soybeans, Hogs		Georgia: Peanuts		Washington: Wheat	
Acres	Net worth ($)	Acres	Net worth ($)	Acres	Net worth ($)	Acres	Net worth ($)
400	1,784,397	320	1,269,064	580	984,292	1,280	1,989,051
1,360	3,785,149	760	1,904,389	1,880	1,805,845	4,679	4,341,017
400	61,589	320	54,705	580	72,406	1,280	111,465
0	913,880	0	446,262	300	748,979	0	1,318,040
400	214,544	320	131,822	580	189,673	1,280	359,139
99	1,240,829	0	631,746	514	926,619	505	1,845,050
0	572,441	0	302,177	74	540,409	385	1,370,435
0	952,123	0	480,440	274	806,798	505	1,640,353
0	740,457	0	451,725	194	631,447	105	1,096,421
20	1,025,613	0	470,059	354	780,972	505	1,650,248
59	1,179,624	0	576,331	474	883,993	505	1,802,142

[b] The baseline case minimizes net worth and maximizes acres and assets owned, with debt capital subject to zero cash flow and at least 20 percent equity in owned property. Selected assumptions for the baseline case are relaxed one at a time, noncumulatively, below.

SOURCE: Charles Eginton, "Impacts of Federal Tax Policies on Potential Growth in Size of Typical Farms," *American Journal of Agricultural Economics*, vol. 62, no. 5 (December 1980).

6. Elimination of the investment tax credit, perhaps the most widely recommended measure to restrain growth of large farms, has a modest impact on growth in net worth. Although it may influence the purchase of machinery to substitute for labor, that is not apparent in acreage expansion as compared with the baseline case.

7. Failure to index tax rates restrains growth more than elimination of the investment tax credit. All calculations in table 3 assume 6 percent inflation. Nonindexed federal income tax rates simulated with 12 percent inflation (not shown) severely restrained farm growth.

8. Table 1 indicated that farms needed to grow in scale by about

3 percent annually in the 1980s and 1990s. Each typical farm in table 3 grows at less than this rate under the baseline scenario and at greater than this rate under the full-owner scenario. The implication is that the tax features are needed for growth of the low-equity base-line farm. Perhaps tax provisions need to be revised to enhance their use by entry-level and expanding modest-size farms and to restrain their use on established, high-equity, large farms.

9. Current estate tax provisions permitted a family with two children (one son, one daughter) to pass on to the next generation at least as much real equity as the current generation began with.

In short, results in table 3 confirm many of the tax cliches. Established farmers indeed have a major advantage over neophyte farmers in com-peting for farm resources.

Influence of commodity program policies. Markets and technology have been the principal forces shaping the structure of the farming industry, but government commodity programs also exert explicit and implicit influences on farm size. Explicit provisions of the Food and Agriculture Act of 1977 are (1) payment limitations, (2) special provisions for haying and grazing, and (3) research and extension directed to small farms. These explicit provisions of the 1977 act have had little impact on farm structure.[10]

A major objective of commodity programs is to provide an eco-nomic climate in which well-managed family farms of adequate size can operate efficiently to provide adequate supplies of food and fiber for domestic and foreign consumers at reasonable cost. In achieving this objective, implicit, often unintended, effects on farm structure emerge over time that dwarf the explicit provisions regarding farm

[10] With payment limitations for wheat, feed grains, and upland cotton at $50,000 for 1980 (Title I, section 101), the Food and Agriculture Act of 1977 had no significant impact on economies of farm size through payment limitations. Title X, section 1004, authorized the secretary of agriculture to administer a special wheat grazing and hay program, which was implemented in 1978. A producer was per-mitted to designate for haying or grazing out a portion of the acreage on the farm intended to be planted to wheat, feed grains, or upland cotton for harvest, not in excess of 40 percent of that acreage or 50 acres, whichever was greatest. Par-ticipants received a payment on this acreage for hay or grazing. Because producers with less than 125 acres intended for planting of wheat, feed grains, or upland cotton could still graze or hay up to 50 acres, the small producer received some benefits not available to the large producer. Title XIV, sections 1440-43, of the Food and Agriculture Act amended the Rural Development Act of 1972 to strengthen and extend research and education programs for small farms, defined as farms with sales of $20,000 or less per year. Funds not to exceed $20 million were authorized but not spent to carry out the research and extension programs.

size stated in the legislation. Table 4 contains estimates of government program dollar benefits among farm sales classes in 1970, a year of sizable benefits, and in 1978, a year of modest benefits. Dollar benefits arise from two sources: direct payments and additions to receipts induced by production controls. Production controls raise product prices for all farmers and commodities and hence for all economic classes. This short-run benefit contributed 10 percent to farm receipts for each class of farms from 57 million diverted acres in 1970 and 3 percent from 18 million set-aside acres in 1978. Diversions have considerably greater impact on income than direct payments except for small farms. The table probably overestimates the contribution of production controls to farm receipts on large farms because such farms produce a higher proportion than family farms of fruits, vegetables, and livestock, which are not directly influenced by set-aside programs.

Both receipts and program benefits were concentrated on large farms, but receipts were more concentrated than program benefits. Direct payments, including government payments for conservation and disaster as well as for commodity programs, constituted a smaller percentage of receipts on large farms than on small farms both in 1970 and in 1978. Program benefits were the largest proportion of net farm income on moderate-size farms in 1978, a departure from their significance to large farms in 1970. Large farms use a higher ratio than small farms of purchased inputs to farm equity capital and operator and family labor. A given percentage drop in gross income of the farming industry is associated with a larger percentage drop in net income on large farms than on small farms, because large farms have a smaller amount of net income to equity and family labor relative to gross farm income. Because income from farm sources is a high proportion of total net income from all sources on large farms, termination of commodity programs reduces total income by a greater percentage on large than on small farms. The result would be a more even distribution of income from all sources among farms. The greater equality would come not from increasing income on small farms but from a sharp drop in income on large farms. Large farms not only benefit most in dollars from commodity programs, but they also experience the greatest short-term setback from termination of programs. Table 4 indicates that if program benefits are to be denied to large farms, then benefits must be in the form not of production controls but of direct payments to small and moderate-size farms.

Long-term effects can be decisive, however. In 1968, Tyner and I advanced the hypothesis that "forward pricing and income security provided by [government commodity] programs have encouraged sub-

TABLE 4

Distribution of Government Program Benefits among U.S. Farms Classified by Sales, 1970 and 1978

	Farms with Sales							
	$100,000 and over	$40,000 to $99,000	$20,000 to $39,999	$10,000 to $19,999	$5,000 to $9,999	$2,500 to $4,999	Less than $2,500	All Farms
1970								
Share (%) of all farm:								
Operators	1.9	6.1	11.1	13.2	13.6	14.3	39.8	100.0
Direct payments	14.2	19.4	22.7	18.4	11.0	6.9	7.4	100.0
Receipts	33.4	22.1	19.5	12.3	6.5	3.4	2.8	100.0
Realized net income from farming	16.3	21.8	24.0	16.1	9.2	5.1	7.5	100.0
Benefits of government programs (in dollars per farm operator)								
Addition to receipts (10% of receipts)	32,088	6,818	3,281	1,734	885	437	129	1,858
Direct government payments	9,263	4,056	2,583	1,754	1,010	608	235	1,260
Total benefits	41,351	10,874	5,864	3,488	1,895	1,045	364	3,118
Benefits as percentage of:								
Farming receipts	12.9	16.0	17.9	20.1	21.5	23.9	35.4	16.8
Net income from farming	98.0	62.3	56.4	59.6	58.7	61.6	40.4	65.0

1978

Share (%) of all farm:								
Operators	7.0	14.6	12.1	11.1	10.5	10.4	34.3	100.0
Direct payments	21.5	36.0	21.5	9.0	5.5	3.7	2.8	100.0
Receipts	56.3	25.0	9.9	4.6	2.2	1.1	0.9	100.0
Realized net income from farming	36.5	31.5	14.2	6.5	3.4	2.0	5.9	100.0
Benefits of government programs **(in dollars per farm operator)**								
Addition to receipts (3% of receipts)	10,463	2,228	1,059	533	275	139	35	1,300
Direct government payments	3,476	2,800	2,012	926	598	401	92	1,134
Total benefits	13,939	5,028	3,071	1,459	873	540	127	2,434
Benefits as percentage of:								
Farming receipts	4.0	6.8	8.7	8.2	9.5	11.7	11.0	5.6
Net income from farming	26.6	23.2	26.1	24.7	26.6	28.3	7.3	24.3

SOURCE: U.S. Department of Agriculture, *Farm Income Statistics*, for data on operators, direct payments, receipts, and net income. Estimates of benefits by author.

stitution of capital for labor."[11] Government programs provided payments that helped farmers purchase machinery and diverted acres from cropland, which necessitated an expansion in acres per farm to restore the efficient-size operating unit. Acreage allotments caused land prices to be bid up, creating a barrier to entry by aspiring young operators and providing windfall equity to established owners so that they could outbid others for land. On the basis of simulated operation of the economy over the 1930–1960 period, Tyner and I were unable to reject the hypothesis that programs encouraged consolidation and out-migration: slightly more labor was estimated to be used in farming without government commodity programs than with them. Later studies by Ray and Heady[12] and by Nelson and Cochrane[13] also found that commodity programs displaced farm operator, family, and hired labor in the long run.

The Tyner-Tweeten hypothesis emphasizes aspects of commodity programs that tend to displace farm labor. Alternative hypotheses emphasize ways in which government commodity programs retain more farm labor and family farms. Commodity programs have helped some marginal and heavily indebted farms remain in agriculture and have slowed adoption of some labor-saving technology, most notably in the case of tobacco. To be sure, government payments are larger on big farms that on small ones, but payments are more equally distributed among farms than receipts. Dividing all costs of farm production by gross farm income on each economic class of farms provides a flatter unit cost curve with than without government payments included in gross farm income. The implication is that commodity programs reduce economies of size. If commodity program payments are viewed as a rate rather than as an absolute amount, that rate or "price" per unit of output is less on large than on small farms. By this reckoning, programs discourage consolidation.

Milton Friedman's permanent income hypothesis states that savings-investment rates are higher out of transitory income than out of permanent income.[14] According to investment equations estimated

[11] Fred Tyner and Luther Tweeten, "Simulation as a Method of Appraising Farm Programs," *American Journal of Agricultural Economics*, vol. 50, no. 1 (February 1968), pp. 66–81.

[12] Daryll Ray and Earl Heady, *Simulated Effects of Alternative Policy and Economic Environments on U.S. Agriculture*, CARD Report 46 (Ames: Center for Agricultural and Rural Development, Iowa State University, 1974).

[13] Fred Nelson and Willard Cochrane, "Economic Consequences of Federal Farm Commodity Programs, 1953–72," *Agricultural Economics Research,* vol. 28 (1976), pp. 52–64.

[14] Milton Friedman, *A Theory of the Consumption Function* (New York: National Bureau of Economic Research, 1955).

by Rogers and me, mean investment is higher for a given mean income when that income is unstable than when it is stable.[15] Farm production, prices, and income are more unstable without than with government commodity programs (see appendix). To the extent that additional investment in capital substitutes for labor and enhances economies of farm size and consolidation, it follows that commodity programs may increase farm numbers and decrease farm size. My conclusion after reviewing the data and logic on both sides of the issue is that the conventional wisdom that government commodity programs contribute significantly to concentration in farming is not well founded. Research provides no compelling evidence that government commodity programs inhibited or accelerated farm consolidation and enlargement; the best guess is that commodity programs had only a modest impact on structure. A policy of direct payments only to low-income farmers, however, could have slowed consolidation.

Do Social Benefits Exceed Private Benefits in Small-Scale Farming?
Early studies revealed that persons on small, low-income farms were characterized by anomie, that is, by feelings of alienation, demoralization, and pessimism.[16] In a recent study, Coughenour and Christenson empirically examined the "small is beautiful" thesis by relating farm size to attitudes about personal well-being, community well-being, and perceived adequacy of services.[17] They found no evidence that small farmers were more satisfied than large farmers with their personal life, with the social aspects of community life, or with the social services available to them. Small differences that did emerge from the study suggest that farmers on commercial, family-size units with sales of $40,000 or more expressed a higher level of perceived well-being than small-scale farmers.

Based on a detailed study of approximately 800 rural families in Iowa and North Carolina from 1970 to 1972, Harper and I found that income, occupation, education, and age were the principal de-

[15] Stanley Rogers and Luther Tweeten, "Farm Investment Behavior under Uncertainty: An Application of the Permanent Income Hypothesis," mimeographed (Stillwater: Department of Agricultural Economics, Oklahoma State University, 1980).

[16] Luther Tweeten, *Rural Poverty: Incidence, Causes, and Cures*, Process Series P-590R (Stillwater: Agricultural Experiment Station, Oklahoma State University, July 1968).

[17] Milton Coughenour and James Christenson, "Is Life on the Small Farm Beautiful? Agricultural Structure and Quality of Life in the United States" (Paper presented at the Fifth World Congress for Rural Sociology, Mexico City, August 1980).

terminants of personal well-being.[18] It seems likely that the feelings of dissatisfaction and anomie prevalent on small farms are the product of low income as much as of small farm size per se. Able-bodied full-time operators of small farms have a high incidence of low income, and it is not feasible to separate positive feelings of independence and pride of ownership of a small farm from negative feelings arising from poverty and underemployment. For small farms with sales of $30,000 or less per year, it is difficult to conceive of operator-family labor income from farming greater than $10,000 per year. In fact, budget studies show that labor income is likely to be much less. Labor income averages approximately 14 percent of receipts over all farms and on large farms averages approximately 5 percent.[19]

If small farms are providing a low quality of life, we should observe a massive exodus from these farms. This is precisely what we do observe (see figure 1). If the 1959–1969 or 1959–1974 trends continue, there will be no full-time small farming by able-bodied farm operators by the early 1980s. In the future we can expect somewhat stable numbers of farms headed by elderly persons, many of whom will receive considerable off-farm income from social security and other retirement sources. The number of part-time small farms with families making substantial incomes off the farm can be expected to grow in the future. Given stability or growth in numbers of small farms with aged and part-time operators and stability or a small decline in the number of small farms with full-time able-bodied heads, the number of small farms can be expected to grow or at least become stable by the late 1980s. These part-time units will not be the back-to-nature farms providing a way of life to the alternative culturists but will be a further extension of the urban-industrial process to the farm, as evidenced by the dominance of part-time operations.

In short, no basis exists for the notion that the social benefits exceed the private benefits of small farms or that conventional measures of output used to appraise economic efficiency do not apply to small farms.

Do Operators of Small Farms and Owner-Operators Take Better Care of Their Land Than Other Farmers? A number of studies before 1960, many of them in western Iowa, suggested that soil conservation was

---

[18] Wilmer Harper and Luther Tweeten, "Socio-psychological Measures of Quality of Rural Life," *American Journal of Agricultural Economics*, vol. 59, no. 5 (December 1977), pp. 1000–1005.

[19] Tweeten and Huffman, "Structural Change," pp. 46, 53.

inhibited by crop share-leasing arrangements, small farm size, low income (high discount rate), and owner resistance to cooperation.[20]

In a recent and more comprehensive study, Lee analyzed merged data from the 1977 natural resource inventory conducted by the Soil Conservation Service and the 1978 landownership survey undertaken by the National Economics Division of the U.S. Department of Agriculture.[21] The two-stage sample of 70,000 primary sampling units resulted in 37,000 completed landownership questionnaires, providing basic data reliable at the state level on land use, land quality, potential cropland, and erosion. The results revealed no significant differences in mean soil losses among different types of ownership groups nationally. In none of the ten regions did average rates of erosion by nonfamily corporations exceed those of other types of ownership. In the Southeast region, family ownerships averaged 6.36 more tons per acre of soil loss annually than nonfamily corporations. Almost 57 percent of land owned by nonfamily corporations was operated using minimum tillage or residue practices, whereas only 36 percent of land owned by families had these practices in effect. Yet the need for conservation practices as measured by erosion hazards was as great or greater on land owned by families.

Nationally, Lee's analysis did not reveal significant differences in soil erosion rates among noncorporate tenure groups. For operators who operated only land that they owned, higher incomes were associated with lower rates of erosion both nationally and within five of ten regions of the United States. Mean levels of erosion for landowners reporting net farm incomes of $3,000–9,000, $10,000–19,999 and $20,000–49,999, for example, were respectively 1.34, 1.49, and 2.31 tons per acre less than for farm landowners reporting annual income of less than $3,000. Net farm income greater than $50,000 did not appear to result in significantly lower erosion rates. In the Corn Belt, landowners with net incomes of $20,000–49,000 averaged 9.4 tons per acre less erosion on cultivated cropland than owners with less than $3,000 of net income. The pattern was similar in the Northeast, Delta, and Mountain regions, where full-owner operators who experienced net income losses

[20] H. O. Anderson, P. E. McNall, and B. C. Inman, *Progress in Application of Soil Conserving Practices, Southwestern Wisconsin*, ARS 42-43 (Washington, D.C.: Department of Agriculture, Agricultural Research Service, April 1957); Burnell Held and Marion Clawson, *Soil Conservation in Perspective* (Baltimore: Johns Hopkins University Press, 1965); and Burnell Held and John Timmons, *Soil Erosion Control in Process in Western Iowa*, Research Bulletin no. 460 (Ames: Agricultural Experiment Station, Iowa State University, August 1958).
[21] Linda Lee, "The Impact of Land Ownership Factors on Soil Conservation," *American Journal of Agricultural Economics*, vol. 62, no. 5 (December 1980).

had the highest reported erosion rates. In the Delta, for example, land-owners with net income losses averaged 26.4 tons per acre soil loss, compared with 3.0 tons per acre by the highest-income landowners in the region. Despite less erosion hazards on land owned by the affluent, 60 percent of cultivated cropland owned by landowners with net income greater than $50,000 had minimum tillage or residue practices in effect, and 47 percent of such land owned by those with net farm income less than $3,000 had these practices.

In short, Lee's results gave no basis to conclude that tenants have more soil losses than full- or part-owner operators. Low income, often associated with the small farms, is a factor in poor soil conservation practices and erosion. The Lee study did not examine the environmental effects of chemical pesticides and fertilizers. The greater economic efficiency of large farms is partly due to greater use of chemicals. Although chemical use could be reduced under proper management without loss of yields, a large reduction in chemical use would severely impair yields and require extension of cropland to erosion-prone soils to maintain output.[22]

Will the Rising Cost of Energy Improve the Comparative Advantage of Small Farms? Scattered facts and logic shed some light on the issue of rising energy prices and their effects on small farms. Large tractors, while saving labor per horsepower-hour, provide as many horsepower-hours per unit of fuel as small tractors. Large farms may use more energy in the form of pesticides and fertilizer per unit of output than small farms, but chemicals reduce the energy needed for tillage and harvest per unit of output. National data presented by David Holland show that fossil fuel energy use per dollar of output is greater on small farms than on large farms.[23] If energy shortages make it economically feasible to fuel farming operations with alcohol produced on the farm, large farms would have an advantage because of economies of size in alcohol production.

Finally, and most important, a population dispersed on many small farms requires greater transportation energy for shopping, school buses, and other trips to town than a small population on larger farms. In summary, higher energy prices will not improve the competitive position of the small farm.

---

[22] Stanley Schraufnagel and Earl Heady, *Supply Control and U.S. Agriculture*, CARD Report 94 (Ames: Center for Agricultural and Rural Development, Iowa State University, July 1980).

[23] David Holland, "Energy and the Structure of Agriculture," *American Journal of Agricultural Economics*, vol. 62, no. 5 (December 1980).

Does the Trauma of Migration from Farms Offset Gains in Earnings?
It is well to recognize that the heaviest migration from farms has been by youth. Comparatively few prime-age families established in farming migrated to urban places in any generation. After reviewing a large number of studies of rural-urban migrants, Brinkman and I stated that:

> migrants substantially increased their real income and na-
> tional income. Farmers who remained at home also received
> higher incomes because they could farm larger units and did
> not have to share the home farm operation with others.
> Available data also show that migrants in vast majority im-
> proved their housing and medical and welfare service oppor-
> tunities, as well as educational opportunities for their children.
> Very few became part of the urban unrest problem.[24]

Inadequate human investments in the form of job information, training, and public schooling created undue friction in the great rural-urban exodus. Given the choice between the poverty, underemployment, and squalor and the exodus with inadequate preparation, the exodus was more attractive to the disadvantaged and disfranchised.

Can Publicly Supported Research and Extension Save the Small Farm?
The payoff from agricultural research and extension has been exceed-
ingly high, typically averaging a 50 percent rate of return on investment.[25] This return is achieved by savings in conventional inputs such
as land and irrigation water, by lower food and fiber costs to consumers, and by foreign exchange earnings through exports. Early
adopters benefit from research and extension, but the competitive farming industry as a whole is unable to retain the benefits of research and
extension. Farm productivity gains averaged 1.7 percent per year from
1970 to 1978, or over $2 billion annually, of which nearly half was
from private sources.

Because publicly supported research and extension are mainly
biological and focus on increasing output, their impact on farm structure
is modest compared with that of the business sector. Machinery firms
and other private industries emphasize labor-saving technology, which
has massively influenced farm size and numbers. This private investment
would continue to expand farm size and diminish numbers even if public
research and extension were terminated for large farms. We would,

---

[24] Luther Tweeten and George Brinkman, *Micropolitan Development* (Ames: Iowa State University Press, 1976).

[25] For a summary of estimates, see Vernon Ruttan, "Bureaucratic Productivity: The Case of Agricultural Research," *Ag World*, vol. 5, no. 3 (March-April 1979), pp. 1–7.

however, lose the benefits of research and extension from the land grant university system, benefits that lower real spending for food, expand exports to earn foreign exchange, and save soil.

Research and extension are not a welfare program or an effective tool to redistribute income to small farms. Part-time farmers are often distracted from improving farm productivity by other responsibilities, by lack of scale, and by lack of need for additional income; aged farmers have too short an earnings horizon to make needed investments in greater productivity; and full-time, able-bodied operators often have limited human and material resources to raise output and income substantially.[26] I am by no means contending that research and extension should not be directed at small farmers, but rather that they must be accompanied by general education, vocational-technical training, labor information, off-farm job creation, and welfare programs if standards of living are to be markedly improved. Research and extension provide the highest payoff to society when made available to all farms.

Is Farm Ownership Falling into the Hands of Nonfarmers and Foreigners? A 1978 survey of U.S. landownership patterns—the most comprehensive information we have—states that "ownership of U.S. land is concentrated in the hands of a few; the top 5 percent of all landowners own 75 percent of all land, while the bottom 78 percent of all landowners own 3 percent of the land."[27] These figures, pointing to high concentration of ownership and wealth, are grossly misleading because they include a large number of residential and commercial properties that have small acreages per unit.

Farmland ownership is becoming more concentrated, but the degree of concentration is less than that of farm receipts and liabilities. Ownership concentration is mainly in the hands of farm operators. We know too little about the nature and extent of nonfarm ownership of farmland. Ambiguities in the census of agriculture and lack of a benchmark for the 1978 survey preclude estimating changes in farmland ownership over time. The proportion of farmland owned by nonfamily corporations and partnerships and by foreigners is small. From 35 percent to 50 percent of farmland is owned by nonfarmers, but a significant proportion of these—we do not know exactly how many—are retired farmers or spouses of farmers.

[26] Jerry West, Van Harrold, K. C. Schneeberger, and Lionel Williamson, *Missouri Small Farm Program*, SR 176 (Columbia: Cooperative Extension Service, University of Missouri, 1975).

[27] James Lewis, *Land Ownership in the U.S., 1978*, Agricultural Information Bulletin no. 435 (Washington, D.C.: Department of Agriculture, Economics, Statistics, and Cooperatives Service, April 1980).

Is the Optimal-Size Farm a Small Farm? Many studies of economies of size indicate that most production economies are realized by farms with sales of approximately $60,000 per year, although modest market economies continue to accrue to sales of $100,000 and more. Of course, economies of size differ greatly by type of farm and characteristics of the operator. Tew and others found that, on the average, variable costs of production did not appear to vary systematically by size of farm. This suggests that small farmers are adopting technology about as fast as other farmers.[28] Miller showed that variability among individual farmers vastly outweighs economies of size as a factor determining costs of production.[29] We do not know whether the large variation in cost of production among farmers is the result of systematic differences in management abilities or is a random element traced to uncontrollable uncertainties of nature and markets.

The 1980 farm output could be produced with approximately 2 million family farms producing $60,000 per farm and obtaining 40 percent of their income from off-farm sources (to obtain a satisfactory living) or by 1.2 million economic farming units producing $100,000 per farm and relying solely on the farm for their livelihood. This is a far greater number of family farms than the 600,000 shown in table 1. The optimal size of farm varies a great deal by individual and commodity. In cattle and broiler feeding operations, for example, the size needs to be larger, as it does in processed fruits and vegetables. In tobacco and selected fresh fruit and vegetable production, economies of size are few, and an adequate income can be realized on smaller farms.

The optimal size of farm depends not only on production and market economies but also on the marginal utility of resources and income. As the size of a farming business expands until it reaches sales of approximately $100,000 on the average, efficiencies are obtained that are passed on to consumers and increase their utility. As farm size expands further, efficiencies are nominal, but the marginal utility of income to farmers declines. Thus $1 billion of labor-management income produces more utility when received by 60,000 farm operators than by 1,000 farm operators. At some point utility gains to consumers equal utility losses to farmers as earnings per farm are pushed to high levels.

Most production and marketing economies are achieved on farms with $100,000 of sales, but labor income and utility per farm family

[28] Bernard Tew, Stan Spurlock, Wesley Musser, and Bill Miller, "Some Evidence on Pecuniary Economies of Size for Farm Firms," *Southern Journal of Agricultural Economics*, vol. 12, no. 1 (July 1980), pp. 151–54.

[29] Miller, "Economies of Size," p. 111.

increase as sales are expanded even further. Because costs to consumers remain similar with 1.2 million farms or fewer, only the impact on farmers' utility is considered. Using estimates of the marginal utility curve estimated by Harper and me, updated to the 1979 price level, utility to the farming industry is reduced 15 percent by having 600,000 farms marketing $200,000 per farm rather than 1.2 million farms marketing $100,000 per farm.[30] The reduction in total utility with fewer farms that arises from the declining marginal utility of income is slightly less estimated by a marginal utility curve derived from the federal income tax schedule. Having a system of smaller farms would not reduce the utility of the farm population from the optimal level of $100,000 per farm because farm people take off-farm jobs to bring the average income of smaller farms to that of farms of optimal size. Consumers, however, experience a substantial loss of utility because of lower farming efficiency.

In summary, optimal farm size varies widely, and certainly no one size fits all conditions. The size of farm consistent with increased well-being is not a small or a very large farm, but rather a moderate-size family operation.

Will Power and Wealth Be Concentrated in the Hands of a Few? Measures of concentration presented earlier have raised fears that production and marketing will be manipulated to raise food prices and restrict supplies. Concentration of production within the farm sector, highest in egg, fed cattle, vegetable, and fruit production,[31] could increase by several magnitudes before it would reach levels found in many nonfarm industries. Some price enhancement has occurred in fruits, vegetables, and dairy products with government help in the form of marketing orders. Despite concentration of ownership and vertical integration in broiler production, the industry is characterized by rising efficiency and falling real prices.

Although at some point a few might gain control of the agricultural market, it is unlikely in the foreseeable future unless government provides the necessary legal framework for a cartel. If the government turns from fostering cartels to enforcing existing Sherman and Clayton antitrust laws, the cartel problem is not of concern. The 50,000 producers who may produce nearly two-thirds of farm output by the year 2000 will be a long way from the dozen or so producers needed to control output for monopoly profit without government help.

[30] Harper and Tweeten, "Socio-psychological Measures," p. 1003.
[31] Barry Carr, "A Profile of the Commercial Agriculture Sector," in Senate, *Farm Structure*, p. 28.

Is Farmland Overpriced in Relation to Its Prospective Earning Capacity?
Farmland that was overpriced in relation to prospective earnings would
constitute an unwarranted barrier to aspiring family entrants into farming and would pose a threat to financially leveraged landowners if the
speculative bubble burst and land values collapsed. For many years the
perception has been widespread among laymen as well as agricultural
economists that farmland is overpriced in relation to its potential earning
capacity. The superficial evidence seems clear—earnings from three
acres of farmland are required to pay the interest on one acre.

Those who buy and sell farmland have had a keener feel for rational real estate pricing in an inflationary economy than many agricultural economists. Rates of return from current earnings of farm equity
capital, primarily real estate, averaged 5.2 percent from 1968 to 1978.[32]
Real capital gains averaged 6.7 percent over the same period, bringing
total real returns to 12 percent. This return compares favorably with
rates of return on alternative investments.

Current earnings to farm real estate have averaged approximately
4 percent of investment for decades and continue to do so. One must
add to these earnings the nominal capital gains equal to inflation, because land earnings are expected to increase as fast as inflation. The
result is nominal capital gains equal to the inflation rate, zero real
capital gain, and real returns equal to current earnings, approximately
4 percent per year. Many investors would be pleased to receive such
real rates of return. Prospective earnings from farming alone warrant
current land values; one need not invoke justifications such as speculation and urban encroachment to account for current land prices. Current
land prices seem in line with prospective earnings, but land seems to
have been underpriced in the past.

Economists have confused overpricing of land with a cash-flow
problem. Land is clearly overpriced for a would-be young owner-
operator with a few dollars of equity. The cash-flow problem, which
is the result of inflation, is probably the most serious farm problem of
today and is a major factor in the demise of the moderate-size family
farm.

**Is the Social and Economic Vitality of Rural Towns and Small Cities
Drained by Farm Enlargement?** Since the famous Goldschmidt study

---

[32] Carson Evans, *Balance Sheet of the Farming Sector 1979*, Agricultural Informa-
tion Bulletin no. 430 (Washington, D.C.: Department of Agriculture, Economics,
Statistics, and Cooperatives Service, February 1980). For other estimates of rates
of return, see Carl Gertel and James Lewis, "Returns from Absentee-Owned Farm
Land and Common Stock, 1940–1979," *Agricultural Finance Review*, vol. 40
(April 1980), pp. 1–11.

of the California towns of Arvin and Dinuba in the early 1940s, the socioeconomic relationship of the rural town or small city to its surrounding farming area has been of interest.[33] Output and employment multipliers estimated by economists have quantified the relationship between basic industry, such as farming, and secondary and tertiary industry, such as banks, grocery stores, and lumberyards, in local communities. In 1963 Walker and I studied the impact on southwest Oklahoma of the declining numbers and increasing size of farms.[34] We estimated a long-term multiplier of farm and nonfarm employment that indicated that 2.25 nonfarm workers were associated with 1.0 farm workers. We projected the impact of adjustment to farms of economically optimal size from the many farms that were earning low incomes. Our projections of reductions in number of farms were off the mark, as were projections by social scientists for other rural areas, primarily because we did not foresee the rise of the nonfarm economic base with its employment opportunities for part-time farmers and for nonfarm people.

The issue of whether public policy should be invoked to slow or stop farming adjustments that affect local communities involves many economic, social, and political dimensions, not all of which can be considered here. From a reading of the literature, I reach these conclusions:

• Vast misinformation surrounds the question of interaction between the farm and nonfarm sectors. This distortion was perhaps first engendered by the failure to realize that Dinuba was a town surrounded by family-size farms (slightly larger than average size), not by small farms. Many towns in the South are surrounded by small, low-income farms. These communities are characterized by an egregious lack of economic and social vitality and are hardly models to be emulated. Given the importance of income and employment to well-being, the farm of optimal size from the standpoint of the community is not a small, low-income farm.

• Much of the decline in rural nonfarm population attributed to the decline in farm population would have occurred in the absence of farm consolidation and enlargement. The principal reason for the decline of the small town is the improvement of transportation, that is, the devel-

[33] For reference and critique of the Goldschmidt and related studies, see Steven Sonka, "Consequences of Farm Structural Change," in *Structure of Agriculture and Information Needs Regarding Small Farms* (Washington, D.C.: National Rural Center, 1980), pt. 2.

[34] Luther Tweeten and Odell Walker, *Estimating Socioeconomic Effects of a Declining Farm Population in a Sparse Area* (Raleigh: Agricultural Policy Institute, North Carolina State University, 1963), pp. 101–19.

opment of automobiles and roads. They influenced not only the local general store but also schools and medical facilities because they enabled people to travel greater distances to obtain a higher quality and variety of educational, medical, and other services.

• Rural communities have shown remarkable vitality in the face of declining farm employment. The well-documented demographic transition is characterized by employment and population growth not only in counties adjacent to metropolitan counties but also in hinterland counties. The probability of growth for towns of 1,000 inhabitants has been as great as that for larger towns and cities in recent years because of the movement of nonfarm industry to rural areas.

• It has been feared that the rural turnaround is threatened by rising costs of energy. Although commuting patterns are only one dimension of energy costs in nonmetropolitan areas, they are important. Recent work by Bowles and Beale indicates that such areas are not so burdened by energy consumption or time in the journey to work that their competitive advantage will be eroded with rising energy prices.[35] In 1975 the effort required to get to work was less for nonmetropolitan residents (4.6 miles, 14 minutes) than for metropolitan residents (7.6 miles, 22 minutes).

About one-fifth of employed nonmetropolitan household heads worked in counties in which they did not live, and less than half this group commuted to metropolitan area jobs. Only 17 percent of all household heads who had moved into nonmetropolitan counties between 1970 and 1975 were still working in metropolitan locations in 1975, and they traveled an average of 26 miles to work. Their median family income was $15,248, or $2,228 more than that of movers who did not commute in 1975. If these groups were comparable in other respects except in their commuting pattern, the net cost in transportation alone could be as high as twenty-two cents a mile to break even on this income difference. Whereas more fuel-efficient means of transportation and car pools can reduce the cost of commuting, the important point is that nonmetropolitan residents appear on the average to require less energy and effort to get to work than metropolitan residents. The major cost of commuting is time, and the more favorable opportunities to improve public transportation in metropolitan areas may add to time even as they reduce energy costs. The rising cost of energy thus would appear to curtail economic activity as much in metropolitan as in other

[35] Gladys Bowles and Calvin Beale, "Commuting and Migration Status in Non-Metro Areas," *Agricultural Economics Research*, vol. 32, no. 3 (July 1980), pp. 8–20.

areas. The effect of rising energy costs will be to inhibit part-time farming, however, because it will be cheaper for workers to reside in towns and small cities closer to their work.

Other Myths. Other commonly held views of agriculture need to be critically examined. One is that improved farming productivity has been a subsidy to metropolitan corporations rather than a benefit to lower-income consumers.[36] Examination of trends in corporate profits and the real cost of farm food ingredients to low-income consumers refutes the myth.

Another myth is that the exodus of farmers erodes the tax base of rural communities. In fact, since better managers take over when farms are consolidated, output and the tax base usually expand. The per capita tax base has mushroomed in many farming communities.

Other contentions, such as that the small farm is essential to a democratic form of government and to stability in output of food, have no substance in reality.

Summary and Conclusions

The record of American agriculture is a drama of unparalleled socio-economic success. Its successes include sharply higher quality of life, improved nutrition, lower real food prices, the role of the United States as breadbasket of the world, and the farming industry's position as the greatest source of foreign exchange earnings. Extreme care should be taken in tampering with this proven record of performance. The pathos of the drama includes concern over the projected shrinking numbers and shares of moderate-size family farms in the farming sector.

This paper reaches the following conclusions about the structure of agriculture:

1. Commodity programs have probably had no major impact on the size and number of farms, but federal income tax policies give a distinct advantage to the established farmer and to the part-time small farmer. Termination of favorable federal income tax features would be a severe blow to farmers who have invested in reliance on their continuation. If the goal is to promote family-size farms, one possible strategy would be to continue the tax features, perhaps making them even more favorable for young farmers but restricting the amount and duration of deductions.

2. Operators of small farms appear to receive less personal satis-

---

[36] See Flinn and Buttel, "Sociological Aspects of Farm Size."

faction from life than operators of moderate-size or large farms, other things being equal. Intangibles, such as subsidies for small farms, do not warrant special consideration.

3. Persons operating moderate-size and larger farms appear to take at least as good care of the environment, measured mainly by soil conservation, as small farmers, and there is no indication that sole proprietors take better care of the land than corporations. Externalities do not warrant special subsidies to small farms.

4. There is no indication that the increasing cost of energy will improve the comparative advantage of small farms, although this issue is clouded by lack of empirical evidence.

5. There is no indication that persons who have left farming have experienced a degree of trauma that would offset the economic and social benefits of mechanization and consolidation of farms; there also is no basis to conclude that a speedup of emigration from farms would be desirable. There is continuing concern by social scientists that farmers be given adequate access to education, training, and labor market information so that they have options in deciding how to use their human resources.

6. Considerable public agricultural research and extension have focused on the small farm since the 1930s. Some of the research has been conducted on topics such as rural development, poverty, and underemployment. One conclusion of the research is that a major re-direction of public agricultural research and extension to small farmers would have a low payoff, raising incomes of small farmers by only a modest amount. The payoff to society is highest from continued public research and extension without regard to farm size.

7. The optimal size of farm to increase well-being appears to be consistent with typical commercial farms of today—approximately $100,000 in sales and $1 million in assets. The nation could support approximately 1.2 million such farms, approximately twice the existing number of family-size farms.

8. Fears that farm production will become concentrated in so few hands that prices will be manipulated at the expense of consumers appear to be premature. There is no indication that any sector of the farming economy will be able to aggrandize itself substantially at the expense of the public in the foreseeable future.

9. Current land prices are justified by prospective future earnings from farming alone, although farmland appears to have been under-priced in the past. This is not to deny that some land is now overpriced and other land underpriced in relation to prospective earnings.

10. The social and economic vitality of many rural towns and small cities has declined but on the whole has been maintained remark-

ably well in the face of declining farm employment, in part because the economic base has been expanded by manufacturing and other industries.

There may be sound reasons for overriding the market system to preserve small and family farms, but this report shows that many of the reasons traditionally given for doing so are not grounded in fact.

Appendix

The magnitude of instability in production, prices, and farm value of receipts is measured in tables 5 and 6 by the coefficient of variation, defined as the standard deviation divided by the mean (in a normal distribution, 67 percent of random outcomes fall within one standard deviation above and below the mean). Coefficients for selected crops in table 5 and for selected livestock and all farm output in table 6 indicate patterns in variability over time.

No consistent upward or downward trend in variability is apparent since 1930 among crops. The relationship between instability and government commodity programs, especially prominent in the 1950s and 1960s, is apparent. In each of these decades, commodity programs were associated with low coefficients of variation in wheat and corn production, price, and farm value. Soybean production, which was not controlled by commodity programs, continued to exhibit high production variability from 1950 to 1969. The variation for crops as a whole was much higher in periods of uncontrolled production than in periods of extensive commodity programs.

Coefficients of variation for livestock and livestock products in table 6 also show no consistent trend over time. Although production of livestock was not controlled by commodity programs, variation in the hog market might have been influenced by efforts to stabilize feed grain production. The measures of variation for hogs suggest that commodity programs were a stabilizing influence on production, price, and farm value. Stability for all livestock and all farm products appears to have been enhanced in the 1950s and 1960s.

Trends in farm outcomes, if unanticipated, can be a source of uncertainty and inefficiency to farmers and to others. Trends have not been removed from most of the coefficients of variation shown in tables 5 and 6, but the coefficients in parentheses were estimated with a linear trend removed for each decade. The magnitude of the coefficient of variation is substantially reduced in later decades, but the conclusions remain the same: the decades of most intense government involvement in farming (1950–1959 and 1960–1969) were also the periods of some stability.

TABLE 5: COEFFICIENTS OF VARIATION FOR PRODUCTION, PRICE, AND VALUE OF SELECTED CROPS FOR FIVE PERIODS, UNITED STATES, 1930–1978

	1930–1939	1940–1949	1950–1959	1960–1969	1970–1978
Wheat					
Production	20.8	16.7	15.7	11.7	15.1
Price	30.7	33.8	6.7	18.3	39.8
Farm value	30.2	48.1	13.9	10.4	45.0
Corn					
Production	23.9	13.5	11.7	10.6	15.4
Price	37.3	36.5	15.2	6.3	30.7
Farm value	19.1	34.2	8.4	12.2	32.7
Cotton					
Production	21.4	19.3	15.4	22.9	16.8
Price	23.9	31.9	9.2	17.2	34.1
Farm value	19.9	40.5	16.5	36.1	35.9
Soybeans					
Production	39.9	27.4	28.8	23.9	18.7
Price	33.0	31.9	13.0	7.3	29.2
Farm value	66.4	44.4	16.4	26.6	39.6
All crops[a]					
Production	12.3 (12.3)	6.6 (4.2)	5.2 (3.0)	4.7 (2.2)	8.4 (3.8)
Price	22.7	30.9	6.7	3.4	27.7
Farm value	20.3 (20.0)	37.7 (9.6)	5.9 (5.9)	8.0 (1.8)	32.6 (15.4)

[a]Coefficients in parentheses are estimated from data with linear trend for the decade removed.

SOURCES: U.S. Department of Agriculture, *Changes in Farm Production and Efficiency, 1978*, Statistical Bulletin no. 628 (Washington, D.C.: Department of Agriculture, Economics, Statistics, and Cooperatives Service, January 1980); and U.S. Department of Agriculture, *Agricultural Statistics* (Washington, D.C., 1979).

TABLE 6: COEFFICIENTS OF VARIATION FOR PRODUCTION, PRICE, AND VALUE OF SELECTED LIVESTOCK AND LIVESTOCK PRODUCTS FOR FIVE PERIODS, UNITED STATES, 1930–1978

	1930–1939	1940–1949	1950–1959	1960–1969	1970–1978
Milk					
Production	2.1	2.7	3.0	3.3	2.7
Price	16.4	29.8	6.8	12.1	23.0
Farm value	15.0	29.7	5.4	8.8	24.8
Hogs					
Production	15.4	107.4	7.3	4.3	9.2
Price	36.3	38.3	15.3	16.5	30.9
Farm value	31.7	126.6	13.5	15.6	24.7
Beef cattle					
Production	5.1	6.8	9.1	8.6	2.6
Price	23.7	36.5	19.0	10.7	18.9
Farm value	26.1	38.2	19.0	17.8	22.1
All livestock[a]					
Production	5.0 (5.0)	7.0 (6.7)	4.8 (1.6)	4.7 (1.5)	1.6 (1.6)
Price	21.7	30.8	12.6	9.7	25.1
Farm value	21.1 (12.0)	34.7 (10.6)	8.0 (8.2)	14.5 (5.4)	21.9 (8.9)
All farm products[a]					
Production	9.3 (9.3)	7.0 (4.0)	5.4 (1.8)	4.4 (1.6)	5.9 (2.9)
Price	20.9	30.6	9.5	4.3	25.0
Farm value	20.4 (20.1)	35.9 (10.0)	5.9 (5.9)	11.4 (3.1)	26.1 (1.6)

[a]Coefficients in parentheses are estimated from data with linear trend for the decade removed.

SOURCES: U.S. Department of Agriculture, *Changes in Farm Production and Efficiency, 1978*; and U.S. Department of Agriculture, *Agricultural Statistics, 1979*.

Commentary

John W. Mellor

These comments address the dynamics of third world food relationships as they bear on U.S. agriculture and the optimal U.S. policy for effectively increasing agricultural exports in this context.

Josling correctly points to growth in per capita income as the key dynamic element in third world demand for food. As populations increase, they tend to provide for their own additional food requirements through additional labor input into an agricultural sector that is still somewhat responsive to more intensive husbandry. Insofar as rural labor productivity declines in response to population growth on a limited land base, so too do per capita income and the derived demand for food. It is the dynamics of agricultural technology and the rise of urban industry, with its rising labor productivity and income, that make a net addition to the demand for food. As I spelled out a decade and a half ago, in the early stages of rapid economic growth the increase in demand for food is virtually certain to overcome even the most productive agricultural capacity to grow.[1] When countries commence rapid growth, their population is still usually growing at more than 2 percent per year, consumers use food expenditures almost proportionately to per capita income growth, and income per capita may grow at 4 percent or more. Thus, although the demand for food may grow by 5 to 7 percent, agricultural growth rarely increases by more than 4 to 5 percent a year. Eventually rates of population growth decline to near zero, and little added income is spent on food. But in the transitional phase, imports are likely to rise substantially.

We see portents of the future in Taiwan, the classic success story in agricultural production, which has gone from a net grain exporter in the prewar period to an importer of more than a third of all its grain consumption today. Much of this, of course, is for livestock consumption. In a recent study by the International Food Policy Research

[1] John W. Mellor, *The Economics of Agricultural Development* (Ithaca, N.Y.: Cornell University Press, 1966).

Institute it was found that imports of agricultural commodities increased in sixteen third world countries with rapid agricultural growth. Among developing countries, fast growth in agriculture is usually accompanied by fast growth in the overall economy and hence in per capita income.

Rapid economic growth is becoming a reality for more and more people in the third world. Some benefit substantially from rapid increases in raw material prices, as was the case for the over 200 million people of Nigeria and Indonesia. The phenomenon of rising raw material prices is undoubtedly an expanding one. Third world countries with larger aggregate populations are also experiencing growth from increased efficiency in production, particularly from rapid industrialization. Taiwan, South Korea, Singapore, and Hong Kong are being joined by Malaysia, Thailand, and the Philippines, which together have close to 100 million people. Other third world countries, some of immense population, are poised at the edge of an accelerated growth period. These developments will create new, rapidly growing export markets for agriculture, with the United States having a powerful comparative advantage.

The prospect of large new agricultural markets in the third world depends largely on how quickly the developing countries grow. Their own agricultural successes are likely to increase their demand for imports. There is a dominant pessimistic view of prospects for third world economic growth today, but this is because that growth is seen as linked to growth in the countries of the Organization for Economic Cooperation and Development (OECD). It is recognized that growth in the OECD countries will continue to be slow in response to rising raw material prices. Thus imports from the third world will at best grow slowly, and the third world capacity to import the essential producer goods of agricultural and industrial growth will be slow. This analysis misses the widespread diversification of third world economies and hence the rapidly rising scope for rapid growth of third world trade.[2] Realization of the potential for such trade expansion and the development of the necessary institutions and financing become essential to this overall growth and hence to growth in agricultural markets.

There is considerable scope for growth of agricultural commodity trade between third world countries. As livestock, fruit, and vegetable production, consumption, and trade rise, using low-cost labor in generally labor-intensive processes, the pressure for large net imports of grain will rise. There are few third world countries with the physical resources to respond to large export demands for grain. Argentina is

[2] W. A. Lewis, "The Slowing Down of the Engine of Growth," *American Economic Review*, vol. 70 (September 1980), pp. 555–64.

probably one of the few with such potential. Thus the United States is likely to face a strong demand for agricultural exports, particularly grain.

What might the United States do to facilitate such growth in markets? Obviously it must encourage third world growth. This calls for technical assistance to develop trained people and effective institutions; financing for infrastructure and industry, in both concessional and commercial forms; and facilitation of intra–third world trade and growth in third world–OECD trade. Though surprising, encouragement of agricultural growth helps to provide agricultural markets by fostering faster overall growth.[3]

Encouraging a broad-based, employment-oriented strategy of growth is a humane approach that is skewed toward food consumption. Stabilizing food supplies through stocking, food aid, and loan facilities works very much to that end. Food aid or financial aid to subsidize food to the poor on a long-term basis serves to encourage employment growth in third world–OECD trade. Though surprising, encourage-

U.S. policy toward third world countries has overtly emphasized the charitable, humanitarian aspects of poverty abatement on the one hand and short-run geopolitical objectives on the other. Both have served to mask the long-term economic interests. The U.S. farm sector has been unaware of this potential despite strong indications. Foreign aid to agriculture has been seen as charitable or as generating competition. Food aid has been viewed as either charity or dumping. There has been a particular failure to note that humanitarian concern for alleviating hunger and an interest in developing long-term commercial markets for agricultural commodities may be pursued simultaneously through employment-oriented development and that food aid and other forms of foreign assistance as well as trade can play a strong positive role in those processes.

Peter M. Emerson

Professor Tweeten's paper on farm structure covers a wide range of materials, identifies some important issues, and demonstrates a reasoned approach to a sometimes controversial topic.

The general theme of the paper reflects the notion that farming must change, that it cannot be held in a mold of the past. Others before him have concluded that, if farm people are to share in the fruits of

---

[3] John W. Mellor, *Three Issues of Development Strategy: Food, Population, Trade* (Two conference papers from 1978 and testimony presented to the U.S. House of Representatives Select Committee on Population, Washington, D.C., April 19, 1979) (Washington, D.C.: International Food Policy Research Institute, 1978).

economic growth, there must be steady resource adjustment involving an outflow of labor from agriculture.[1]

Professor Tweeten argues that for the most part farming has adapted itself very well, citing an impressive record of increasing productivity, rising incomes for farm people, and steady or declining real food costs. Changes in the number and size of farms, tenure patterns, capital-labor requirements, decision-making responsibilities, and key coordinating linkages with the nonfarm economy are described as a consequence of the joint interaction of many diverse factors: new technology, rising nonfarm wages and salaries, inflation, tax policies, commodity program provisions, and life-style preferences.

Professor Tweeten foresees a continuation of current structural trends over the next ten to twenty years. Farms will be less numerous but larger, and a distinct bimodal distribution is expected to emerge, of many small, part-time farms and an increasing proportion of very large farms. On the other hand, he believes that current farm output could be produced by 1.2 million "moderate-size family operations"—more than double the actual number of such farms—and that this would result in a substantial increase in the combined well-being of farmers and consumers. Given this strong argument, it is indeed surprising that the paper does not contain a careful discussion of alternative policies that would shift future structural change in favor of moderate-size family operations. Instead, the reader is left with the impression that the traditional family farm is best viewed as an endangered species.

This conclusion is a direct result of the manner in which Professor Tweeten chooses to define different types of farms. In my opinion, the typology of farms presented in table 1 is unnecessarily rigid and does not highlight a key distinction between types of farms. Perhaps my reaction is due to the fact that the paper provides few definitions. Nevertheless, I do *not* think it is logical to classify small and part-time farms as nonfamily farms or to omit industrial-type farms as a separate category. For many purposes, it is sufficient simply to recognize that we have evolved a farm sector that combines family and industrial farms. Family farms are unique because they combine the functions of capitalist, manager, and laborer. This attribute allows for direct feedback and adaptability in decision making but does not preclude modern family farms from using hired labor and borrowed capital. As a group, family farms are numerous, but they differ widely with respect to capital and labor requirements, annual sales, production practices, and sources of income.

[1] See D. Gale Johnson, *Farm Commodity Programs* (Washington, D.C.: American Enterprise Institute, May 1973), pp. 16–19.

Industrial farms, on the other hand, are characterized by a high degree of differentiation between capital ownership, management, and labor; they often use assembly-line production techniques; and they have a distinct managerial hierarchy. The chain of events associated with gathering data, making decisions, and evaluating the outcome of decisions extends through several managerial layers that provide intermediate inputs and serve as an information filter.[2] Industrial farms are few but account for a relatively large share of total output in animal production and in a few crops where they seem to have an advantage in raising large amounts of capital, carrying out standardized tasks, and providing highly specialized technical skills.

Given this classification scheme, the long-term outlook for family farms, particularly in crop production, is not necessarily bleak.[3] To remain economically viable, many family farms will grow in size to take advantage of new technology and to generate adequate family income. Others will supplement income from nonfarm sources. Public policy can play an important role in helping family farms remain competitive. Key public policy objectives may include providing access to technical and market information, ensuring that new technologies and production practices are available to all sizes of farms, providing price stability, monitoring and regulating the performance of input and product markets, and encouraging continued rural economic growth. In this environment many family farms will be able to produce food and fiber at a very low cost, and society will benefit from an agriculture of competing institutional forms.

Within the category of family farms, some people—most often residing on small farms—merit special attention. Using the current definition of the U.S. Department of Agriculture, there are 1.2 million small farm families in the United States. As a group, three-fourths of their total family income is derived from nonfarm sources. It is estimated that only 35 to 40 percent of the small farm families have wage earners working off the farm more than 100 days per year and that about 30 percent of the families fall below the poverty line.[4] In short,

[2] For a discussion of some consequences of managerial layering in agricultural production, see Philip M. Raup, "Some Issues in Land Tenure, Ownership, and Control in Dispersed vs. Concentrated Agriculture," in National Public Policy Education Committee, *Increasing Understanding of Public Problems and Policies— 1980* (Oak Brook, Ill.: Farm Foundation, September 1980), pp. 4–7.

[3] See Don Paarlberg, *Farm and Food Policy: Issues of the 1980s* (Lincoln: University of Nebraska Press, 1980), chap. 16, "The Future of the Family Farm," pp. 184–203.

[4] Based on information provided by Thomas A. Carlin, U.S. Department of Agriculture, from the 1973 Farm Family Living Expenditure Survey, 1975 Farm Production Expenditure Survey, and other data sources.

some of our lowest-income people remain closely tied to farming, yet do not benefit from commercial agriculture policy. These people need specific human resource development programs and, in some cases, direct income supplements. It would be unfortunate if the debate about the structure of agriculture (family farms versus industrial farms) were to direct attention away from those people most in need of public assistance.

In assessing the influence of commodity programs on the crop sub-sector, Professor Tweeten is justifiably cautious. He concludes that commodity programs have "had only a modest impact on structure," slightly enhancing the trend toward fewer and larger farms. In review, I would like to emphasize three specific structural effects that tend to underline and add a degree of precision to Tweeten's general conclusion:

• Higher market prices, direct payments, and reduced uncertainty resulting from price and income support activities have benefited producers who would otherwise have gone out of business.

• Incremental income derived from higher market prices and direct payments tends to be distributed among farms in direct proportion to the amount of commodity sold. Therefore, it is highly likely that commodity programs have encouraged high-volume, low-cost producers to expand relative to low-volume, high-cost producers.

• Windfall profits generated by commodity programs tend to be capitalized into cropland values and distributed in direct proportion to landownership.

It is probably impossible precisely to quantify the net effects of commodity programs on farm structure. Nevertheless, I remain convinced that producers who use income gains and reduced uncertainty to acquire new technology and additional land are the primary farm sector beneficiaries of commodity programs. Of course, the increasing market orientation of many commodity programs since the mid-1960s has tended to reduce their impact on the number and size of farms, food prices, exports, and other farm sector variables.

And some people will judge structural impacts to be less important than other consequences of commodity programs. Nelson's simulation of the farm economy, for example, shows that elimination of commodity programs between 1953 and 1972 would have slowed the trend toward fewer and larger farms but would have increased the variability of farm prices and incomes and reduced the rate of productivity growth.

Given the caution Professor Tweeten exercises throughout his paper, I am surprised to find the rather strong statement, presented without much conceptual reasoning and no empirical evidence, that "high energy prices will not improve the competitive position of small farms." The trend toward fewer and larger farms is based on a substitution of capital inputs, energy-intensive inputs, and scientific knowledge for physical labor and land. Therefore, higher energy prices might slow the trend and will certainly alter farm production practices, as well as food processing, packaging, and shipping patterns. How these adjustments will ultimately affect the farm sector—the competitive position of conventional farms versus organic farms, large farms versus small farms—appears to be unknown.

In closing, I would like to mention two issues relating to farm structure that Professor Tweeten did not emphasize. First is the control of decision making in agricultural production. Traditionally, farmers have enjoyed much independence and made many decisions solely according to their own intentions. Continuing technological change and increasing capital requirements have brought a steadily growing pressure for closer coordination in the use of resources. Today more and more farmers find that they must give up some of their independent decision-making responsibility to participate in contractual agreements or other arrangements that create vertically integrated systems. In this situation, public policy may be useful in strengthening the negotiating position and protecting the interests of individual farmers relative to large agribusinesses, financial institutions, and other concentrations of power. Such policies might include government participation in standardizing the terms of contracts, reporting prices paid to farmers, supporting producer bargaining associations, using cooperatives to maintain alternative market outlets, blocking mergers of large firms, and monitoring consumer prices.

A second farm structure issue that should not be overlooked is the human agent—the men and women actually involved in farming. It is generally agreed that education and experience are very important in determining the rate of response to changing circumstances—our willingness to seek information, to experiment with new production practices, and so on. It is noteworthy that the farm sector is characterized by a huge educational gap between generations of farmers. For those farm operators at, or close to, retirement age, it is likely that less than 40 percent have finished high school.[5] On the other hand, nearly 80 percent of the farm operators under thirty years of age have a high school education, and many have college training. These data reveal that in the years ahead farming will be directly affected by an expanded supply of skills derived from formal education. It seems plausible to hypothesize that these younger, more highly educated farmers will greatly accelerate the future rate of structural change.

[5] Based on information provided by Calvin L. Beale, U.S. Department of Agriculture, from the U.S. Department of Commerce, Bureau of the Census, *Current Population Reports*, no. 225, June 1976, p. 20.

Part
Three

U.S. Agriculture in an Interdependent World Economy: Policy Alternatives for the 1980s

G. Edward Schuh

U.S. agriculture is emerging at the beginning of the 1980s into a world dramatically different from the world of the early 1970s. It is now an integral part of a world agricultural economy. General economic policies affect it differently than in the past. The sector is characterized by instability in contrast to stability. And sustaining strong international markets is now a policy imperative.

The food and agriculture legislation of 1973 and 1977 brought substantial changes in agricultural policy, most of them giving market forces a greater role in determining agricultural prices and farm incomes.[1] My paper has two premises: (1) in the decade ahead we should move to even greater dependence on market forces than we now have, and (2) general economic policies are now more important to the welfare of agriculture and rural people than agricultural-specific or commodity policies. Among general economic policies that are important are monetary and fiscal policies, exchange rate policy, labor market policy, and general trade policy.

I shall argue below that much of what affects agriculture in today's world comes from forces external to the farm sector. Moreover, strictly sectoral policies are relatively blunt means of dealing with the problems these external effects or forces create. Unless we recognize the new structure of the economy and the importance of these external forces in the design of policy, both U.S. citizens and policy makers will be frustrated and disappointed with the results.

My paper is divided into two parts. In the first part I attempt to

[1] This trend actually started in the mid-1960s. For an excellent history of the evolution of agricultural policy, see Willard W. Cochrane and Mary E. Ryan, *American Farm Policy, 1948–1973* (Minneapolis: University of Minnesota Press, 1976).

characterize the new economic environment in which agriculture finds itself. In the second I sketch out a new policy perspective for the 1980s. At the end I make some concluding comments.

Important aspects of agricultural policy will be neglected or slighted in this paper. Among these are resource and energy policy, the problem of structure, food and nutrition policy, and dairy policy. I neglect these aspects of policy not because they are unimportant but because I wish to present a tractable paper around a central theme. Some of these topics will be discussed tangentially, others by implication. I hope that some of the other participants in the conference will give them a more careful treatment than I have been able to provide.

The New Economic Environment for Agriculture

In the past decade, agriculture has undergone some dramatic changes, including: (1) an increased integration with the international economy, (2) a fuller realization of its inherent comparative advantage, (3) increased instability, (4) increased dependence on market forces, (5) the near completion of the agricultural transformation, and (6) a fuller integration with the rest of the domestic economy. Each of these changes is examined in the sections that follow.

Increased Integration with the International Economy. U.S. agriculture has experienced an increasing integration with the world economy over the past decade, and we can expect to see that integration increase further in the decade ahead. This increased integration has at least four dimensions: (1) a rapid growth in trade in agricultural commodities, (2) a growth in the trade of modern inputs, (3) a sustained growth in the number of undocumented workers entering this country, and (4) a remarkable evolution of the international capital market, which has important implications both for monetary and fiscal policy and for commodity policy per se. Let us consider each of these in more detail.

The growth in commodity trade, especially the trade in grain and soybeans, receives most of the attention of policy analysts. Trade for some individual commodities has been important for a long time. It was only in 1963, however, that this nation became a net exporter of agricultural commodities in the aggregate.

Since 1963 our agricultural exports have sustained a high growth rate. During the 1970s the growth rate was truly remarkable. Exports are now expected to hit a record $40 billion for fiscal 1980, that total being 25 percent higher than the previous record of $32 billion, set last year. The volume of exports is expected to be a record 162 million metric tons in fiscal 1980, up 18 percent from the previous high of 137.5 million tons, set in fiscal year 1979.

The surplus of exports over imports in fiscal year 1980 is expected to be $22 billion. With an expected petroleum import bill alone of $60 billion in 1980, the importance of this trade surplus to the economy as a whole can hardly be underestimated. Strong agricultural exports help to sustain the value of the dollar and thus provide important income gains to the economy as a whole.

Impressive as these figures are, even they do not tell the full story. We export over 60 percent of our wheat crop in most years, approximately 50 percent of our soybeans and rice, one-third of our cotton and tobacco, and some 25 percent of our corn. Put somewhat differently, the output of approximately one of every three acres of cropland is shipped abroad, and roughly 25 percent of the value of cash marketings comes from export sales.

This dependence on export markets has important implications for agricultural policy. Without this strong export performance, the character of our agricultural policies would surely be different. Farm programs would be much more costly, and the degree of government intervention would undoubtedly be substantially greater.

Further insight into the broad ramifications of this increased dependence on trade can be gained by noting where our exports are expanding. The markets that attract attention are the centrally planned economies, especially the Soviet Union. But the more rapid growth this past decade has been with the less-developed countries. The significance of this component of our trade is that it involves U.S. agriculture in all the issues of the North-South debate and the pleas for a new international economic order.

Interdependence with the international economy does not, however, stop with the commodity markets. The United States is both an exporter and an importer of fertilizers. This trade also has grown in the past and can be expected to do so in the future. We are already heavily dependent on imports for potash fertilizers and may find ourselves increasingly dependent on imports of nitrogen fertilizers. This increased trade in important agricultural inputs subjects agriculture to the vagaries of policies and policy makers in other countries in ways very similar to that which results from commodity trade.

The undocumented worker has received a great deal of publicity in recent years. It is less seldom recognized that these workers are important to the agricultural sector, where they do work that many domestic workers are unwilling to perform. For some groups of producers these workers are quite important. As the issue of the undocumented worker become politicized, instability in the agricultural sector increases.

Finally, and perhaps ultimately more important than any of these linkages, international markets for capital now link together the economies of the world in a truly integrated world market. The Eurocurrency markets are now huge, with total credit outstanding of more than $800 billion. The less-developed countries now borrow capital from these markets to finance their development programs, some of which are focused on agriculture, as do the centrally planned economies. Of course the Eurocurrency markets are not the only source of funds. The International Monetary Fund now has numerous specialized windows—different types of credit—in addition to the special drawing rights that it provides as part of its normal operations.

Two aspects of these evolving international capital markets are important to agriculture. In the first place, there is a growing interdependence between financial markets and commodity markets. Commodity forecasters have not fully recognized this interdependence, which is an important cause of their poor forecasting record in recent years.

Equally important, the emergence of these markets, together with a system of floating exchange rates, has taken away a great deal of the autonomy that governments have in managing their economies, contrary to what was expected by most economists when the shift from fixed to floating rates occurred. With well-integrated capital markets, the inflation premium is almost the only component of the interest rate that domestic policy makers can influence. Flows of capital take place in response to interest rate differentials among countries, and these flows continue until the differentials are eliminated or until policy makers in other countries take measures to offset them. These capital flows, of course, cause changes in currency exchange rates, which in turn affect the competitive potential of individual countries. We will return to this issue below.

Fuller Realization of Inherent Comparative Advantage. U.S. agriculture during the 1950s and 1960s presented an important puzzle: Why was a country with one of the most modern and productive agricultural sectors in the world forced to use implicit and explicit subsidies to compete in international markets? The answer to the puzzle came in the early 1970s when the dollar was twice devalued and we shifted to a system of floating exchange rates.[2] Our exports exploded, and our system of export subsidies has been almost completely dismantled as a consequence of these developments.

Clearly, there are other forces at work in international markets that help explain the sustained growth in our exports over the past

[2] G. Edward Schuh, "The Exchange Rate and U.S. Agriculture," *American Journal of Agricultural Economics*, vol. 12 (February 1974), pp. 1–13.

decade. It is noteworthy that our exports have held up well even when world agricultural output was above the trend line and even when Soviet agriculture was having a good year.

Although there are still other barriers to trade, including substantial nontariff barriers, the system of floating exchange rates has reduced an important barrier to the realization of our comparative advantage in international markets.[3] The removal of the implicit export tax that the overvalued dollar represented, as well as the implicit tariff that the undervalued currencies of other countries represented, has enabled U.S. agriculture to realize a great deal more of its competitive potential.

Increased Instability. U.S. agriculture was relatively stable throughout the 1950s and the 1960s. Real prices for many commodities tended to trend downward during this period, and the sector was burdened with a rather severe secular adjustment. Year-to-year changes in prices, however, were fairly small.

There were various reasons for this stability. First, U.S. agricultural output tends to be relatively stable compared with that of other countries. Second, the domestic demand for agricultural output (which dominated total demand) was also relatively stable, with domestic monetary and fiscal policy managed reasonably well and built-in stabilizers evening out whatever fluctuations in demand there might have been from cycles in the general economy. This inherent stability in the system was reinforced by the large stocks of grain in government hands, accumulated as a byproduct of prevailing farm programs, and the availability of a sizable land reserve at price ratios current at the time. When there were significant fluctuations in foreign demand, as occurred in both the mid-1950s and the mid-1960s, the level of stocks could be run down, and additional land could be returned to production to offset it.

These tranquil conditions of the 1950s and 1960s no longer prevailed during the 1970s. We have seen very large swings in agricultural prices, with a great deal of year-to-year, and even month-to-month, instability.

Some of the reasons for this instability are not difficult to find. During the early part of the 1970s our reserve stocks were permitted to dwindle to quite low levels. This reduction in stocks would have created a more unstable situation even if there were no other changes. The problem was exacerbated by a great deal of panic buying by gov-

---

[3] For a thorough treatment of nontariff barriers to agricultural trade, see Jimmye S. Hillman, *Non-Tariff Agricultural Trade Barriers* (Lincoln, Nebraska, and London: University of Nebraska Press, 1978).

ernments attempting to ensure supplies for their domestic economy. These actions tended to aggravate what was already a serious problem.

The pursuit of neomercantilist policies by many countries, including the United States, has also contributed to instability. D. Gale Johnson[4] has focused attention on this issue, and both the logic of the case and the empirical evidence are quite strong. When international prices are not reflected to domestic consumers and producers, very little adjustment can take place. The consequences of a given shock are therefore exaggerated.

The growing dependence of the Soviet Union on trade has been an additional source of instability. Soviet agriculture is one of the more unstable in the world. By attempting to protect its domestic consumers from this instability, the Soviet Union has passed a great deal of this instability on to international markets and in turn to countries that are relatively open to market forces.[5] The 1975–1981 grain agreement with the Soviet Union helped to stabilize their import pattern somewhat but obviously did not completely stabilize it.

Finally, the emergence of a well-integrated international capital market and the shift to a system of floating exchange rates has contributed significantly to the instability of international commodity markets.[6] Before these developments, U.S. agriculture, for example, bore little of the brunt of changes in domestic monetary policy, except insofar as the rate of out-migration from agriculture was quite sensitive to the level of unemployment. In the presence of well-integrated capital markets and floating exchange rates, however, shifts in monetary policy are reflected in shifts in the value of the dollar on international markets, and this in turn affects the competitiveness of our exports. More specifically, the sectors competing in exports and imports bear the burden of adjustment to changes in monetary policy, with resources transferred in and out of the sector in response to changes in macroeconomic policies. Shifts in macroeconomic policies in other countries can have an equally important effect on U.S. agriculture.

This shift in how monetary and fiscal policy affects the economy

---

[4] D. Gale Johnson, "World Agriculture, Commodity Policy, and Price Variability," *American Journal of Agricultural Economics*, vol. 57, no. 5 (December 1975), pp. 823–38.

[5] D. Gale Johnson has noted that up to 85 percent of the fluctuation in trade of cereals and soybeans during the 1960s and 1970s was due to fluctuations in Soviet trade. See D. Gale Johnson, *The Soviet Impact on World Grain Trade*, British-North American Committee, National Planning Association, 1977.

[6] For a more detailed discussion of the issues, see G. Edward Schuh, "Floating Exchange Rates, International Interdependence, and Adjustment Policy," September 1979, Department of Agricultural and Applied Economics, University of Minnesota, St. Paul, Minnesota.

has not been given the attention it deserves, either for the management of agricultural policy or for the management of the economy as a whole. In the case of agriculture, we have shifted from a relatively stable demand for agricultural output to quite unstable demand, the driving force being the instability of foreign demand in response to the twists and turns of monetary and fiscal policy. For the economy as a whole, there are a number of questions about whether sectors such as agriculture are best suited to bearing the adjustment burden of shifts in monetary and fiscal policy.

The last two years have provided ample evidence of the importance of this source of instability. U.S. exports have closely followed the shifts of our own monetary policy, the tightness in money markets, and the changing value of the dollar. Although the embargo on sales to the Soviet Union received most of the blame for the decline in commodity prices earlier this year, the tight monetary policy imposed during that period was the real culprit. As monetary policy was relaxed in the month of August and the value of the dollar fell in international currency markets, prices of agricultural commodities moved up accordingly.

To conclude this section, it should be noted that ultimately it is the instability of government policy and government intervention that causes the instability in commodity markets. In light of that fact it is not likely that just calling for additional government intervention would be of much help or add more stability.

Increased Dependence on Market Forces. The decade of the 1960s already saw strong tendencies toward greater dependency on market forces for agriculture. Nominal support levels for most commodities were either fixed or worked down gradually, with inflation allowed to erode the real values. By the end of the 1960s, agriculture was in approximate adjustment with the rest of the economy at prevailing price levels, and the secular adjustment problem was largely behind us.

Other developments in the 1970s made the dependence on market forces even greater. Greater use was made of deficiency payments in lieu of rigidly fixed price supports, with the result that consumers were able to benefit when supply outpaced demand. The 1977 legislation established the concept of a price corridor, with the lower limit to the corridor approximated by the nonrecourse loan level and an upper level approximated by the call level on the reserves set up by the farmer-owned reserve (FOR) program.

The 1977 legislation also saw the elimination of the rigid allotment system and a shift to a combination of set-aside and paid diversion. Finally, distortions in foreign currency markets were reduced, with the result that this important market can provide incentives for adjustment in response to changing conditions in international capital and trade markets.

Over time, therefore, we have shifted from a system in which prices were rigidly sustained and rather large quantities of land were removed from production by direct government actions to a situation in which prices are free to fluctuate within limits set by a price corridor and land can shift to its highest use in response to changing price relatives. Barring a rapid and unexpected rise in the value of the dollar or substantial additional government interventions in the sector, we can expect to see a continuation of this dependence on market forces.

Agricultural Transformation at an End. Development economists like to talk about something called the transformation of agriculture, which they view as the central process around which the development of an economy takes place. In fact, one of the major contributions of Theodore W. Schultz, who just received the Nobel Prize in economics, was a book called *The Transformation of Traditional Agriculture.*[7]

The basic idea behind this transformation is that an economy starts the development process with the bulk of its labor force employed in agriculture and producing agricultural products. The essence of economic development, then, is to transfer this labor to the nonfarm sector to produce the goods and services associated with rising per capita incomes. For labor to be released, there has to be a steady and sustained rise in productivity in the agricultural sector. For the labor to be absorbed on the nonagricultural side, new nonfarm activities have to be introduced, and existing nonfarm sectors have to expand. If the process goes well, per capita incomes rise in the economy as a whole, as incomes in both the farm and nonfarm sectors rise. Moreover, the share that food and agricultural products make up of the total bundle of goods and services that consumers purchase becomes smaller and smaller, while the share made up of goods and services from the nonfarm sector grows larger and larger.

This process by which an economy transforms itself from an agrarian economy to an industrial society and then to the information society the United States has become is important as a basis for understanding the forces that impinged on agriculture in the past and that might be expected to shape it and influence it in the future. An important cause of the secular income problem in agriculture was this chronic need to transfer labor from the farm to the nonfarm sector. The problem was exacerbated by our unique system of educational finance,

[7] Theodore W. Schultz, *The Transformation of Traditional Agriculture* (New Haven, Conn.: Yale University Press, 1964).

which caused rural people to produce an important share of the human capital for the economy as a whole and export or donate it to the non-farm sector as essentially a free good.[8] The problem was further compounded by the technological revolution in agriculture of the 1950s and 1960s and the implicit export tax represented by the overvalued dollar.

Two points are important in thinking about this process. First, farm programs that had their beginning in the Great Depression were extended, modified, and carried over to help deal with the secular income problems of the 1950s and 1960s. It was in this more recent period that commodity programs essentially became institutionalized.

Second, the agricultural transformation is now nearing an end for the United States in the sense that the agricultural labor force makes up only a very small proportion of the total labor force. In a very real sense, the U.S. economy has reached a form of developmental maturity. We can expect to see a continued drain of labor out of agriculture, but on nowhere near the scale of the past and under conditions in which the migrants can be more easily absorbed into the nonfarm sector. We reached this situation in the early 1970s, at about the time that the implicit export tax was removed from the farm sector.

These developments have far-reaching implications for agricultural policy in the decade ahead. The secular income problem arising from excess labor in agriculture is essentially behind us. In its place are problems of severe income instability and of rural poverty associated with disadvantaged families and regional stagnation. Policies to deal with these problems will be discussed in part 2 of this paper, "A New Policy Perspective for the 1980s."

Fuller Integration of Agriculture with the Rest of the Economy. At the same time that U.S. agriculture has become an integral part of a world agricultural economy, it has also become better integrated with the nonfarm economy domestically. Two aspects of this closer integration merit special attention: (1) the more complete integration of the agricultural labor market with that of the nonfarm sector and (2) the more complete integration of the credit and capital markets.

Perhaps the most significant aspect of the growing integration of the labor markets is the increasing share of income of farm families that comes from nonfarm sources. This share has been in a long-term upward trend throughout the post–World War II period. In recent years roughly 60 percent of the income of farm people has come from nonfarm

[8] G. Edward Schuh, "Out-Migration, Rural Productivity, and the Distribution of Income," in R. H. Sabot, ed., *Essays on Migration and the Labor Market* (Washington, D.C.: World Bank, forthcoming).

sources. Moreover, this share is inversely related to size of farm as measured by value of cash marketings, with the result that families of small farms receive an even larger share of their income from nonfarm sources.

This aspect of the income situation of agriculture was sadly neglected in congressional discussions of the 1977 food and agricultural legislation. Its neglect leads to bad policy. The income problem of agriculture needs to be addressed as a family income problem, not as a sectoral income problem as it conventionally is. The policy mix that evolves will be substantially different if it is viewed from this different perspective.

The consequences of the more complete integration of the credit and capital markets really came to the fore only this year, although the changes have been taking place for some time. Interestingly enough, the changed conditions are due in part to the partial deregulation of the banking sector. This deregulation was motivated in no small part by the accelerated inflation of recent years and the need to let market forces prevail in the credit markets to accommodate that inflation and by the decision to return to a more rational way of implementing monetary policy.

Agriculture has benefited in the past from both the segmentation of credit markets that our banking legislation has caused and the prevalence of usury laws. As usury laws were eliminated and banks were permitted to compete more effectively for funds in national markets, however, the cost of credit to farmers rose rapidly. In effect, the agricultural sector is now forced to compete for funds on the same basis as other sectors and in essentially a more national market.

This situation is not likely to change in the future. Moreover, if the Federal Reserve perseveres in its attempt to stabilize the growth rate in the money supply rather than to stabilize interest rates, conditions in the credit markets are likely to be more unstable in the future, and interest rates are likely to be more volatile. Under these conditions, it may well be that credit may become quite costly or wholly unavailable at the peak of the planting season, just as it was in 1980. Farmers will need to be more knowledgeable about monetary policy in making their production plans, and policy makers will need to be more sensitive to the special needs of the agricultural sector.

A New Policy Perspective for the 1980s

The economic environment that now characterizes U.S. agriculture is substantially different from that which characterized it a decade ago. These changed conditions call for a new approach to agricultural policy, and it is to this new approach that I now turn.

There are seven elements to the new perspective that I shall attempt to sketch. The thrust of the new approach is that agriculture needs less specialized treatment than it has received in the past and that general economic policies and policies outside agriculture are as important as commodity and other policies specific to agriculture or more important.

Stable Macroeconomic Policy Is an Imperative. Agriculture has always benefited from a fully employed economy; hence it has always benefited from proper monetary and fiscal policy. The rate of out-migration from agriculture has traditionally been sensitive to the level of unemployment in the general economy. Given the long-term need to transfer labor resources out of the sector, a fully employed economy enabled excess labor to leave the sector faster, and this in turn helped to improve relative incomes in agriculture.

The importance of monetary and fiscal policy is now even greater than it was in the past, however, and its importance takes on additional dimensions. The fact that monetary and fiscal policy now affect the economy in large part by means of changes in the exchange rate and resource adjustments in the export- and import-competing sectors puts a special burden on agriculture. Even though resources undoubtedly flow back and forth between the farm and nonfarm sectors more easily than they did in the past, the fact that the production process is not continuous and is determined in large part by biological processes gives rise to special adjustment problems. Moreover, the fact that the production period supply elasticity is quite low causes the shifts in foreign demand induced by changes in the exchange rate to create substantial instability in prices.

Much dissatisfaction is now voiced with the system of floating exchange rates. Much of this dissatisfaction is due to the instability in the foreign exchange markets. The ups and downs of the Japanese yen this past year serve as an important example, but the dollar, the British pound, and the deutsche mark have also fluctuated rather widely.

This instability of exchange rates is cause for concern. The important question, however, is why these markets have been so unstable. And here the instability of monetary and fiscal policy, especially of U.S. monetary and fiscal policy, has to take a major share of the blame. Our policy has been characterized as stop and go in the extreme, with the experience of the last year again an important example. The first six months of 1980 were characterized by stagnation and even declines in the monetary aggregates as a tight monetary policy was pursued. In July the policy moved to one of relative ease, with the result that the money supply increased at an annual rate of almost 20 percent through

August and into September. The value of the dollar fluctuated accordingly, and it surely will respond again when the monetary authorities slam on the brakes shortly after the election in November.

Devising more stable monetary and fiscal policies is the key to stabilizing the foreign exchange markets. Stabilizing the foreign exchange markets will contribute significantly to the stability of commodity markets and in turn to U.S. agriculture. With such stabilization, much of the motivation for a stocks policy will be reduced or eliminated.

Failure to stabilize the foreign exchange markets may cause us to revert to a policy of fixed exchange rates, which could make us once again lose our competitive edge in international markets, for the dollar still plays an important role as a reserve currency. A shift to fixed exchange rates would also sacrifice the powerful adjustment mechanism that the exchange rate can be. It is worth noting in passing, of course, that much of the adjustment potential of a floating exchange rate has been perverted by the instability of monetary and fiscal policy in recent years.

The Need to Revitalize Our Science and Technology Policy vis-à-vis Agriculture. The United States is endowed with an unusual set of agricultural resources and the climate to go with them. Our comparative advantage in agriculture, however, is not due solely to our endowment of physical resources, as both our own experience and the experience of countries as disparate as Argentina and Israel amply attest. Appropriate economic policy and investments in education and the production and distribution of new technology are equally important.

The importance of these investments in human capital is amply demonstrated by the fact that the stock of physical resources used in U.S. agriculture is practically the same today as it was in the mid-1920s. All of the increase in output since that date is due to increases in productivity. The sources of the growth in productivity include sizable investments in research, extension, and education; the provision of appropriate economic incentives; and a system of free enterprise that encourages entrepreneurs to take risks, innovate, and undertake appropriate investments.

Much could be said about both productivity growth and science and technology policy.[9] Evidence suggests that the rate of productivity growth in agriculture has declined, although there is room for disagree-

---

[9] For a recent review of some of the issues, see Vernon W. Ruttan, "Agricultural Research and the Future of American Agriculture" (Paper presented at a conference on the Future of American Agriculture as a Strategic Resource, The Conservation Foundation, Washington, D.C., July 1980).

FIGURE 1

PURCHASING POWER OF FEDERAL APPROPRIATIONS AND
NONFEDERAL SUPPORT OF AGRICULTURAL RESEARCH PROGRAMS
IN THE UNITED STATES, 1960–1978

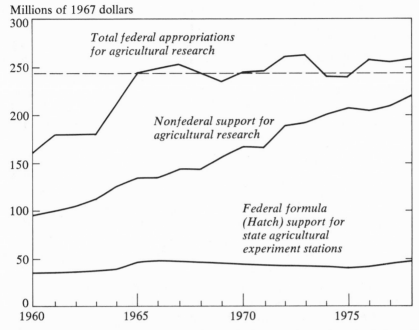

SOURCE: Ruttan, "Agricultural Research and the Future of American Agriculture."

ment about that.[10] A proper science and technology policy has many dimensions, some of which go far beyond the scope of this paper.

The issue I would like to single out for attention here is the stagnation in federal support for agricultural research in the period since 1965 (figure 1). Total support for agricultural research has gone up during this period, but the bulk of the increase has come from nonfederal sources, notably from individual states.

Two points are worth making on this issue. In the first place, an important share of the benefits of new production technology under the present trade regime are passed on to consumers in a very diffuse way. It is true that given the importance of trade to the agricultural sector,

[10] As in all comparisons over time, the result largely depends on the base period chosen. Agricultural productivity data are also affected by weather and weather cycles, and few attempts have been made to separate these effects from the data. For an earlier attempt, see D. Gale Johnson, *Grain Yields and the American Food Supply: An Analysis of Yield Changes and Possibilities* (Chicago: University of Chicago Press, 1962).

the aggregate price elasticity of demand for agricultural output is larger than when a closed-economy model was more relevant. Under these conditions producers receive a larger share of the benefits from technological innovation than they received in the past. It is also true, however, that this nation's increased dependence on trade for raw materials and consumer goods creates a national interest in a strong export performance. Sustained growth in productivity is the key to a strong export performance. An increase in agricultural exports, other things being equal, implies a rise in the value of the dollar. This rise will cause the relative prices of imports to decline, thereby benefiting consumers on a large scale. The fact that an important share of the benefits of increased productivity is realized in this way creates a strong case for federal support of agricultural research.

The second point is equally important. To the extent that agricultural research is financed from local sources, the tendency is to focus the research effort on activities that have a local payoff. This creates a bias in the research effort toward applied research and toward research that is highly specific to a location. Yet basic research—research that has large spillover effects—is an integral aspect of obtaining sustained rates of growth. Hence on these grounds also a case can be made for revitalizing the federal support for agricultural research and with it the agricultural research establishment. If we are to sustain our strong agricultural export performance into the future, revitalized support for agricultural research should have high priority.

The Imperative of Open Markets. An important aspect of U.S. foreign policy through the post–World War II period has been its stance in favor of free trade and more open international trading arrangements. The United States has provided the leadership for successive rounds of multilateral trade negotiations designed to lower barriers to trade. We have been reluctant to join international commodity agreements in part because of a belief that such agreements impeded the free play of market forces, and we have been reluctant to participate in bilateral trade agreements for the same reason.

This posture on international trade is being challenged on many fronts and for a variety of reasons. The sizable realignments in exchange rates during the 1970s have posed new competitive threats to various countries, threats that have been exacerbated by the sluggish and unstable growth that has characterized the economies of the industrialized West. The emergence of vigorous middle-level developing countries with robust industrial sectors has posed new threats to the more developed economies. The growing obsolescence of our own industrial plant and the low savings and investment rates in the United

States have caused us to lose our competitive edge in international markets. We turned against our own tradition by using trade policy as a means of punishing the Soviet Union for its intrusion into Afghanistan and Iran for holding U.S. hostages.[11]

Agriculture now has a vital interest in free trade. Unless international trade is kept open and even further liberalized, this sector will face serious adjustment problems and ultimately a reversion to programs of the past that involved a great deal of government intervention. The increased intervention of government as a consequence of the Soviet embargo should be an object lesson for all.

At least three aspects of a free trade policy are important to agriculture. The first, and perhaps most important, is to resist and turn back the protectionist pressures in our own country. Much is heard these days of the need to reindustrialize the United States. Except for the need to refurbish our obsolescent capital stock and to revitalize our transportation infrastructure, programs designed to reindustrialize the U.S. economy would be misguided. As attempts to turn the clock back, such programs would fail to capitalize on our comparative advantage in world trade and impose real income losses on our society.

With a few exceptions, the comparative advantage of the United States no longer lies in the manufacturing sector. We are becoming a high-technology, information society, and our comparative advantage in trade lies with high-technology industries and activities. Rather than turning back to an outdated economic structure, we should press ahead where our emerging comparative advantage lies and deal more effectively with the adjustment problems that arise as the sectoral composition of the economy changes.

The international division of labor obviously has national security implications, which need to be addressed. We would be foolish to give up a vehicle industry, for example, if such an industry were needed to conduct a future war. By the same token, national security interests should not be used as an excuse for protecting an industry that fails to modernize and keep up with the latest in production technology. International competition may be the most important form of competitive pressure some sectors of our economy face, and such pressure is needed if the vitality of our economy is to be sustained.

An open trade policy for labor-intensive manufactured goods is an

---

[11] This is not, of course, the first time the United States has used trade policy to attain foreign policy objectives. We severed trade relations with Cuba shortly after Castro took control of that country, we participated in the United Nations blockade of Rhodesia, and we pretended that mainland China did not exist for some twenty-five years. These important exceptions essentially prove the general rule, however.

imperative if our markets in most of the Third World and China are to grow. Both of these offer enormous market possibilities for agricultural exports, possibilities that are not likely to emerge unless we are willing to accept imports from them.

Our experience with the Soviet Union has probably misled us a bit on this issue. The Soviets have been able to sell gold into a rising market whenever they wanted to import grain. Hence willingness to accept their exports has not been an issue in the growth of our trade with that country. That will not be the case with China or with the less-developed countries—except for those few who happen to be petroleum exporters or have some other mineral export. For many of the countries with whom we have export potential, the willingness of the United States and other potential trading partners to accept their exports will be the key to expanding our exports to them. Agriculture has a vital interest in a more open trade posture on the part of this nation.

The second dimension of our trade posture is the need to persevere in general trade liberalization on the part of other countries. The key to our maintaining an open trade stance is for other countries to be perceived as relatively open to trade as well. Equally important, we need to persevere in efforts to keep other countries open to exports coming from third countries. The case of beef provides an object lesson, for import pressures increased significantly when Japan and the European Economic Community closed off imports a few years ago. Maintaining a relatively open trading stance domestically is difficult when we are perceived as being the dumping grounds for other countries.

Many observers believe the recently concluded Tokyo round will be the last attempt at multilateral trade negotiations. The multitude of countries involved and the complexity of the issues involved make the negotiations seem almost impossible. Certainly, progress was slow in that round, and the gains, though significant, must seem to the participants incommensurate with the costs and efforts involved.

Unfortunately, a great deal still needs to be done to reduce prevailing barriers to trade and to strengthen and improve the rules of the game. Barriers to agricultural trade are still substantial, despite the considerable progress that has been made.

Clearly there is a role for bilateral negotiations, which many believe must be the basis for future attempts to liberalize trade. The complexity of trade relationships, however, limits what can be accomplished bilaterally. Moreover, the establishment of improved rules of the game requires a consensus of the participants, which will result only from broad discussion among the many countries participating in trade.

An important problem on the international scene is that there is one set of rules for the advanced countries and another set for the less-developed countries. This dual system evolved in part because the trading arrangements that have prevailed through most of the post–World War II period were designed in large part by the United States and its wartime allies. In addition, the less-developed countries have been treated with a deference that was not always in their best interests. They have been shunted onto the sidelines in trade negotiations. Most of them do not belong to the General Agreement on Tariffs and Trade (GATT).

I will return to some of these issues in the section "The Need to Develop New Institutions on the International Scene." The main point I want to make here is the need to persevere in the effort to reduce barriers to trade, the need to encourage participation in both trade negotiations and the membership of organizations such as GATT, and the need to establish uniform rules for all so that trade can be perceived as fair and equitable. This last is perhaps the most important reason to resist protectionist pressures.

Finally, the third dimension of obtaining a system of freer international trade is to establish rules for the management of currency exchange rates. Despite the obvious effects that distortions in exchange rates have on trade, exchange rate policy was not on the agenda of the Tokyo round of trade negotiations. Trade theory teaches us that distortions in exchange rates are equivalent to export subsidies, to tariffs, to import subsidies, and to export taxes, depending on the direction of the distortion. It also teaches us that a given tariff or export subsidy can offset a given distortion in the exchange rate. Given these relationships, it makes little sense to negotiate over trade barriers that are explicit while ignoring those that are implicit.

The system of floating exchange rates has served the trading community quite well. Although it has not given policy makers the autonomy of action that economists long argued it would, it has provided an important means of adjustment to some rather sizable shocks. The system is criticized for the inherent instability that has characterized the exchange markets. But the criticism might better be directed to the underlying instability of monetary and fiscal policy than to the exchange markets themselves.

If the system of floating exchange rates is to be preserved, agreement needs to be reached on rules for managing exchange rate policy so that distortions in the foreign exchange markets are not used as a substitute for direct trade distortions. Free trade must include free, competitive exchange markets.

Commodity Policy to Deal with Instability. Commodity policy as it evolved during the 1970s was something of a neoclassical economist's dream. Market forces were given freer reign, the old rigid system of allotments was discarded and producers were given greater freedom of choice, a system of price bands was established for many commodities to limit the range in which prices could fluctuate, and a farmer-owned reserve was established to stabilize the markets. In addition, greater use was made of deficiency payments, which not only made the subsidy or income transfer more transparent but also enabled consumers to benefit from excess production when it occurred.

It is now time to ask how well this system has performed. I regret to say that in my judgment it has not performed very well, despite the high expectations that many had for the new programs when they were legislated. The indictments are numerous. In the first place, it has really added very little stability to the markets. This is not inherently a fault of the programs, of course. Rather, the programs have not been able to cope with the basic source of the instability, which has been the monetary and fiscal instability of this past decade. It is doubtful whether *any* commodity policy could offset this instability except at enormous program costs. The point, of course, is that we need to attack the source of the instability and not fritter away resources dealing with the symptoms of the problem.

Second, the policies were no less subject to politicization than previous programs, despite the well-defined rules for managing the commodity policy that came with the 1977 legislation. It is possible that the politicization would have been less had there not been a Soviet grain embargo, but the fact of the embargo demonstrated how fragile the equilibrium was.

Third, the farmer-owned reserves have not added all that much to total stocks, with the result that almost any measure of cost effectiveness would give low marks to the rather sizable investments in this program. The data in table 1 suggest that the farmer-owned reserves did little more than displace privately held stocks. Although the reserve program did give policy makers a means of lifting commodity prices off their floors in late 1977 and early 1978 and the means to limit their increases in the second half of 1979, it is not clear that private speculators would not have performed the same function and perhaps more efficiently.

Fourth, some evidence suggests that the reserve program has been destabilizing, especially to the livestock sector. The failure of the cattle cycle to follow its normal pattern is probably a consequence of the price signals created by implementing the reserve policy. One might argue that producers can do a better job of forecasting the behavior of a multitude of private speculators than they can the whims of policy makers or politicians.

Finally, the income transfers made by means of the deficiency

TABLE 1

CARRY-OVER (ENDING) STOCKS OF WHEAT AND CORN, 1970–1979

(in million bushels)

Wheat Stock Data

Marketing Year	Privately Owned	Government Owned	FOR[a] Ending Stocks
1970	470	353	—
1971	628	355	—
1972	591	6	—
1973	340	1	—
1974	435	0	—
1975	665	0	—
1976	1,112	0	—
1977	1,131	46	317
1978	875	50	403
1979	700	200	250

Corn Stock Data

Marketing Year	Privately Owned	Government Owned	FOR[a] Ending Stocks	
			Corn	Other feed grains
1970	570	97	—	—
1971	970	156	—	—
1972	704	4	—	—
1973	484	0	—	—
1974	361	0	—	—
1975	399	0	—	—
1976	884	0	—	—
1977	1,094	10	257	78
1978	1,190	96	552	97
1979[b]	1,386	300	950	110

[a] Farmer-owned reserves.
[b] Estimate.

SOURCE: Department of Agriculture, *Agricultural Statistics* and *Feed Situation*, various issues.

payments and the support of prices by means of the reserve policy have not addressed the basic problem of poverty in the sector but rather have benefited those who are already relatively well off. This problem has been exacerbated by the disaster program, which was an integral part of the 1977 legislation and which, as Secretary Bergland has said, is little short of a disaster itself. This program has induced the production of commodities, especially wheat, in areas where they ought not be produced, as evidenced by some counties' being declared disaster areas year after year. Moreover, the beneficiaries of this program have also tended to be the relatively well off.

It should be noted in passing that the deficiency payment program has the potential to be used as an implicit export subsidy. Although it has not yet been used extensively for that purpose (wheat may be an exception), the extent to which the program has become politicized suggests that it may well move in that direction in the future.

Where does one go from here? My suggestion is that we continue the evolution of the 1973 and 1977 legislation and go even further to a free market commodity policy. The exception to letting free market forces work should be an actuarially sound but subsidized income insurance program that could be developed by extending and improving the crop insurance program recently signed into law by President Carter. Such an insurance program can be devised as a cost-share income insurance program that would enable producers to be good credit risks for the commercial credit system.

The basis for this suggestion is fivefold. First, commercial agriculture is now in relative resource adjustment, with the result that secular income is no longer a problem so long as international markets remain relatively open and the world economy continues to develop. The continuing problem of rural poverty has to be dealt with by means other than commodity policy.

Second, the basic problem of instability in U.S. agriculture is not something inherent to agriculture. It is a problem of monetary and fiscal policy and should be dealt with by that means. The experience of the last decade indicates how little commodity policies can do in the face of monetary and fiscal disturbances. They simply are not worth their costs.

Third, the current use of cost of production as a basis of policy is unfortunate. Cost of production is a poor basis for commodity policy and little better than the discarded parity concept. Cost-of-production pricing results in capital gains to some producers and inhibits regional adjustments within the country. We also are in real danger of pricing ourselves out of international markets.

Fourth, a legitimate case can be made for transferring some fraction of the risk inherent in agriculture to the rest of the economy.

Farmers are subject to the vagaries of the weather, and the biological character of agricultural production processes does limit the adjustment that producers can make within a given period. Hence, there are externalities that producers should be protected against.

Sound policy would address this problem directly by means of an income insurance program. This program could be nothing more than an extension of the program the Carter administration attempted to get through Congress. It would be actuarially sound, but a subsidy would be provided to offset the externalities associated with risk. The premium subsidy would be limited, and the producer would share the cost. Moreover, the producer could choose the level of protection he desired by selecting some percentage of normal yields. The producer could also choose the price for his commodity that he would like to insure, and it is in this sense that the policy becomes an income protection program.

It would not be possible to move immediately to such a program, for actuarial data are lacking. A commitment could be made to move to a full insurance program within a given number of years, however.

The purist might argue that even an insurance program is not needed, since producers can in principle use the futures markets or forward contracting to serve the same purpose. That, of course, is feasible for the large producer, but the transactions costs are too high for the small and medium producer. In fact, eventual evolution of the system might find the subsidized insurance program used by the small and medium producer and other instruments used by the large producer.

The insurance program has two important advantages. First, if devised so as to make maximum use of the private sector, which is feasible if the subsidy is attached to the premium, the program will help to mobilize the private insurance industry to handle the risks in agriculture and to tap the nation's capital markets. Second, by further drawing on the capital markets to stabilize their income streams, insurance would give the small and medium producer greater direct access to credit and capital markets.

The final basis for scrapping the old program and moving to a comprehensive income insurance program is that it would reduce government-induced instability in commodity markets. Key decisions, instead of being made by a handful of policy makers, would be decentralized into the marketplace and to the private speculators. This potential for pooled judgment would most likely add stability to the market.

One additional element is needed in the program. A case can be made for a small reserve of 4 to 5 million tons of food grains in government hands. No pretense should be made that the reserve has any stabilization goal. Its sole intent would be to enable us to meet our food aid commitments, so that we do not have to turn away from the disadvantaged at the very time they most need our assistance. The availability of this reserve would preclude policy makers from having to enter commodity markets when they are at their peak to meet our foreign policy objectives. Preferably, this small reserve would become part of an international undertaking designed to provide food security.

The Need to Develop New Institutions on the International Scene. The growing dependence of the U.S. economy on trade gives this nation a vested interest in effective international institutions. The need for such institutions is perhaps greater now than it has been at any time in the post–World War II period. Agriculture, as much as any sector in the economy, has a vital interest in international institutional reform and in the health of the international economy. Seldom has the opportunity for institutional creativity been so great.

The key to the stabilization of international commodity markets will be the stabilization of international financial markets. The Bretton Woods conventions, which had regulated international monetary phenomena for almost thirty years, were abandoned when the United States devalued the dollar for the second time in 1973 and shifted to a system of floating exchange rates. Nothing has been put in their place, and policy makers have dealt with problems on a day-to-day crisis basis.

What the world needs if it is to stabilize international monetary markets is a true international central bank that would act as a central bank for the world economy. An international monetary system would have to be created, with the central bank as the centerpiece. Rules would need to be established regarding the management of national monetary policy and interventions in foreign exchange and capital markets.

The establishment of such a system would require that member countries give up some of the sovereignty they now have over their national policies.[12] But such a system appears to be the only hope for establishing international monetary stability, which is the only hope of obtaining some stability in international commodity markets.

Our present situation involves serious risks, risks we should try to reduce. The interest rate war the United States has conducted with West Germany and other countries on occasion in recent years is fraught with danger. In some respects it is similar to the competitive devaluations that created serious problems in the 1930s. Of course, the dangers of competitive devaluations are still with us. These dangers are so real,

---

[12] Realistically, nations should realize that they do not have all that much control over their own policies even now. Like it or not, they are forced to respond to changing conditions in their external accounts and in international markets. Cooperation will be in the best interests of all.

and the potential consequences so great, that it seems imperative that we attempt to negotiate a new international monetary system.

Of equal importance is the need to design some response to the low-income countries composing the Group of 77 in the so-called North-South debate. So far, this debate has been a dialogue of the deaf, with neither side apparently listening to the other. An equally bold initiative will be required to help move this discussion out of its present stalemate and onto more constructive turf. Agriculture may provide the basis for a more constructive initiative. It may be over food that the interests of the less-developed and advanced countries finally converge.

Population growth toward the end of this century suggests that the world food problem, though tractable, will be difficult. Unless this problem is solved, the advanced countries face a combination of rising food prices and political instability that threatens our economic and political interests. This instability also threatens the regimes of many less-developed countries.

On the other hand, the less-developed countries offer important market possibilities for the agricultural and other high-technology exports of the developed countries. The realization of these possibilities will depend on the less-developed countries' establishing reasonable rates of growth, however.

As noted earlier, an increased willingness on the part of the United States and other advanced countries to accept labor-intensive imports of manufactured goods is an important means of facilitating that growth and of providing the exchange earnings the less-developed countries can use to buy our exports. But providing expanded trade opportunities alone will not be sufficient. The capital and labor markets have to be opened up as well. Freer labor markets may border on the impossible, but more open capital markets are certainly feasible, and we should press for the reforms that would make that possible.

Institutional developments associated with the establishment of an international central bank will undoubtedly contribute to a freeing up of capital markets. But an essential element of the negotiations for freer trade on the part of the advanced countries should be more liberalization of capital markets on the part of the less-developed countries. This may sound like wishful thinking, but, by the same token, no one would have thought some ten years ago that the low-income countries would be making the extensive use of international capital markets they now are. The negotiation of reasonable rules of the game may give further impetus to present trends. The crisis created by high petroleum prices may stimulate needed reform.

Limited reforms of the labor market may also be possible. Highest priority should be given to opening the markets for skilled professionals

179

and researchers. There is now general recognition of the importance of human capital and of the production and distribution of new production technology in obtaining more rapid economic growth and development. Aside from the system of international agricultural research centers, however, there has been little attempt to develop institutional arrangements whereby the market for skilled professionals could be opened up and international capital markets more effectively used to serve the human capital needs of developing countries. Attempts in these directions are long overdue.

There has been some concern in Congress that technology transfer is not in the best interests of this nation. This view is misguided. Technological change is the key to faster rates of growth in those countries, and faster rates of growth are in our best interests.

Focusing our attention on improving international factor markets would be a bold new initiative. Such improvements would not come easily, but they might well establish the basis for a dialogue. Economic and political pressures may now be such that progress can be made if we are creative enough and if we have the courage to put forth new proposals and implement change.

The Problem of Rural Poverty in U.S. Agriculture. My remarks here will be limited. The main point to be made is that the core problem of poverty in rural America does not lend itself to solution by commodity programs. Completely different policy instruments are required.

Similarly, most of what passes for community development in this country is equally ineffective. Most of these programs focus on physical infrastructure when they should concentrate on providing formal schooling and vocational skills to the disadvantaged. Little progress will be made in the war on rural poverty until a substantial shift in policy comes about.

The Farmers Home Administration is now, incredibly, the third largest bank in the United States. It provides loans for rural telephone systems, electric power systems, rural housing, and other physical infrastructure. Were just half of the resources of this agency allocated to schooling and training programs and to facilitating relocation of workers and their families, there seems little doubt that significant progress could be made in eliminating rural poverty.

The elimination of poverty is important both as a goal in its own right and as the basis for improved commodity policy. The rural poor dominate the aggregate income data on the agricultural sector. Until the problem of rural poverty is reduced or eliminated, it is not likely that we will make much progress toward a more rational commodity policy.

Energy. My original intent was to say nothing about energy policy other than to note its obvious importance to trade issues. But the distortions now being introduced in the form of the gasohol program cannot be neglected. The potential budget costs and economic waste associated with these programs promise to dwarf the costs of any of the commodity programs, past or present.

The gasohol program will have far-reaching effects on our food and agricultural system. Commitments to subsidies for this program have already been extended up to 1992. Fred Sanderson[13] estimates that the cost to the federal treasury could exceed $30 billion over the next ten years if the present goal of 10 billion gallons of alcohol a year by 1985 is reached. This does not include the costs of state tax exemptions or of higher food prices to consumers or the loss in foreign exchange earnings as a consequence of reduced exports.

A preliminary analysis we have made at Minnesota[14] suggests that the diversion of corn from exports into alcohol may well have deleterious consequences for the balance of payments. Using October 1979 prices, which favor the conversion of corn to gasohol, attainment of the gasohol goal set by the Carter administration will result in a net gain of $32 million on the balance of payments if all processing energy is derived from domestic sources. If all processing energy comes from imported energy inputs, however, the net loss to the balance of payments would range from $262 to $329 million.

Concluding Comments

The changed economic environment in which U.S. agriculture now finds itself suggests the need for a new approach to commodity policy. The program sketched out above responds to those changed conditions. It recognizes the need to implement policies that attack the causes of problems now reflected in agriculture, and it proposes a commodity policy that directly addresses the problem of risk inherent in agriculture. It also recognizes that new international arrangements are needed if we expect to stabilize international commodity markets and ensure growth in our markets in the years ahead.

---

[13] Fred H. Sanderson, "Gasohol: Boom or Blunder?," *The Brookings Bulletin*, vol. 16, no. 3 (Winter 1980).

[14] Dave Orden and G. Edward Schuh, "Trade and Balance of Payment Implications of Agriculturally Produced Motor Fuels and Other Aspects of Higher Petroleum Prices," USDA/Universities Agricultural Trade Research Consortium (Roseville, Minn., July 1980). Summary available in U.S. Department of Agriculture, Economics and Statistics Service, *Consortium on Trade Research*, ESS-2, December 1980, pp. 25–7.

Some of these policies will not come overnight, and the negotiations for others will be complicated and demanding. The effort to create and establish these arrangements is needed, however, if we are to develop more rational commodity policies and to reestablish this nation's long-term growth rates.

Agricultural Policy Alternatives for the 1980s

D. Gale Johnson

Looking ahead is often assisted by looking back. This is certainly the case for U.S. agricultural policy for the major crops. For the past two decades, the farm programs for crops have shown a quite remarkable pattern of gradual adjustment toward important goals. Vacillations and setbacks have been minor, although political forces on more than one occasion tested the resolve to push on toward the explicit and implicit objectives of agricultural policy.

Starting in the late 1950s, successive farm programs for the major crops increased the role of the market in the pricing and distribution of output while simultaneously reducing the influence of the government over short-run price developments. Beginning in 1961 the government attempted to influence farm prices through managing supplies rather than by direct intervention in the market.

It is not obvious how political considerations influenced farm programs in the past two decades. There is fairly general agreement that the conflicts over agricultural programs that prevailed during the Eisenhower administration between the executive branch and the Congress created the legacy of costly programs deemed ineffective in improving the income of farmers and responsible for the accumulation of enormous quantities of farm crops by the Commodity Credit Corporation (CCC).

During the Eisenhower administration the executive branch pressed for lower price supports to discourage production and expand utilization. Congress voted to maintain price supports at relatively high levels. Programs that were adopted to restrain output were generally ineffective. When, in the late 1950s, some of the price support levels were reduced, Congress was disappointed that output did not decline immediately and domestic use and exports did not respond in a year or two. Thus the 1950s ended with no apparent progress in finding a solution to the problem of excess resources engaged in agriculture.

Eight years of conflict and experimentation were seemingly ended by the election of both a Democratic president and a Democratic Congress in 1960. Such did not prove to be the case, however. Although President Kennedy believed the large governmental costs of the farm programs could not be sustained, he proposed an increase in the government's role through strict mandatory supply management covering most farm commodities. Congress refused to support the president in his call for mandatory controls. During the 1950s Congress persisted in its efforts to achieve a balance between supply and demand at unrealistically high prices through the use of voluntary measures. Farmers were induced to remove land from cultivation by payments. As surpluses in the hands of the CCC mounted during the last half of the 1950s, there was recognition that price supports had been maintained at unrealistic levels, and downward adjustments were made, especially for corn, as the decade ended.[1] In spite of the apparent failures of the prior voluntary programs, Congress maintained its adherence to voluntarism.

President Kennedy desired mandatory controls because he believed that in this way government costs could be substantially reduced. Congress was reluctant to give up the credit for the distribution of substantial payments to farmers and, at the same time, accept the onus for approving mandatory controls that would displease the majority of their farmer constituents. In the end the conflicts between the administration and Congress were resolved by a series of costly voluntary programs designed to limit crop production and a gradual reduction of almost all price supports for crop products to or below world market levels. With most crop prices at world market levels, a transition that was largely completed by 1964, farm incomes were maintained at politically acceptable levels by direct payments.

The major features of the compromise farm policies that evolved after 1955 were included in the Food and Agricultural Act of 1965. This legislation has been modified in a number of ways by three succeeding farm acts, but most of the basic ideas remain unchanged. These basic concepts are price supports at levels that permit the market to allocate supplies among the various markets, income support to be achieved through direct payments, and voluntary methods of achieving supply management when deemed necessary. The farm acts of 1970,

---

[1] See Willard W. Cochrane and Mary E. Ryan, *American Farm Policy, 1948–73* (Minneapolis: University of Minnesota Press, 1976), chap. 6, for an objective and illuminating discussion of support price policies during the 1950s and the impact of those policies on the stocks of major farm commodities owned or controlled by the Commodity Credit Corporation.

1973, and 1977 differed in detail from the 1965 legislation and from one another, but the basic concepts remained unchallenged.[2]

Price Support Levels

The price support levels established after 1965 were substantially lower than the levels that prevailed during most of the 1950s (table 1). The support levels for wheat were reduced by almost one half in a decade; the reductions for corn and cotton were a third or more. In each case the price supports established for 1965 and subsequent years were usually low enough to permit U.S. farm products to compete in international markets. U.S. farm products were exported in increasing quantity and value. After World War I, U.S. agriculture apparently lost its comparative advantage; for two decades starting in 1922 (except for one year), the United States imported more agricultural products than it exported. Exports exceeded imports during World War II and during the early postwar years, but by 1950 imports again exceeded exports. This lasted until 1957, even with the substantial export disposal programs that were undertaken. It was not until the early 1960s that commercial exports of agricultural products exceeded agricultural imports in value.[3]

The competitive pricing of farm crop products was associated with a significant growth in the quantity of our agricultural exports during the latter part of the 1960s and early 1970s. A variety of factors were responsible for the export growth—devaluation of the dollar, expansion of grain imports by the centrally plannned economies, and increased food demand in the middle-income developing countries, including the members of the Organization of Petroleum Exporting Countries (OPEC). The other factors in the growth of our exports were the increase of farm output and the slow growth in domestic demand for all farm products after 1973. The United States became the major supplier for the growth in demand for grains in the world markets after 1973, supplying more than 80 percent of the growth in world grain exports during the 1970s.

The competitive pricing of farm products was associated with direct payments to farmers for the major crops. Such payments were made as a part of acreage control and diversion programs. For wheat

---

[2] Ibid., chap. 3, gives a concise history of agricultural legislation from 1965 through 1973.

[3] See D. Gale Johnson, "World Agricultural and Trade Policies: Impact on U.S. Agriculture" in William Fellner, ed., *Contemporary Economic Problems 1979* (Washington, D.C.: American Enterprise Institute, 1979), pp. 313–15, for a discussion of the shifting patterns of the trade surplus of U.S. agriculture.

TABLE 1

PRICE SUPPORT OR LOAN RATES, 1950–1980

(in 1967 dollars)

Year	Wheat ($/bu)	Corn[a] ($/bu)	Soybeans ($/bu)	Manufactured Milk ($/cwt)	Cotton[b] (cents/lb)
1950	2.31	1.71	—	3.57	32.44
1951	2.29	1.65	—	3.79	32.06
1952	2.32	1.68	—	4.05	32.54
1953	2.48	1.80	2.88	4.20	34.61
1954	2.52	1.82	2.49	3.54	35.48
1955	2.39	1.82	2.34	3.62	36.43
1956	2.30	1.72	2.47	3.68	33.72
1957	2.22	1.56	2.32	3.61	32.01
1958	1.98	1.48	2.27	3.33	33.95
1959	1.95	1.20	1.99	3.29	32.68
1960	1.93	1.15	2.01	3.47	31.49
1961	1.92	1.29	2.47	3.66	34.28
1962	2.13	1.28	2.39	3.31	33.92
1963	1.92	1.13	2.36	3.31	33.39
1964	1.38	1.17	2.39	3.35	29.30
1965	1.30	1.09	2.34	3.38	29.43
1966	1.25	1.05	2.50	3.75	20.21
1967	1.25	1.10	2.50	4.00	20.25
1968	1.25	1.05	2.50	4.28	20.25
1969	1.20	1.01	2.16	4.12	19.47
1970	1.16	0.97	2.08	4.31	18.75
1971	1.11	0.93	1.99	4.36	17.26
1972	1.03	0.87	1.86	4.07	16.16
1973	0.86	0.72	1.54	3.38	13.36
1974	0.94	0.66	1.36	3.96	15.22
1975	0.75	0.60	—	3.98	18.83
1976	1.17	0.78	1.30	4.21	19.23
1977	1.12	0.88	1.75	4.50	22.32
1978	1.09	0.93	2.08	4.57	22.32
1979	1.01	0.85	1.81	4.63	20.25
1980	1.10	0.82	1.84	4.53[c]	17.00

NOTE: Dashes indicate that there were no price supports in those years. Loan rates used in this table are actual loan rates deflated by prices paid by farmers for production items; do not include any direct payments.

[a] Other and lower loan rates prevailed in 1950 and 1954 through 1958. For details see Cochrane and Ryan, *American Farm Policy*, p. 179.

[b] For 1950 through 1960, basis 7/8-inch middling; from 1961 to date, 1-inch

and cotton, the direct payments were large relative to their market prices and applied to nearly all the output. For corn, the direct payments were more modest and applied to approximately half the output (table 2).

The United States relied on export subsidies for several commodities during the 1950s and 1960s. The reduction in price support levels did not entirely eliminate the use of export subsidies. As shown in table 2, however, the magnitude of export subsidies diminished during the late 1960s and early 1970s. After 1973 explicit payment of export subsidies was halted and has not been revived. Implicit export subsidies—the export at a loss of products owned by the Commodity Credit Corporation—continue for dairy products.

Agricultural Adjustment

In a monograph written in late 1972, I argued that most of the excess resources retained in U.S. agriculture during the 1950s and early 1960s had been eliminated, primarily through adjustments in the labor market and the significant abandonment of farm land.[4] The labor market adjustment before 1950 had occurred primarily through migration away from farms, but, starting in the 1950s, part-time nonfarm employment played an increasing role in labor adjustment in agriculture. In 1960, the first year for which we have data for farm operator families, 42 percent of the income of such families came from off-farm sources; the percentage had increased to 55 by 1970 and to 62 percent in 1976 and 1979. Primarily as a result of the reduction in the number of farm workers and the increase in off-farm income, the per capita disposable income of farm people increased from less than 50 percent of that of nonfarm people in the late 1950s to about 75 percent in 1970 and 1971.[5] Given the characteristics of the data and the fact that capital gains are not included in the income data, farm per capita disposable

---

middling. Before 1971 loan rate was on gross weight basis, after 1970 on a net weight basis. Loan rates after 1970 should be reduced about 4 percent to be comparable to loan rates for 1970 and earlier years.

c From April through September 1980; as of October 1, 1980, price support level increased in current dollars.

Sources: Department of Agriculture, *Agricultural Statistics*, various issues, and *Wheat Situation, Feed Situation, Fats and Oils Situation, Cotton and Wool Situation*, and *Dairy Situation*.

4 D. Gale Johnson, *Farm Commodity Programs: An Opportunity for Change* (Washington, D.C.: American Enterprise Institute, 1973), especially pp. 29–49 and 83–88.

5 U.S. Department of Agriculture, Economics, Statistics, and Cooperatives Service, *Farm Income Statistics*, Statistical Bulletin no. 627 (October 1979), p. 36. Since 1971 the ratio has varied between 78 and 110 percent; in 1978 it was at 91 percent.

TABLE 2

MARKET PRICES, SUPPLEMENTARY PAYMENTS, AND EXPORT SUBSIDIES, WHEAT AND FEED GRAINS, UNITED STATES, 1968/1969–1978/1979

(\$ per metric ton)

Year	Wheat			Feed Grains		
	Prices received by farmers	Average payment	Export subsidy	Prices received by farmers	Average payment	Export subsidy
1968/69	45.56	17.68	—	39.68	8.84	—
1969/70	45.56	21.88	5.51	45.67	10.22	0.12
1970/71	48.86	23.65	8.45	52.36	10.39	0.61
1971/72	49.23	20.11	5.14	42.52	5.62	0.50
1972/73	64.66	21.04	12.86	61.81	10.27	—
1973/74	145.12	10.21	16.91	100.39	6.28	—
1974/75	150.27	2.10	—	119.29	2.18	—
1975/76	130.79	0.88	—	100.00	0.62	—
1976/77	100.30	2.49	—	84.60	1.16	—
1977/78	104.40	22.46	—	79.50	2.81	—
1978/79	120.50	16.81	—	83.50	4.71	—

SOURCES: Department of Agriculture, *Wheat Situation*, various issues; *Feed Situation*, various issues; *Agricultural Statistics*, 1973 and 1977.

income that is 75 to 80 percent of nonfarm income is probably not far from an equilibrium level. By equilibrium level I mean one that provides approximately the same return to farm resources, both labor and land, as is received by comparable nonfarm resources.

In the same monograph I argued that the impact of the acreage diversion programs during the late 1960s and early 1970s was quite small—approximately 2 percent of total agricultural output.[6] Since the acreage diversion programs affected the output of crops that were exported in substantial amounts, the price impact of this small reduction in farm production was also rather small. It must be noted that during the late 1960s and early 1970s direct governmental payments averaging about $3.5 billion annually were paid to farmers and landowners. An offset to the small increase in price due to output restraint and the governmental payments was the significant overvaluation of the dollar during the 1960s and early 1970s. Since the U.S. prices of major farm crops were at international market prices or changed in response to international market prices, the overvaluation of the dollar amounted to a tax on the output of these products. The devaluation of the dollar in 1971 eliminated this implicit tax and increased the income of U.S. farmers by an amount comparable to the direct governmental payments relative to total cash income from sales.

Farm prices were high in 1973 and 1974 and seemed likely to remain at real levels above those realized before 1972. This induced some additional capital resources to enter agriculture and reduced the usual flow of labor out of agriculture. A sharp decline in farm prices that started in 1975 and continued through 1977 resulted in a major reduction in net income from agriculture. In constant dollars, net farm operator income declined by nearly 60 percent between 1973 and either 1976 or 1977. While the significance of this decline is easy to exaggerate given the abnormally high income of 1973—more than double that of 1971—it remains true that total net income for farm operators in real terms in both 1976 and 1977 was the lowest since 1940.[7]

To a considerable degree, the 1977 agricultural legislation was a political response to the sharp decline in farm incomes from 1973 through 1976. The general pattern of the 1977 legislation, however, did not differ significantly from the 1973 legislation. True, there were differences in detail, such as the abandonment of acreage allotments, which in most cases were related to land use almost two decades earlier.

[6] Johnson, *Farm Commodity Programs*, pp. 41–42. As noted in the monograph, other economists, including Luther Tweeten, estimated the amount of excess resources in agriculture at a significantly higher figure.

[7] Department of Agriculture, *Farm Income Statistics* (October 1979), p. 33.

The 1977 legislation did introduce two important innovations—a criterion for establishing target prices and the farmer-owned reserve (FOR) program for grains. The criterion for establishing target prices was that of production costs, although one must admit some degree of puzzlement over a target price for wheat for 1978 that was established at $3.00–3.05 for 1978 in the 1977 act but was increased to $3.40 by Congress in the Emergency Agricultural Act of 1978. The use of changes in production costs to modify target prices over time has apparently not had the desired effects, as viewed by the Carter administration, since legislation was supported by the administration and passed by Congress to increase the 1980 target prices for corn to $2.35 per bushel and for wheat to $3.63.[8] Presumably the reason for lack of enthusiasm for the provisions of the act for changing target prices is that the rather significant increase in grain yields in the past two years meant that variable production costs failed to increase significantly and thus there was no basis, under current legislation, to increase the target prices for grains significantly.

Farm Policy Issues

What I have said so far serves as a long introduction to my discussion of farm policy alternatives for the 1980s.

My discussion of policy options is organized by policy issues rather than by commodities. For the most important crop products, the general pattern of the farm programs is quite similar, although, as will be noted, not all crops receive equal treatment. The following policy issues will be addressed: (1) price support levels, (2) target price levels, (3) storage and reserves, (4) supply management, (5) export policies, (6) disaster payments and insurance programs, and (7) gasohol. There are, of course, other important policy issues that I will not cover, such as marketing orders, farm credit programs, the food stamp plan, environmental controls, and agricultural research.

Price Support Levels. The United States has no alternative but to set price support levels for major export products low enough to have a minimum impact on the capacity of the market to allocate supplies among the alternative demanders. This approach to price policy has been adhered to now for more than a decade and a half for the grains,

---

[8] U.S. Department of Agriculture, Economics, Statistics, and Cooperatives Service, *Feed Situation*, FdS-277 (May 1980), p. 5, and *Wheat Situation*, WS-252 (May 1980), p. 5. Lower target prices will prevail if a farmer exceeds his "normal crop acreage" as established—$2.05 for corn and $3.08 for wheat. The lower target price for corn is meaningless since the loan rate will be $2.10 per bushel.

cotton, and soybeans. The effects of the policy have been the desired ones: our export markets have grown, and yet the price support levels through loans for storing crops have served to assist farmers in the orderly marketing of their crops, as well as to assure farmers of a minimum level of prices for their output.

If price supports are set at levels that usually become the market prices, the United States will lose much of the competitiveness and responsiveness that have characterized our export activities during the 1970s. The United States is, in any case, likely to be the substantial residual supplier in the world market for grains because of its huge size, supplying as it does almost half of world grain exports. The United States has an even stronger argument, however, against setting international market prices at levels above those that will clear the market, if not every year, then certainly over a period of three or four years. Such higher support prices would have output effects, both in the United States and in other major exporting countries, that would soon lead to excess production, diminished consumption, and stock accumulations. The inevitable consequence of price support levels set above market clearing levels is the need to limit output to keep governmental cost at an acceptable level. Farm people paid the price of resource adjustments during the 1950s and 1960s. It would be most unwise to create an artificial need for resource adjustment through unwarranted price support incentives.

For the grains, cotton, and soybeans, the current price support levels are a continuation of recent practice. For dairy products and sugar, on the other hand, we continue to follow the very same price support and trade policies we criticize so strongly in our major trading partners, Japan and the European Economic Community (EEC). The EEC has its butter mountain, and we will soon have ours or at least a rapidly growing hill for surplus disposal at home and abroad, given the current criterion for establishing price support levels. The criterion is one of the few still tied to parity prices, with a range of 80 to 90 percent. Dairy products are one of the very few products whose market price has been determined by governmental price supports set at fairly specific percentages of parity. As a result, dairy prices have been lifted, both by the U.S. Treasury, which has provided the financial resources required to put a floor under dairy product prices, and by our trade negotiators, who have valiantly maintained strict quantitative restrictions upon dairy imports.

Past and current price support operations influence future parity prices for dairy products and, in turn, future price supports. Parity prices are no longer tied directly to the 1910–1914 prices received by farmers. For all farm products, the parity ratio—the prices-received

191

index divided by the parity index—is still based on 1910–1914, but for individual commodities there is an adjusted base (1910–1914) price which is the average price of the commodity for the most recent 120-month average of prices received, divided by the average of the index of prices received for all commodities for the same period of time. This calculation is made annually. For the 1980 calendar year, the milk adjusted base price is $1.91 per hundredweight, or 19 percent above the actual 1910–1914 price. But for corn the adjusted base price is $0.478 per bushel, 26 percent below the 1910–1914 price. While the corn adjusted base price reflects whatever direct payments were received during the most recent ten years, most of the relative price relationships for the 120-month period reflected the fact that corn prices were determined in the international market, while dairy prices were determined in a highly protected domestic market and as part of a price support program involving substantial government purchases and disposal. Put simply, an effective price support for dairy products influences future price support levels by increasing the parity price. This is probably not what Congress had in mind in revising the parity formula, but it is exactly what has happened and will continue to occur.

For farm products that we import, or would if trade barriers were reduced, it would be reasonable to expect price supports to be established at levels designed to achieve politically acceptable levels of producer incomes and hence encourage production. The two most important products for which such price support levels may be anticipated are dairy and sugar, although at the time of this writing, there is no significant protection of sugar in the United States.

Target Prices. The major policy debate in the formulation of the 1981 agricultural legislation, in my opinion, will be on the level of target prices. Quite frankly, an economist has little to say about that level. What little he has to say is as follows: (1) do not set the target prices too far above long-run equilibrium prices, and (2) set the target prices for each commodity at approximately the same percentage above support prices.

These two criteria reflect the view that target prices and the associated deficiency payments should not be used to influence production decisions significantly. Some production effect cannot be avoided, although its magnitude would be minimized if the target prices were approximately the same as market prices received over a period of years. The view that there should be approximately equal ratios of target to support prices is based on the assumption that target prices should not have differential effects on output. In other words, high target prices create resource adjustment problems by encouraging increased output and transfer part of the adjustment problem to crops with relatively low target prices.

The 1977 act does not, however, provide for target prices that are approximately proportional to the support prices. The act set the 1978 target price for wheat at 28 percent more than the loan level, even though for corn the difference between target and loan levels was only 5 percent. Before 1978 wheat crops came to market, however, the target price for wheat for 1978 was increased significantly by the Emergency Agricultural Act of 1978 to 51 percent more than the loan level, which was left unchanged at the announced level of $2.25 per bushel. The target prices for grain sorghums and barley were established by the secretary of agriculture under the discretion permitted in the act at 20 and 32 percent above their respective loan levels.

The criterion that was said to have been used to determine target prices in the formulation of the 1977 act was cost of production. The target prices for wheat, corn, and cotton were set in the legislation, though not without considerable jockeying about what constituted an appropriate measure of the price of the land input. What actually emerged in the legislation, quite naturally, represented a series of compromises. The target price levels specified in the act assumed a return to land of 3.5 to 4.0 percent on its then current price. The cost-of-production formula that was to be used to change the target prices over time, however, considered only changes in variable costs and thus ignored changes in land values. Subsequent target price changes have been legislated rather than calculated. I do not want to be interpreted as implying that one process is necessarily inferior to the other.

The limitations of cost of production as a criterion for determining target prices are very great.[9] Measurement problems are insuperable. There is no way to determine a meaningful measure of the cost of production to establish a price that would provide appropriate guidance for production decisions. A price set above the level that would equilibrate supply and demand in a market will become self-fulfilling,

[9] A workshop on the estimation of costs of production was organized by the Economics, Statistics, and Cooperatives Service of the U.S. Department of Agriculture in June 1978. The papers and discussion were published in *Estimating Agricultural Costs of Production—Workshop Proceedings*, ESCS–56 (June 1979). The various papers note the weak basis of many assumptions, such as the magnitude of the charge for management; the wide variation in costs for different farms and in different regions; the weak empirical base for the cost estimates; the difficulties of estimating the price or cost of such inputs as family labor or owned capital; and the insuperable problem of arriving at an appropriate charge for land since the rent of land depends on the price of the produce of the land.

in the sense that the cost of production will increase until it equals that price. As is well known, the prices of some factors of production are derived prices, or prices that depend on the prices of the products produced by those factors. This is principally true of land in agriculture, but it can also influence the price of labor and management. In addition, a price greater than the market equilibrium price will influence the amounts and productivity of resources used in the production of the product. The amount of fertilizer used and its marginal cost per unit of output, for example, is a function of the product price. Consequently, if the price of wheat is set at $5.00 per bushel, that price will greatly influence the costs of producing wheat. Given time, the cost of producing wheat would increase, and measurements of that cost would cluster around $5.00.

Now that cost of production has been accepted in agricultural legislation, it is not going to be easy to remove it. Part of the difficulty, as I have already indicated, is that there are no established criteria for determining the level of target prices. Target prices and deficiency payments are methods of transferring income. How much income is to be transferred is a political decision. Why, then, did the 1977 legislation rely on cost-of-production estimates to arrive at the magnitude of the income transfers? It is possible that the answer to this question is a very simple one, namely, that the average costs of production available in 1977 gave the politically desired target prices. This explanation is based on the pattern of income transfers that have persisted in the past and the target prices that were specified in the Agricultural Act of 1973, without the sanction and support of cost-of-production data.

In the 1973 act the target price for wheat was set for 1974 and 1975 at 49 percent more than the target price for corn; the farm prices for the decade from 1964 through 1972 were $1.41 per bushel for wheat and $1.20 for corn, a difference of 19 percent in favor of wheat. The 1978 target price for wheat, as established in the 1977 act, was $3.00 per bushel and $2.00 for corn; that is, the wheat target price was 50 percent larger. In the Emergency Agricultural Act of 1978, however, the target price for wheat for 1980 was increased from $3.00 to $3.40 per bushel; the increase for corn was from $2.00 to $2.10. Thus in 1978 the effective target price for wheat was 62 percent above that for corn.[10]

---

[10] U.S. Department of Agriculture, *Feed Situation*, FdS-269 (May 1978), pp. 42–43. This issue provides a good summary of the differences between the 1973 and 1977 agricultural acts.

I have so far discussed only the relationships between the target prices for wheat and corn under the 1977 legislation. Cost-of-production estimates were used by the secretary of agriculture to justify target prices for barley and grain sorghum that were significantly higher in relation to the target price for corn than the relative farm prices of the three products during the 1970s. From 1970 to 1979, the average market prices per bushel for barley, grain sorghums, and corn were, respectively, $1.83, $1.83, and $2.02. The average prices per bushel of barley and grain sorghum were each equal to 91 percent of the corn price. The target price set for 1977 for barley was 107.5 percent of the corn target price, and the target price for grain sorghum was 114 percent of the corn target price.

Why should the target prices for the three small grains—wheat, barley, and grain sorghum—be so much higher than the target price for corn relative to past market price relationships? The favoritism, if that is what it can be called, for wheat relative to corn has been a longstanding feature of our commodity programs, but the favored position of barley and grain sorghums is of recent origin. For the decade 1963 through 1972, the average loan rates plus direct payments per bushel to the participants in the feed grain programs were $1.32 for corn, $0.98 for barley, and $1.18 for grain sorghum.[11] I find it hard to believe that the supply prices of these three grains changed as radically between the 1960s and the 1970s as the relative target and price support levels. What these changes in relative charity seem to indicate is that farmers in the Great Plains have significantly greater political influence than farmers in the Corn Belt. Alternatively, the differences could indicate greater sophistication on the part of corn farmers concerning the long-run effects of target prices significantly above equilibrium market prices.

Cotton producers have clearly opted for a target price that would come into effect only if there were a serious decline in market prices. The 1980 target price for cotton is only 12 percent above the 1977 target price and substantially below recent market prices.

As economists we must recognize that the target prices and the associated deficiency payments represent the political price we pay for support prices that interfere little, if at all, with the functioning of the market. It is evident that the political price is not uniform—it is highest for wheat and modest or nil for corn and cotton. The grains that compete with wheat for resources, barley and grain sorghum, fall in an intermediate position.

---

[11] U.S. Department of Agriculture, Economics, Statistics, and Cooperatives Service, *Agricultural Prices*, Pr 1 (1-80), January 31, 1980, p. 30.

The growing disparity in relative target prices has reached a level that is cause for concern. The target prices can have an influence on resource allocation, both aggregate allocation and the allocation of resources among the various grains. We must hope that the current disparities do not grow but rather that differences are reduced.

The most immediate effective limit on target prices is budgetary cost. Price support or loan levels are limited by the desire to export freely and by the rapid accumulation of stocks when levels are set too high. The stimulating effects of high target prices on output become apparent rather slowly. For a brief period, perhaps two or three years, the output effects can be contained by set-asides and acreage diversion programs. Recent experience indicates, however, that expenditures required to elicit voluntary participation in acreage diversion programs can be substantial if significant output effects are desired. It needs to be recognized that the magnitude of the required output adjustment is a function of the level of the target prices. Consequently, high target prices impose two budget costs—the deficiency payments and the costs of achieving additional diversion.

Relative Levels of Target and Support Prices. Although corn farmers may well believe that it is in their interest to have target prices at or below expected market prices most of the time, they have an interest in both the absolute and the relative levels of the target prices and loan levels for the other grains. With rather minor exceptions, the price support or loan levels for wheat, barley, and grain sorghum have been set in terms of their feed values in relation to corn. This means that when these small grains are produced in excessive amounts, perhaps in part because of the high target prices, the adjustment problems for all of the grains are imposed on Corn Belt producers.

In election years the pattern of loan levels of wheat and corn has been modified on two occasions. Before the 1976 election the Ford administration announced substantial increases in the price support levels for grains for both 1976 and 1977. The increase for wheat, however, was much greater than for corn, and the new loan level per bushel was 50 percent greater for wheat than for corn. As J. B. Penn noted in describing this action:

> The Ford administration was . . . criticized for distorting the wheat/corn price support relationship which had been maintained for many years. While the world market tends to accord wheat a price premium (over corn) as a food grain, the U.S. loan levels for many years had been set in such a manner that when wheat was in excess supply, its price could

move to levels enabling wheat to compete as a feed grain in domestic markets.[12]

The 1977 legislation reestablished the approximate equality of the loan rates per ton for wheat and corn.

In January 1980 the loan rate for wheat was increased from $2.35 to $2.50 per bushel while the loan rate for corn was increased by $0.10 to $2.10. At the end of July 1980, loan rates were increased for all grains, but more for wheat than for the others. The new loan rates were $3.00 for wheat and $2.25 for corn. The relative loan rates for wheat and corn now depart significantly from the relative feed values, as did the changes made before the 1976 election. Apparently the urge to tinker with price supports before elections is irresistible. It needs to be recognized, however, that if wheat prices weaken and approach the new higher price support level, the response may be to bring the wheat and corn loan rates into approximate equality and again shift wheat adjustment problems to corn producers.[13]

Storage Programs. The farmer-owned reserve program for the grains surely must be counted as one of the success stories of agricultural legislation during the 1970s. This program was designed to take the Commodity Credit Corporation out of the grain storage business and, until recently, was successful in doing so. The recent entry of the CCC into grain storage and ownership has been due to efforts to minimize the price impact of the suspension of grain exports to the Soviet Union.

The farmer-owned reserve program should be maintained for the grains throughout the 1980s. The program functioned well in a significant test during the spring and early summer of 1979, when grain prices increased significantly in response to the anticipated increase in Soviet import demand. The reserve functioned as anticipated: when market prices increased during the late spring and early summer, significant quantities of grain were removed from the reserve. The wheat reserve was at 403 million bushels on June 1, 1979; about 150 million bushels were removed by October.[14] The corn reserve stood at

[12] J. B. Penn, "The Federal Policy Process in Developing the Food and Agricultural Act of 1977," *Agricultural-Food Policy Review*, U.S. Department of Agriculture, ESCS-AFPRO-3 (February 1980), p. 11.

[13] With the increase in loan rates for sorghum, barley, oats, rye, and soybeans as well as for wheat and corn, there were new release and call prices for the major grains. In fact, there are now multiple release and call prices for wheat. Depending on the time the wheat was put into the farmer-owned reserve, the release prices per bushel are $3.50, $3.75, and $4.20. Call prices for wheat are $4.38, $4.63, and $5.25. The new call price for corn became $3.26 and the release price $2.81.

[14] Department of Agriculture, *Wheat Situation*, WS–251 (February 1980), p. 15.

729 million bushels on May 2, 1979, and 188 million bushels were removed by October.[15] For neither wheat nor corn did market prices go high enough to result in a call of these commodities from the reserve.

Some significant changes in the reserve program were announced immediately after the suspension of grain exports to the Soviet Union. For corn the call price was increased from 140 to 145 percent of the loan level. Since the loan level was increased from $2.00 to $2.10, the call price was increased from $2.80 to $3.05. The reserve release price was also increased but solely because of the increase in the loan rate, the release price remaining at 125 percent of the loan rate. Even more substantial changes were made in the reserve and call prices for wheat. The reserve release price was increased from 140 to 150 percent of the new loan level and the call price from 175 to 185 percent. Given the significant increase in the loan level for wheat, the reserve and call prices were increased by about 14 percent.

Why were these changes made? Was there evidence that the earlier relationships among loan rates, release prices, and call prices led to undesirable consequences? If so, I do not know what that evidence was. One effect of these changes is to increase the size of the farmer-owned reserve, at least for a transition period. The penalty for withdrawal of grain from the reserve when the price is less than the release price is a substantial one—repayment of storage costs and the payment of a penalty. Since the prices must now rise higher than before, the amount of grain in the reserve will be larger than it would have been under the previous rules. It is not obvious that increasing the release and call prices will increase the average prices of grain received by farmers or will otherwise be to the advantage of farmers. There seems to be the mistaken impression in many governmental policies and programs that more is better. This is often not the case, however, and the increase in release and call prices may be an instance in which more is not better. It may well be that the increase in the spreads over the loan rate will make the farmer-owned reserve less rather than more attractive.

With the changes in release prices, the farmer has a greater risk of having to keep his grain in the reserve for the period of his contract, say three years, and then repay the loan at whatever the price may be at that time. The increase in release price is the cause of this greater risk. I find it difficult to understand why, if it were believed necessary to make some change for political reasons, only the call price was increased rather than both the call and the release price. The judgment of the farmers and the market generally in response to the crop short-

15 Department of Agriculture, *Feed Situation*, FdS–273 (May 1979), p. 33.

fall in 1979 was clearly superior to that exhibited by government officials on prior occasions. I can see no justification for assuming that the tinkering with release and call prices of early 1980 will result in improving the operation of the farmer-owned reserve.

The reserve should be continued as part of the new legislation, but it should be modified, if at all, on the basis of careful thought and analysis, not as part of a response to short-run phenomena. There should also be consideration of whether the present division of the costs of storage between the farmer and the government is reasonable given the objectives. The current sharing of costs results in a higher level of storage than is socially optimal.

Supply Management. It is far from obvious whether the 1977 act provides for a significant capacity for supply management, at least at governmental costs that are politically acceptable. It is fair to say that the supply management features of the current legislation have not yet been tested.

The crude empirical evidence seems to support the conclusion that the wheat set-aside and diversion features can have some influence on the area in wheat. In other words, the harvested area was less in 1978 and 1979, when there was an effort to limit acreage, than in the prior years, when there was no effective effort. Yet so crude an analysis should make one uneasy. The acreage of wheat harvested does respond to expected prices, and there was a substantial reduction in the wheat area harvested between 1976 and 1977. Expected prices would have called for further reductions in the wheat area in 1978, and this is what occurred.

The potential slippage in the system is indicated by the increase in area harvested between 1978 and 1979 of almost 6 million acres while the diverted and set-aside area decreased by only 1.4 million acres. The feed grain program appears to have as much or more potential for slippage.[16]

The changes in supply management tools that started with the 1973 legislation and continued in 1977 have provided farmers with significantly greater flexibility. The abandonment of acreage allotments removed an anachronism but probably reduced an already limited capacity to manage supply. In any case, it is difficult to imagine voluntary supply management programs that can have a significant impact on agricultural output for more than one or two years. Even these programs may involve larger budgetary costs than are politically acceptable.

[16] Department of Agriculture, *Feed Situation*, FdS–277 (May 1980), p. 2, for data on harvested area and set-aside and diverted area.

I am not about to recommend that more effective tools for supply management be devised and included in the new legislation. Even if it were possible to achieve more effective supply management, I would not favor it. In the present economic circumstances of U.S. farmers—their wealth and total family incomes—there is no rational basis for using output limitation as a means of increasing farm incomes. Even if effective supply management were possible, it would be quite ineffective in achieving a long-run increase in the prices received by farmers. Our agriculture's dependence on exports is now so large for the major crops that our ability to increase market prices through output limitation is very small indeed. The economic viability of American agriculture depends on further growth in our exports and not on restricting them by supply management that would result in quite small increases in prices but quite substantial reductions in exports if such policies were pursued over an extended period.[17]

Export Policies. The general trend of agricultural policy during the past two decades has reduced governmental intervention in agricultural exports. The reduction in support levels, the minimization of the use of export subsidies, and the restraints on Commodity Credit Corporation acquisitions of major export crops have worked to free the market to allocate most farm products between domestic and export use. This general trend has contributed substantially to the striking growth of U.S. agricultural exports. Without the growth in exports achieved during the 1970s, the economic position of American agriculture would have been dire indeed.

One other important trend in our export policy has been the diminishing role of food aid and barter arrangements. Public Law 480, the legislative authority for our food aid program, no longer represents a major part of our total agricultural exports, as it did during the latter part of the 1950s and the first half of the 1960s. In fiscal year 1979 our grain shipments under Public Law 480, both as gifts and on concessional terms, accounted for only 5 percent of our total grain exports. Yet we remain by far the world's largest supplier of grain as food aid.

Even though the general trend has been toward reducing the role of government in the export of agricultural products, the past decade has seen a number of specific interventions. There are those who argue that exports or trade should not be manipulated in pursuit of our national security or foreign policy goals. For four decades we have used food, to a greater or lesser degree, in the pursuit of these goals. We need only look at our food aid to realize how extensively food

[17] Johnson, "World Agricultural and Trade Policies," pp. 313–18.

has been used in pursuit of political objectives—we so used food during and after World War II, during the Vietnam War, and in recent years in the Middle East for political as well as for humanitarian ends.

There is an important distinction to be made between the recent suspension of grain exports to the Soviet Union and the three other interventions of the mid-1970s. The other interventions were the brief export embargo on soybeans in 1973 and the suspension of grain exports to the Soviet Union in 1974 and to the Soviet Union and Poland in 1975. Each of these three interventions was undertaken for domestic political purposes—to minimize domestic price effects of large export volumes. The interruptions of exports that occurred during the 1970s were not designed to influence the political behavior of any other nation. Of the four significant restrictions on exports of agricultural products, only the 1980 suspension of grain sales to the Soviet Union was intended to support our foreign policy objectives.

On the whole, our agricultural export policy of the past two decades has been remarkably successful. I am puzzled by repeated efforts to shift the locus of our agricultural export trade from the private sector to substantial participation by government. Some of the support for this view is based on a mistaken impression that the U.S. private trading system has been less successful in dealing with the Soviet Union than, say, the Canadian Wheat Board. Support for greater governmental control over farm exports may be based on the mistaken impression that the limited effect of the Soviet grain sales suspension was caused by unpatriotic and profit-seeking behavior of the American grain exporting firms. Even though there is no firm evidence that the exporting firms have in any way violated U.S. regulations, the general tendency on the part of some to assume that private markets serve only the interests of the marketing firms has resulted in unfounded accusations and claims.[18]

[18] In testimony before the Committee of Agriculture, House of Representatives, June 25, 1980, Dale Hathaway, under secretary of agriculture, described the role of the private grain firms in carrying out U.S. policy of limiting exports of U.S. grain, whether the grain was located in the United States or outside it, to the Soviet Union to 8 million tons. He noted that there is a general misunderstanding "that if the dozen companies that were asked to participate in the third country sales restrictions continued to abide by it, the Soviets would be prevented from obtaining grain from non-U.S. sources. Given the large number of companies which operate entirely outside U.S. legal jurisdiction, and that are capable and experienced in trading grain, this is just not true. Moreover, we cannot exercise jurisdiction over foreign corporations not owned or controlled by U.S. persons, when they trade in foreign origin grain."

Had U.S.-origin grain been readily available to the Soviet Union, as some uninformed individuals seem to believe, Argentina would not have been able to realize substantial premiums over U.S.-origin grain. For example, in December 1979 before the U.S. suspension, Argentine wheat was selling for $6 to $8 per ton less

We had substantial governmental control over the exports of important farm products during the 1950s and 1960s. From 1949 through 1972 it was not possible to export a bushel of wheat without some intervention by the government; throughout the 1950s and until 1968 cotton exports were determined to a large degree by the Commodity Credit Corporation.[19] Any dispassionate review of the record of agricultural exports during this period hardly supports any return to large-scale governmental intervention.

Disaster Payments and Insurance. One of the more costly features of the 1977 Agricultural Act has been the provision for disaster payments. For at least two years, the Department of Agriculture, through the secretary and other officials, has promised a new crop insurance program. The difficulties with the current disaster payment program are well known. Among other things, farmers are induced to use resources in a manner that they know would be uneconomic for them if the disaster payments did not exist. This is the moral risk problem, and it appears to be significant in this program. Perhaps of equal significance, the disaster payments subsidize crop agriculture in marginal areas.

The basic idea of crop insurance is an appealing one. Except for certain specialized risks such as hail, however, few farmers are willing to pay a premium that comes close to covering the actuarial risks. Any crop insurance program that included as much as three-fifths of total cropland would require a heavy subsidy; one study puts the rate of subsidy needed at 50 percent.[20] If this is the case, and experience does not contradict it, does a highly subsidized crop insurance program serve a useful social purpose? If we say it does, I believe that we are saying that we know more about the real interests of farmers than they do. Given the capabilities of American farm operators, I find this a dubious proposition at best.

Gasohol. If I had been asked a decade ago if two particular ideas would by 1980 represent major elements in agricultural policy discussions, I would have said that it was clearly impossible. The two ideas are that price supports or targets would be determined by costs of production and that we would solve the problem of long-term demand

---

than U.S. wheat at Gulf ports; by March Argentine wheat was selling for export at $50 per ton more than U.S. wheat for export. Substantial price differentials also existed for corn exports. (U.S. Department of Agriculture, Foreign Agricultural Service, *Foreign Agricultural Circular: Grains*, FG-21-80 [July 15, 1980], p. 29.)

[19] Cochrane and Ryan, *American Farm Policy.*

[20] Congressional Budget Office, *Protecting the Farmer against Natural Hazards: Issues and Options*, March 1978, p. 29.

for grain by using it for alcohol. I would have been even more amazed had I been told that the alcohol produced from grain would not only take care of the actual or potential output from all set-aside or diverted land but also go some distance toward reducing or eliminating oil imports. Obviously I am a person of insufficient imagination.

The production of gasohol requires very substantial subsidies, even when oil is priced at $35 per barrel and corn at the rather modest price of $2.50. And substantial subsides are available, including exemption from the four cents per gallon federal gasoline tax for gasohol; this means forty cents per gallon for the alcohol (ethanol). As of September 1979, twenty-two states provided exemptions of at least forty cents per gallon of ethanol; in some cases the exemption was as much as $1.00. Thus in these twenty-two states the combined federal and state subsidies to ethanol range from eighty cents to $1.40. In addition, there are subsidies through subsidized credit, accelerated depreciation, property tax exemptions, and loan guarantees. Fred Sanderson estimates that, in addition to the exemption from the federal tax on gasoline, federal subsidies amount to at least eighty cents per gallon of ethanol.[21]

The alcohol program announced early in 1980 calls for the production of 10 billion gallons of ethanol by 1990; this is approximately 10 percent of current gasoline consumption. In 1979 the United States produced almost 300 million tons of grain; by 1990 our grain output may be projected at 400 million tons. If we used 100 million tons of that grain and produced ethanol, what would we realize?

First, we would produce the 10 billion gallons of ethanol; a ton of corn produces 100 gallons of ethanol. Second, in producing, harvesting, and transporting the corn to the processing plant, we would use approximately 3.3 billion gallons of high-quality petroleum fuels, such as diesel fuel for tractors and trucks and natural gas for producing fertilizer. This estimate assumes that no oil or natural gas is used to produce the alcohol from the grain, an assumption that is generally incorrect for the plants now producing alcohol for use in gasohol. Third, federal and state governments would be paying subsidies approximating $10 billion per year for a net savings of 6.7 billion gallons of imported oil. This amounts to $1.49 per gallon of gasoline saved or more than $55 per barrel of crude oil. Fourth, we would have used a net of 60 million tons of corn (100 million tons minus the feed value of the feed byproduct). If the corn is priced at $2.50 per bushel at the alcohol plant (perhaps $2.25 per bushel at the farm), the value of

[21] Fred Sanderson, "Gasohol: Boon or Blunder?," *The Brookings Bulletin*, vol. 16, no. 3 (1980), p. 11.

the corn used would be about $6 billion. Fifth, the estimated costs of producing a gallon of alcohol, excluding the value of the feedstock (grain), is about $0.60 per gross gallon.

The cost of the grain and the costs of transforming the grain into alcohol are here conservatively estimated at $1.20 per gallon of alcohol. Since it takes three gallons of ethanol to replace two gallons of imported oil, because of the high-quality energy required to produce the corn, the resource or real cost per gallon of gasoline saved by producing ethanol is not $1.20 per gallon but approximately $1.80 per gallon. Consequently the real or resource cost of reducing imports of oil required to produce 6.7 billion gallons of gasoline is $12 billion per year. The subsidy cost, under present programs, is almost as great at $10 billion. In terms of real cost, gasoline must have a price or marginal cost at the refinery of almost $1.80 per gallon, net of federal and state gasoline taxes, before gasohol will yield a positive net social return.

It needs to be borne in mind that while we would import less oil under a gasohol program, we would almost certainly export less grain. How much less would be exported and how much the price of grain would increase is uncertain. Whatever the change in exports and the change in price, the effects would be felt worldwide. The amount of grain we have been discussing—100 million tons gross and somewhat more than 60 million tons net—amounts on a net basis to more than 4 percent of world grain production. Even though major grain producing countries might respond by increasing grain production, that amount of grain could not be diverted from feed and food to alcohol without having a major impact on the world food situation, especially the food situation in low-income countries.

Achieving the president's goal of 10 billion gallons of alcohol from grain and other biomass would have one modest effect: the production, price, and exports of soybeans and soybean products would be adversely affected by the highly subsidized competition of the feed byproduct derived from the production of alcohol. If all the alcohol were produced from corn (or other grains), there would be approximately 30 million tons of high-protein feed. This is equivalent to the soybean meal produced on approximately 40 percent of the existing soybean-harvested area.[22] Part of the enormous quantity of high-

---

[22] I have relied on data and analysis drawn from Wallace E. Tyner, *The Potential of Using Biomass for Energy in the United States*, Institute for Interdisciplinary Engineering Studies, Publication Series no. 80-3, Purdue University, May 1980, and Ronald Meekhof, Mohinder Gill, and Wallace Tyner, *Gasohol: Prospects and Implications*, U.S. Department of Agriculture, Economics, Statistics, and Cooperatives Service, Agricultural Economic Report no. 458, June 1980. In both of these

protein feed derived from alcohol production would be exported in competition with soybeans or soybean products. There would also be a reduction of nearly a billion pounds (4.5 million tons) of soybean oil as soybean production was displaced by corn production.

Opposition to the heavy subsidization of gasohol seems to be diminishing as time goes by. Politicians appear to be more and more reticent about questioning the value of large and growing subsidies. Nor does there seem to be much consideration of some of the side effects of the push for rapid expansion of alcohol production. Has anyone stopped to ask, for example, what effects the current incentives for alcohol production are going to have on the structure of agriculture or the processing sector? For those who are interested in the survival of the family farm, the *Christian Science Monitor* of July 7, 1980, carried a quite remarkable story. It told of a 20-million-gallon-a-year ethanol plant to be built in Oregon on the shores of the Columbia River. The complex will cost $60 million to construct and will provide "100 new jobs and a growing market for the nation's corn." It is being built by a farm that now owns 37,000 acres of land; the farm will produce part of the 7.7 million bushels of corn used to produce 20 million gallons of alcohol. The project is to be built in a district represented by Congressman Al Ullman, a person of some significance in Washington. The story noted that the plan was to receive not only tax credits and exemption from the federal gasoline tax but apparently also some grants, loans, and loan guarantees. And then it noted: "Future legislation in Oregon will call for property tax and corporate income tax exemptions for alcohol fuel plants."

Have we lost all perspective? Apparently we have when it comes to using grain to produce fuel. The present wild emphasis on gasohol seems to have been one of the side effects of the suspension of grain exports to the Soviet Union. After that suspension occurred, there was a scramble to seek alternative outlets, and gasohol, although it could have no immediate effect on demand or use, was one possibility that was seized upon. Before January 1980 officials of the Department of Agriculture took proper positions with respect to gasohol. Since then they have expressed views either equivocal or supportive of using

---

studies it is indicated that if more than 2 billion gallons of alcohol is produced from corn the price impacts become quite significant. Meekhof, Gill, and Tyner indicate that with crude oil at $35 per barrel and a corn export price of $3.00 per bushel (approximately the same as $2.50 in the Midwest), the U.S. balance of trade would be adversely affected by the production of 500 million gallons of alcohol per year. What happens to the trade balance should not be given much weight, though it is likely that most supporters of gasohol assume that its production would affect only our imports and not our exports—a clearly erroneous assumption.

grain products for the production of alcohol. Perhaps once the president announced a goal of achieving 500 million gallons of alcohol fuel capacity by the end of 1981 and 10 billion gallons by 1990, the Department of Agriculture had no choice but to fall in line. Whatever the reason for the change in position, we now have our government embarked upon a program of expanding the production of a highly subsidized commodity at an enormous annual cost. The contribution of this very expensive program to the nation's energy supply, to the reduction of petroleum imports, or to the improvement of our balance of payments will be minimal while the potential is very great for disruption of world food supplies.

The quantities that are envisaged for the alcohol-from-grain program are enormous and probably far beyond what is generally recognized or understood. The 1990 goal will require 500 alcohol-producing plants with an annual capacity of 20 million gallons at a total investment cost in 1980 dollars of $30 billion, if the costs of the facility in Oregon can be taken as a guide. But the investment cost is only a minor part of the total diversion of resources. In the 1990s, if the goal of producing 10 billion gallons of alcohol from grain were achieved, the sum of the annual subsidies for the decade would exceed one hundred billion dollars. As Senator Dirksen used to say, "a billion dollars here, a billion dollars there, and pretty soon you are talking about real money." If grain were the feedstock for the alcohol—and there is no other feedstock that is available in such enormous quantities or at comparable cost—the last decade of the twentieth century would use a billion tons of grain as fuel and recover as feed approximately 40 percent of that amount.

What I have written does not address the issue of the economic effectiveness of producing alcohol from grain or how such alcohol would fare in an unsubsidized setting. Clearly there is some price of crude oil at which it would be economic to produce alcohol from corn if corn prices were in the general range of $2.50 to $3.00 per bushel. Alcohol would also make a contribution to the supply of liquid fuels if the energy used to produce it were derived from sources other than petroleum or natural gas.[23]

[23] My discussion of the gasohol program has been criticized as being overdrawn because of three assumptions that have been questioned. One such assumption is that all the current subsidies for gasohol production will be continued through the 1990s. Once gasohol production capacity is in place, it is argued, some or most of the subsidies would be withdrawn. Perhaps so. History indicates, however, that it is a lot easier to introduce a subsidy than it is to withdraw it. A second assumption is that the natural gas used to produce fertilizer can be equated with oil. It was on the basis of that assumption that I argued that the net contribution to our liquid energy supply from producing 10 billion gallons of alcohol was only

With our presently distorted petroleum prices, it is difficult to say how far alcohol production, if not subsidized, is from being economic. A decision to invest in the production of alcohol from grain depends on price expectations for both crude oil and the grain. If one believes that the price of imported oil will be at approximately $33 per barrel and corn will remain at approximately $2.50 per bushel, gasohol may not be far from a viable economic alternative. But even if this is the case, there are absolutely no grounds for the current frenzied effort to expand alcohol production with subsidies approaching the actual value of the net saving in gasoline. If the present program of encouraging alcohol production from grain is carried out through the 1980s and reaches the 1990 objectives, we can be certain that there will be enormous income transfers. These transfers would be significantly higher than any that we have had under all of the farm commodity programs in any one year.

Concluding Comments

With the exception of the dairy and peanut programs, my conclusion is that the major agricultural commodity programs do not require significant modification or improvement. The evolutionary change and adjustment that have occurred over the past quarter century, if continued, seem most of what is required for the near future. A primary danger in the 1981 revision of the basic agricultural legislation is that the lessons of the past will be forgotten. Somebody's law says: "If it ain't broke, don't fix it." It seems to me that recent experience indicates a tendency to fix such things as loan rates and target prices even though there is no evidence that anything is broken.

While it could perhaps be argued that the changes in loan rates and target prices made in January 1980 after the suspension of grain exports to the Soviet Union were required as part of the effort to offset the negative impact on farmers, it is hard to explain the changes that were made at the end of July as anything other than pure domestic politics in a presidential election year. The changes have potential

---

two-thirds of that amount. Perhaps my assumption is extreme, but by the end of the 1980s, as natural gas becomes available in more areas of the country that now use oil for home and commercial heating, some account should be taken of this substitution possibility by even the most ardent supporter of gasohol. The third assumption that I made, that the dollar savings can be estimated on the basis of the market price of oil, overstates the case against gasohol. The amount of oil imported by the United States affects the international price of oil. Thus cutting oil imports by a significant amount would reduce the price of oil. If we take account of this effect in evaluating gasohol, however, we should do so for all efforts to reduce oil imports, including conservation and expanded use of coal.

long-run effects on the allocation of agricultural resources and adjustment problems. The effects of the significantly greater increase in July 1980 in the loan, release, and call prices for wheat than for feed grains will extend beyond the election of 1980.

At the same time, programs that could stand some fixing are left largely unattended or are made more expensive and disruptive of the efficient use of resources. We have not been able either to replace or to abandon the disaster payments program although virtually everyone would agree with the secretary of agriculture, who has described the program as a disaster.

Whatever theory or rationale there may have been for the establishment of loan, release, and call prices for the farmer-owned reserve now seems to have been abandoned for reasons of political expediency. The changes all appear to be in the direction of providing greater access to federal funds for wheat producers than for corn producers. By saying this, I do not mean to imply that the wheat producers will gain as a result, but merely to indicate at least one criterion that may determine how our tax resources are distributed. The increase in the differentials between the loan and release rates for wheat compared with those for corn, if maintained, could work to the advantage of corn producers. The differential in the loan rate for wheat over corn is much greater than the difference in the feeding value of the two grains. Consequently, less wheat would be fed at the new loan rates than at the old ones. Any oversupply of wheat that might result from the higher support prices would create increased wheat stocks, rather than subsidized competition for corn and other feed-grain producers. An important policy issue would then arise concerning the response to the increase in wheat stocks. One response is to require more stringent set-aside and diversion conditions for wheat than for the feed grains. An alternative is to lower the loan rate for wheat while maintaining the same target price; this would force some part of the wheat adjustment problem upon feed-grain producers.

It is appropriate to close by making explicit my assumption concerning the future course of real or deflated prices of the major grains and soybeans. The process of eliminating excess resources from U.S. agriculture was largely completed by 1972. Thus regular excess production capacity, such as existed during the 1960s, no longer exists. I expect that during the 1980s the growth rates of supply and of demand for agricultural output of the United States will be approximately the same. This means that, on average, the real or deflated prices of grain and soybeans will be approximately constant, and I would not be surprised if the long-term trend of a small rate of decline in the prices of these products continued throughout the 1980s.

That I expect approximate equality of growth rates for supply and demand does not rule out significant variability of prices in international and domestic markets. To a large extent such price variability is a consequence of the agricultural and food policies of many countries that prevent their internal prices from reflecting variations in world supply and demand.

In the context of these assumptions, I believe that the 1981 agricultural legislation should continue the process of increasing the market orientation of our agricultural programs, a path followed for at least two decades. I also believe that the agricultural policy issues for the 1980s will continue to be the traditional ones of price supports, target prices, storage and reserves, export policies, and disaster or insurance programs. It should not be assumed that the price increases of 1980 negate the need to be concerned about setting support prices that will not interfere with the functioning of the market if farm prices return to the real levels of, say, 1979.

If I am wrong and real farm prices increase during the 1980s, little will have been lost by continuing to be concerned about market-oriented agricultural programs. If farm prices were to increase significantly, the prices of some or most of the grains would move above target prices, release prices, and perhaps call prices. The holding of grain reserves would then be entirely in the private sector, as it was very largely from 1973 through 1976. For the 1981 agricultural legislation, which will extend through the middle of the decade, we must be concerned with the traditional components of our agricultural policy. No evidence can be accumulated between October 1980 and early 1981 that will definitively delineate the trend of real farm prices for the 1980s.

A Framework for Food and Agricultural Policy for the 1980s

John A. Schnittker

Four broad subjects or issues will dominate food and agricultural policy discussions during the 1980s. They will not necessarily be prominent in the debate on the 1981 farm bill, however, since they may develop slowly during the decade. These issues are:

• A perceptible shift toward commodity shortages and rising real prices for agricultural commodities as the norm for the food and agriculture sector. The agenda for food and agricultural policy during the 1980s will be determined largely by the way this situation develops.

• The declining role of price and income supports and production adjustment programs. Long the mainstream of federal agricultural policies, these programs will remain in the law but will greatly decline in importance. Occasional commodity surpluses may still require attention, however, in a general climate of strong demand and rising real prices for food and agricultural products.

• Shortages and rising real commodity and food prices. How to cope with them to the satisfaction of farmers, domestic consumers, foreign customers, and budget planners will become the focus of domestic and international agricultural policy.

• A grab bag of concerns, including how to get beyond rhetoric in the discussion of farm size, farm and rural life, and other areas that have been collected under the unfortunate heading of farm structure; how to bring the price support and marketing programs for dairy products into the mainstream of food and agricultural policy; how to manage and conserve natural resources; and how to get other nations to provide part of the world grain reserve. A host of agricultural policy trivia will also come up for discussion, including how to estimate cost of production; what to do with the estimates once they have been made; how to set loan and target prices that farmers will have little interest in under the circumstances anticipated; how to operate our grain reserve programs without making them entirely incomprehensible; whether the food stamp and school lunch programs are agricultural or welfare programs; and how to proceed on various food safety issues in the wake of the abortive nitrite experience.

Continuity and Change in U.S. Food and Agricultural Policy

There has been far more continuity than change in farm policies and programs for many years. These policies and programs have remained largely unaffected by the introduction of a grain reserve policy or by the impact of energy problems on agricultural and food production, and they will not be altered quickly by a tendency toward shortages instead of surpluses. Some new issues will emerge each year: what federal agricultural officials do from day to day will continue to change, the role of grain reserves in stabilizing exportable supplies and prices will mature during times of reduced supplies, and the social and economic role of food distribution and supplemental income programs will remain large. Nevertheless, there will be few fundamental policy changes early in the 1980s, no matter who is elected president, which political party controls the Congress, or who is the secretary of agriculture.

Continuity in U.S. agricultural policy has survived the occasional announcement by a president or secretary of agriculture that "farm policy has been changed dramatically and irreversibly" or by members of Congress hailing some passing legislative achievement as "a completely new and revolutionary farm policy." Changed market circumstances, which have occasionally caused the operation of farm price support and production adjustment programs to be suspended for a season or two, and pride of authorship in a bill passed by Congress explain most such pronouncements.

Significant changes in policy direction have occurred, of course, during the past twenty years, including the policy commitment to food aid and export promotion under pressure from grain surpluses in the 1950s and 1960s, the realization that mandatory acreage controls were no longer acceptable to most U.S. farmers, the decision to compete directly in world markets without direct export subsidies and provide income support for producers of many important crops through federal payments to supplement market prices, and the metamorphosis of grain surpluses into reserves. Such changes in policy and program have usually followed events, not determined them. Some of these new policies may also have run their course or may at least enter a new phase in the 1980s. Transitional change, however, has not altered the underlying federal commitment to a relatively stable agriculture or changed the basic methods by which farm price support and income stability have been pursued whenever the need arose.

Changes in the Political Process. One of the greatest changes in the fifty-year history of farm policy has been in the people and organizations involved in policy making. As the House of Representatives became more representative in the 1960s and 1970s, new voices were heard. Farm bills were soon called food and agriculture acts, in contrast to the earlier agricultural adjustment acts.

This change came about in part because of a transformation in the Congress that reflected dramatic changes in the electorate and in part because of a decline in the number of farmers, which required farm groups to form coalitions with other groups seeking political help. Such coalitions were formed especially in the 1960s and 1970s, when farmers constituted a very small share of the population, to gain passage of favorable agricultural support and stabilization legislation, as well as food distribution and food safety programs. High turnover in Congress, especially in the House of Representatives after the decline of the agrarian, one-party South, also contributed to changes in the way food and agricultural policy was made.

Agricultural policy making once depended on the president and the leadership of the secretary of agriculture. This is no longer the case, although the executive branch is still capable of overwhelming Congress with data, budget estimates, and legislative language. As the executive branch declined to lead, the agriculture committees of Congress, now with a number of consumer and public representatives, became more important, and this tendency is likely to continue.

Since about 1960 various new groups in and outside the government have developed interest in and influence over food and agricultural policy. Church-based associations are concerned about world food supplies; consumer groups seek food price stability; conservation groups decry soil and water depletion; foundations urge research and political action on alternative world futures; and analysts study alternative U.S. economic policies. These divergent voices and forces must be reconciled if there is to be an orderly development of food and agricultural policies consistent with national economic policies.

The Shift to Commodity Shortages

The 1960s and 1970s were dominated by commodity surpluses, with occasional mild remissions and one three-year period of severe shortages. During the 1970s food price increases became a significant factor in overall inflation for the first time in the twentieth century apart from war periods. This began during the so-called world food crisis, but it continued afterward, even as record crops were being harvested.

Assuming that the 1980s are relatively peaceful and modestly prosperous, demand for agricultural resources and commodities, especially land, technology, livestock products, and grains and oilseeds, will be very strong. Some developing nations will neglect their agriculture because they have oil to sell; others will eat foodstuffs as rapidly as they produce them and will still need more food. Rising incomes in relatively advanced developing countries, in central plan countries, and even in the poorest countries will cause the demand for food, including livestock and poultry products, to outstrip those countries' food production. The demand for grain and other agricultural products for use as energy and sweetener feedstocks will add fractionally to an already strong overall demand.

Real prices of agricultural products seem likely to rise under such circumstances, both to help ration the limited agricultural products among various users, nations, and processes and to let farmers know that more production is needed. Managing and responding to this phenomenon will be a challenge with which the United States has had little experience. It will change what agricultural officials and users of agricultural commodities worry about from day to day, both in the United States and abroad. It need not require a vast array of programs or a new army of administrators in the federal government, although we will do well to be watchful on that score.

Price and Income Supports and Production Adjustment Programs in an Era of Commodity Shortages

The adjustment programs have been important to food and agricultural policy for many years but will not continue to be important in the 1980s. Experience from the 1970s tells us that conventional price and income support and production adjustment programs will be put in mothballs, but not discarded, for the next decade. If conditions change for a few years for one commodity or another, some of them may be needed again.

The basic farm program instruments, such as price support loan and purchase programs and authority to limit acreages of major crops and to store and later dispose of surpluses, will probably be continued for a decade or more, even in the economic climate I have suggested. Intense but usually meaningless debates will erupt occasionally in the next five to ten years in the U.S. Department of Agriculture and among farm groups over loan and target price levels and acreage diversion programs. They will seldom be important.

213

Even if this is an accurate prognosis, the debate on the Food and Agriculture Act of 1981 may well focus on the programs that have dominated the past. The farm policy debate in 1980, following the limitation on grain sales to the Soviet Union, provides a useful illustration of legislative action on issues that had already been left behind by events. When the administration's actions after the embargo failed to support grain and soybean prices at preembargo levels as promised, members of Congress introduced legislation to require substantial increases in price support loan levels for grains; the administration opposed those bills. Before Congress recessed in October 1980, long after market prices had risen far above loan and target price levels and at a time when grain was about to be pulled out of the reserve by higher prices, Congress nearly passed a bill to increase loan rates for reserve grain. The administration, after opposing such measures when they were potentially relevant in early 1980, became a strong supporter once the bills had become irrelevant after mid-1980.

In 1981, it will be important to remember that:

- loan levels for grains are important principally because, under the law, they substantially determine how grain reserves will be accumulated and used
- the role of target prices (direct federal payments to farmers) will be negligible during periods when market prices are usually above direct production costs and support levels, and when acreage limitations are not in effect
- allowing the executive branch some discretion in operating federal programs is extremely important during watershed periods, when one cannot be sure that past experience is a very good guide to future actions.

Managing Shortages of Agricultural Resources and Commodities

Food and agricultural policy in the 1980s will focus on managing shortages. Its principal components will be grain reserves and export arrangements, and land and water use and agricultural research could become major policy areas if shortages are severe and extended. Adoption in 1977 of a program to isolate certain amounts of grain from the market until prices rise well above support levels represents an important beginning toward managing shortages in the 1980s. The reserve is now the principal price support program for grains, a fact that is not yet clear to farmers or to the marketplace. It has helped stabilize prices in the face of severe crop losses and record demand in 1980. It will provide the government some time to prepare for the more direct actions that may be required to achieve national economic objectives if commodity shortages are as severe and as chronic in the 1980s as surpluses were in the 1950s, the 1960s, and half the 1970s.

U.S. experience in managing commodity shortages during peacetime has been chaotic. It began in 1973 with official misstatements of U.S. policy on export controls of agricultural commodities. Repeated promises never to limit exports were followed by imposition of export embargoes (the worst form of export restraint) or informal export limitations on certain agricultural commodities when shortages appeared to be more severe than had been expected.

The ability and willingness of the United States to limit the volume of exports of feedstuffs, especially to countries with high meat diets, and the means it chooses to do so may become key elements in maintaining adequate domestic grain supplies at reasonable and competitive prices if (1) U.S. and world demand for grain generally outpaces even large increases in production or (2) poor harvests in a number of seasons dissipate reserve stocks in the 1980s, after the anticipated large decline in feed grain reserve stocks in 1981.

Since it has long been U.S. policy to expand the volume of agricultural exports, it will require a major effort by the U.S. government and by farm groups to address the question of limiting exports in a rational way. The relatively recent introduction of domestic price stabilization to the objectives governing U.S. agricultural exports following serious food price inflation and the addition of sweeteners in the 1970s and ethanol production in the 1980s as high-priority domestic uses for grain threaten the achievement of the traditional objectives of export policy. The recent use of agricultural exports as a diplomatic tool has taken us even further from past hopes and practice in regard to unlimited exports of all agricultural products to all countries under all circumstances.

In this climate, the development of arrangements with a number of countries under which the United States would agree to supply a certain volume, but not unlimited quantities, of agricultural exports seems likely to become a major element of agricultural and trade policy. The 1975 grain agreement between the United States and the Soviet Union may well become a pattern for future bilateral trade agreements with our large customers. One central feature of the agreement is the provision under which the United States decides each year, on the basis of various considerations, whether or not to allow further grain shipments to the Soviet Union, once 8 million tons have been shipped. Chronic supply shortages in conjunction with agreements of this type would lead inexorably to limits on the volume of exports under certain circumstances as a matter of policy in the 1980s. Use of such measures would not exclude but would supplement multilateral trade agreements and the actions of international organizations such as the General Agreement on Tariffs and Trade (GATT).

The United States has had a policy for many years of limiting exports for economic, national security, and foreign policy reasons. Policy on the use of restraints on agricultural exports was stated in the report dated May 25, 1976, of the Senate Committee on Banking, Housing, and Urban Affairs (to accompany S. 3084) and the report of the House of Representatives Committee on International Relations dated September 2, 1976 (to accompany H.R. 15377). As stated in the Senate report:

> Under the Export Administration Act, it is expressed U.S. policy to use export controls, including controls on agricultural commodities, for both foreign policy and national security purposes, as well as for purposes of protecting the domestic economy from the excessive drain of scarce materials and reducing the serious inflationary impact of foreign demand.

This bipartisan policy was informally ratified during the 1976 presidential campaign. Candidates Carter and Ford emphasized their determination to avoid the use of export controls on agricultural products wherever possible but cited the need to use such controls whenever the national interest required it or when serious shortages threatened undue inflation in the United States.

The language of the Export Administration Act seems to authorize limiting the export of agricultural commodities on the basis of supply or price stabilization criteria. The wording of the act is ambiguous, however, stating that exports may not be limited for that purpose if supplies of the commodities in question exceed domestic needs. A narrow interpretation of the act would never permit export controls on grounds of adequate supply, since we have large exportable surpluses every year, giving us more than we need domestically. A practical interpretation of present law would require the secretary of agriculture to make allowance for expected exports before judging if the remaining supply is adequate for all domestic uses, presumably at acceptable prices. This language will require early clarification if the conditions I have described for the 1980s prevail.

If it becomes necessary during the 1980s to determine and announce the conditions under which agricultural exports will be limited on a continuing basis in pursuit of domestic price stabilization objectives and a fair apportionment of our export supplies among all claimants, that would constitute a fundamental modification of our policies and our rhetoric on free and unlimited exports. Our position as the world's most reliable supplier of agricultural commodities would be called into question. Such actions would precipitate a big political fight, but they may well be inevitable under the circumstances I have postulated.

Our methods of pricing agricultural exports would surely come into question under such conditions, as larger export earnings become essential and possible. Relatively short supplies would probably increase market prices by a greater percentage than any reduction in exports and thus add to export earnings through the market, but the possible need to think the unthinkable and to design procedures for selling our products into a very demanding world market at a premium over prices prevailing in the United States should not be overlooked. I do not refer here to some kind of federal export board or corporation. Such a procedure is out of character with our history and is demonstrably beyond the ability of our government to manage. It is not needed since present law and existing private marketing institutions could be adapted to the modest revisions in our export marketing methods that would be required to differentiate between domestic and export prices.

Other Policy and Program Issues

Farm structure is important even if the results of its consideration are mostly talk and the thrill of participation. Perhaps some steps can be taken in the 1980s to get this issue beyond rhetoric and to help a few thousand farmers. We have known for thirty years that big farmers get most of the benefits of the commodity program, that displacement of small farmers is often accelerated by federal programs, that a very small number and percentage of farmers market most of our food commodities, and that certain people are more aggressive than others in using debt and the tax laws to ease their relatives and neighbors out of farming.

The clock will not be turned back by policy measures on fifty years or more of farm technology, farm consolidation, and the abandonment of small towns and other rural infrastructure built by our great-grandfathers. But incentives that speed farm consolidation can be limited or removed; help can be provided for a few more young and small farmers; old farmlands can be reclaimed; and new energy and fertilizer sources can be encouraged. Such measures are important, but they will have little relationship to commercial agricultural production in the 1980s.

Neither the price support program nor the marketing order program for dairy products is in harmony with the programs for other major agricultural commodities. Since the 1960s continual and successful efforts have been made by Congress and several administrations to reduce government activity affecting major commodity markets, especially grains and cotton. Restraint in increasing price supports has resulted in market prices generally above support prices for most commodities. These program changes were made to take account of the changing structure of these producing sectors and of gains in production efficiency, to compete more actively for world markets, to provide more opportunity for market forces to perform their traditional functions, and to insulate the overall economy from inflationary impacts arising from agricultural price and income support programs.

Congressional actions on dairy programs in recent years have moved dairy policy in the opposite direction. Dairy products are losing out in the market. Milk programs are visibly inflationary. Both problems need to be remedied in the 1980s. It is a curious anomaly that, when grain and soybean prices move well above support levels, federal programs are shelved and forgotten but, when milk prices do the same, that is taken as a signal to raise support levels. It will require a hard political fight to modernize U.S. milk programs in the 1980s, even with large surpluses and expenditures, but it needs to be done.

Commentary

William R. Pearce

Dr. Schuh's paper contributes importantly to our understanding of the relationship between farm (or commodity) policy and the agenda of broader public policy issues facing the United States. His paper makes several points that I agree with and would stress.

First, Dr. Schuh notes, as others have, the increasing importance to agriculture of domestic monetary and fiscal policies and international exchange rate and trade policies. He argues persuasively that overvaluation of the dollar in the last years of Bretton Woods limited U.S. grain and oilseed exports and that the regime of floating exchange rates introduced after 1971 was instrumental in our grain export expansion during the 1970s. Similarly, bringing stability to U.S. monetary and fiscal policies and greater coordination to international monetary policies will make important contributions to commodity price stabilization in the future.

Dr. Schuh also makes a persuasive case for agriculture's stake in more open trade policies in the United States and for the international system. There are several key issues here. The growth markets for U.S. agricultural exports are centrally planned and newly industrializing countries that must expand their manufacturing exports to the United States and other developed countries to be able to pay rising food and fuel import bills. Second, domestic farm policies and related trade barriers of major importing countries tend to export price and supply instability, increasing adjustment burdens borne by the United States and developing nations. Third, a rational system requires multilateral consensus on trade rules and institutions. The temptation to substitute import restraints and bilateral trade agreements for a liberalizing, multilateral trade policy should be resisted by those interested in continued growth of U.S. agriculture.

One final thesis in Dr. Schuh's paper deserves approving emphasis. The commercial farm sector—with some obvious exceptions—has accomplished a successful transformation to market-oriented policies in an environment of rough resource balance. The remaining farm income problems are largely of two sorts: (1) the need to stabilize (as contrasted with supporting) the incomes of commodity producers and (2) the need to attack rural poverty through retraining and relocation. His recommendations for increasing federal support for research to boost agricultural productivity and for a more direct attack on rural poverty deserve study and support.

In general, I have few quarrels with Dr. Schuh's analysis and recommendations. They map out a general policy direction that strikes me as the right one for the 1980s. I would, however, like to focus on several specific issues where either a different emphasis or the necessity of staging progress toward market-oriented goals brings me to additional recommendations.

First, it is important to stress the role our private marketing system has played in the past decade's achievements. U.S. grain exports have nearly trebled in volume and increased fivefold in value over the past ten years. Many new customers, both centrally planned and newly industrializing countries, have been added. Trade flows have fluctuated sharply from year to year around the rising trend line of growth.

The U.S. private marketing system's strengths—flexibility, investment, innovation, and the capacity to assume risks in gearing up for anticipated demand—have enabled this country to outperform all of our competitors. We have captured three-fourths of the growth in world grain trade. The export industry has built exports from 1.8 billion bushels in 1971 to more than 5 billion bushels this year and at the same time expanded our export elevator capacity to an estimated 6.5 billion bushels by the end of 1980. It has also attracted new entrants, including cooperatives, that promise to preserve competition in future years.

These strengths are important to highlight because they are not well understood. The increasing market orientation of U.S. commodity programs has encouraged substantial investments in handling facilities throughout the grain marketing system. These investments have not been matched in any other exporting or importing country in which market forces have been given a more limited role. Advocates of system changes, such as grain boards, grain cartels, and bilateral grain agreements, have not attracted much support. Nevertheless, the marketer is always an attractive target for those uncomfortable with market results.

Second, while I share Dr. Schuh's conclusion that general monetary, fiscal, and trade policies have become more important to agriculture's future than commodity policies, that generalization needs qualification. I believe Schuh's analysis does not give enough weight to supply swings in explaining instability in commodity markets. Although tight monetary policy contributed to commodity price declines in late 1979 and 1980 and relaxed monetary policies aided price increases this summer, the basic market factor was U.S. supply. The estimate of the 1979 U.S. corn crop rose in several large steps between August 1979 and January 1980, causing prices to weaken. Similarly, 1980 corn crop estimates were revised downward sharply in July and August as the drought persisted, giving strength to prices.

More generally, it is important to recognize that U.S. grain output can and does fluctuate significantly because of weather. The initial price directions imparted by these developments are accentuated in the short term by import barriers, export subsidies, and consumption practices of other countries; so, while consistent application of appropriate monetary and fiscal policies could help us exploit agriculture's comparative advantage in the longer term, supply management tools remain important for stabilizing supplies and prices in the short term.

In the area of trade policy, I think it is important to stress that bilateral agreements offer at best a false promise. While the long-term agreement between the Soviet Union and the United States has been useful in some ways, it has done little to stabilize prices. Year-to-year Soviet import needs seem unlikely to fall much below 20 million tons, and total Soviet imports are prevented from exceeding 35 to 38 million tons annually by physical capacity constraints. Many other countries face similar circumstances, with minimum annual needs and maximum handling constraints beginning to provide more stable annual commodity flows.

To me this suggests the need for several trade policy steps. First, more cooperation is needed to adjust grain usage and trade flows to changes in supply. The European Economic Community, the Soviet Union, Japan, and several other developed nations have a larger contribution to make here. This should be the first priority of U.S. trade diplomacy. It should be disturbing that trends in international trade are reducing the importance of the U.S. exports subject to international rules and increasing the importance of those that are not. Success here would both reduce the volatility of world prices by broadening the base of adjustment to changed supply conditions in the short term and contribute to the long-term growth of foreign markets for U.S. commodities.

Second, government credits continue to be important in sustaining market expansion. The recent shift to loan guarantees will limit our ability to maintain export volume in years of plentiful supply.

Third, the largely unused intermediate-term credit program should be given more emphasis as a vehicle for financing construction of handling, storage, and distribution facilities. In many importing countries, such capacity constraints are limiting demand.

Finally, market development funding, like funding for agricultural

221

research, has failed to grow in real terms. A larger, more diversified demand base would provide a better framework for stabilizing prices.

Supply management at home is also important. Although the 1973 and 1977 farm acts greatly strengthened producer decision making and overall flexibility, problems remain. Linking production controls to participation in loan, target price, and reserve programs has limited flexibility. The problems in offsetting the effects of the Soviet grain embargo only highlighted these risks. Moreover, as both D. Gale Johnson and Edward Schuh point out, management of wheat loan and target price programs has added politically based distortions.

I am skeptical about the feasibility of Dr. Schuh's subsidized income insurance program. Commodity prices reflect not just the effects of weather in major production areas but also largely unpredictable government actions—for example, decisions by governments to restrict exports to protect domestic supplies or to increase imports rather than adjust consumption to compensate for domestic crop shortfalls. While the advantages he identifies justify further study, it is not clear how private insurers could be persuaded to assume these risks at reasonable cost.

In my judgment, the farmer-owned reserve program can be a more useful, cost-effective supply management tool. But it needs to function on its own merits, free from cross-compliance requirements with land diversion programs. Moreover, the corridors or bands between loan and release and release and call levels need to be widened to provide more room for market-induced adjustments before program levels are triggered.

A special word needs to be said about the role "costs of production" have come to play in implementing the 1977 farm act. Costs of production now serve as the rationale for setting release and call levels, distorting and limiting the farmer-owned reserve. Costs of production as a basis for calculating loan levels and target prices also create real risks for treasury exposure on the one hand or pricing our commodities out of world markets on the other hand. If basic grain and oilseed policies are to remain market oriented, calculation of government intervention and protection levels must be related to market values, not to production costs.

Food aid programs also continue to be an important policy instrument. Emergency reserves to backstop our food aid obligations now seem accepted as a political necessity. I continue to question, however, their economic justification. Schuh's recommendation for better access by less developed countries to capital markets and special funding windows makes sense. I continue to believe that a "food fund" located in an international institution and built up from subscriptions by wealthy countries offers much promise for providing more meaningful supply assurances to needy countries. In my view, greater certainty that food aid recipients will not be "bid out of the market" in time of rising import needs would trigger a constructive response by farmers in their production and stock management decisions.

The attractiveness of subsidizing the use of corn for gasohol production was roundly criticized by both Schuh and Johnson, who draw heavily on the work of Fred Sanderson. All of us have, I believe, a great concern about the potential for conflict between food and subsidized fuel. I tend to share the skepticism expressed in these papers over the wisdom of this policy.

On the other hand, it is clear that the energy-importing nations, including many developing countries, are badly hurt by America's heavy dependence on imported oil. There is ample evidence that failure to curb U.S. oil imports increases everyone's oil import bill by perpetuating a level of demand that encourages price increases. These are applied not on the margin but across the board for all oil imports.

U.S. energy policy now contemplates large subsidies for many alternative energy sources. More should be done, through price and incentive, to encourage substitutes for imported oil, including conservation. When all the consequences of marginal reductions in oil import demand are considered, it may not be clear that corn for ethanol has no useful role to play. The problem is one of balance, and I do not think that we have yet found the final policy answers.

Although I sympathize with the conclusions of Schuh and Johnson on gasohol, I think that we need to go past our current level of analysis on this subject. The only clear conclusions in my mind are (1) that real price increases for corn should and will set a limit to corn use for ethanol production and (2) that corn for ethanol can only be justified at any level if the process fuel is nonliquid.

Conclusion

Let me conclude with two observations, both borrowed from Johnson and Schuh. The first, stressed more explicitly by Johnson, is that resources are roughly in balance for grains and oilseeds. This increases the importance of building demand and limits the usefulness of restricting supplies in sustaining a healthy farm economy.

The second observation, stressed more explicitly by Schuh, is that U.S. agriculture has gained by the shift in decision-making authority from government to the private sector. Today, government's largest contributions are likely to come from a more stable set of broad economic policies that yield a healthy, more predictable environment for the private farm economy.

Dale M. Hoover

John Schnittker has given us a forward-looking view of agricultural policy based on the assumption that commodity prices are going to rise in real terms over the next few years, a projection heard in a number of other presentations of this conference. If he is right, too much attention has been given and will continue to be given to relative support prices among crops, support mechanisms, and the other income transfer and "supply management" paraphernalia. He emphasizes the problems of rationing increasingly scarce output among alternative users and the means of choosing among foreign and—when price advances are substantial—domestic users. He implicitly rejects the price system and assumes that the objective function is too complex to be handled outside Washington.

In this review I will sketch some of the policy problems that will occur (1) if real prices rise and (2) if real prices do not rise. Finally, I will consider the problems associated with changing dairy policy in the direction suggested in papers by Schnittker and several others.

Agricultural Trade Intervention

If real prices of farm goods rise fairly continuously over the next decade, as predicted, there will be real income losses for consumers and gains for producers. The pattern of effects is similar to that created by increases in real energy prices. If the advance in average real farm prices were as much as 15 percent, about half of the income gains from technological advance of the last two decades could be nullified. Because low-income households spend a greater proportion of their income on food, the income losses would tend to act as a regressive tax. Two responses can be expected. Such a change would serve as a stimulus to investment in public research and extension. It would be surprising if consumers working through the political process did not urge a massive investment in agriculture, a counterpart to the synthetic fuels development bill. The subsidization of ethanol production from corn would probably be stopped, and exports might be limited to protect domestic consumers.

Schnittker advocates managing shortages, maintaining reasonable domestic prices, and limiting exports rationally, while maximizing export earnings from reduced shipments. These injunctions suggest the development of an optimum tax on exports for a situation in which the objective function has several arguments. The idea of an optimum intervention in trade in the form of a tariff has been around for a long time, but there is considerable doubt that it can be applied efficiently on behalf of some collective set of values. Writing in the *Economic Journal* in 1908, Edgeworth had the following warning about the potential abuses of Bickerdike's optimum tariff argument:

> Thus the direct use of the theory is likely to be small. But it is to be feared that its abuses will be considerable. It affords to unscrupulous advocates of vulgar Protection a peculiarly specious pretext for introducing the thin edge of the fiscal wedge. Mr. Bickerdike may be compared to a scientist who, by a new analysis, has discovered that strychnine may be administered in small doses with prospect of advantage in one or two more cases than was previously known; the result of this discovery may be to render the drug more easily procurable by those whose intention . . . is not medicinal. . . . Let us admire the skill of the analyst, but label the subject of his investigation POISON.[1]

Given the constitutional ban on an export tax, it seems highly unlikely that the U.S. Treasury would be able to collect the benefits of an optimum domestic-foreign price differential. That leaves us with the problem of designing an optimum set of quotas as the operational counterpart of an optimal export tax. How would one set out to obtain collective benefits for the United States? There probably would be a strong urge to offer food aid in the form of lower prices for consumers in poor countries. Surely this would contribute to price distortions already practiced in a number of countries.

An alternative would be to use lower prices as a form of food aid to support particular friendly foreign governments, as Tim Josling suggests in his paper. If we wish to aid particular governments, there is a question of who should pay for it. If export rationing lowers product prices, farmers lose while a diplomatic goal is being sought. Furthermore, the effectiveness of our use of economic favors in earlier food distribution programs, as well as of import quotas, is questionable. The difficulties involved in a worldwide income redistribution scheme are extremely complex, and the use of cheap food to promote national political goals is frightening.

If the allocation of quantities among foreign buyers is likely to be one problem, the optimum distribution between domestic and foreign consumers is another. It is here that Edgeworth's "vulgar Protection" is most likely to be seen. Instead of producers acting to gain financially by exploiting foreign consumers through the political process, it is likely that consumers will be the active force. The history of recent

---

[1] F. Y. Edgeworth, "Appreciations of Mathematical Theories," *Economic Journal*, vol. 18 (1908), pp. 541–56, at pp. 555–56.

embargoes, excluding the most recent suspension of sales to the Soviet Union, shows that consumers have political clout under some circumstances.

We may be on the verge of repeating the kind of food price interventions seen in many countries. A frequent form is the offering of a subsidy either directly or through foreign exchange allocations for imports. J. M. Davis of the International Monetary Fund reports that "in Egypt, Korea and Sri Lanka, food subsidies accounted for as much as one-fifth of total (government) expenditure in 1974 or 1975, while several other countries devoted approximately one-tenth of expenditure to this component."[2] Lance Taylor reports that in 1975 subsidies on wheat, maize, sugar, and edible oil amounted to over 11 percent of gross domestic product.[3] In general, it is easier to transfer income politically through altered product prices than through explicit tax collections and subsidy payments. Hence U.S. consumers may find it easier to obtain benefits (avoid losses) than consumers in importing countries in recent years simply because the United States is an exporter of agricultural products.

If export limitation is employed, a number of spurious justifications are likely to be used. As Schnittker has noted, the U.S. Senate justifies intervention in trade for the purpose of "protecting the domestic economy from the excessive drain of scarce materials and reducing the serious inflationary impact of foreign demand."[4] This is unfortunately not an isolated or even unusual example of bad theorizing about the source of inflation. Frequently the results of excess demand are identified as the cause of inflation, rather than acknowledged as the measure of its magnitude. Another argument that may be used to support lower-than-equilibrium consumer prices is the conservation of our soil and water resources. After using the political process to transfer income to themselves from consumers, farmers may see the process manipulated to transfer income in the reverse direction through product price manipulation.

Policy Problems If Real Prices Fall

If real prices fall, or perhaps even if they stay constant, the price support mechanism will probably be important again, as Gale Johnson

[2] J. M. Davis, "The Fiscal Role of Food Subsidy Programs," *International Monetary Fund Staff Papers*, vol. 24 (1977), pp. 100–127.

[3] Lance Taylor, "Research Directions in Income Distribution, Nutrition, and the Economics of Food," *Food Research Studies in Agricultural Economics, Trade, and Development*, vol. 16 (1977), pp. 29–45.

[4] U.S. Senate, Committee on Banking, Housing, and Urban Affairs, Report to accompany S. 3084, 94th Congress, 2d session, May 25, 1976.

suggests. As long as there is a mechanism for support, Congress and the president are likely, at least when crops are large, to continue to modify it for their own political gain until intervention in markets distorts resources. I agree with Johnson that the level of support is a political process but argue that the form it takes may be important. The concept of parity, whether modernized or not, was a bad means of determining price supports because it connotes fairness and was therefore more likely to be taken seriously politically. For the same reason, "cost of production" is bad, whether or not land prices, which are simultaneously determined with prices, are included in its measurement. While a formula is an "objective" measure useful to program administrators, it might be better for the electorate if all price supports were to be determined by sheer political strength alone.

Probable Milk Policy in the Years Ahead

Schnittker and several others have suggested that dairy policy is out of line and will be adjusted in the decade ahead. There is general agreement that the classified pricing system for fluid milk has created surpluses and waste. I have argued elsewhere that dairy policy will not be changed easily unless it is done by court action to allow reconstitution of dry milk powder and its mixture with fresh milk for retail sales.

Current dairy policy favors grade A production over grade B production through the classified pricing mechanism of federal and state orders. It also protects domestic producers of nonfluid dairy products from foreign producers. Price supports are continually adjusted so that the government is always on the verge of accumulating stocks. To move from an analysis of the current programs to a prediction about political action, the gainers and losers from a change in policy must be identified. Generally producers can be expected to oppose a change in policy. Consumers are generally not effective political participants because the gains from political action are smaller for the individual than the possible benefits. In the dairy situation, consumers of manufactured products benefit at the expense of fluid milk consumers. We are unlikely to observe a pitched political battle between these two groups of consumers. Interregional rivalry among producers is not likely to be a factor since producers in all regions benefit from classified pricing. Grade B producers are now too small a group to oppose classified pricing and, in any case, have been "bought off" through price supports. Foreign producers have virtually no influence on U.S. policy, since they cannot offer expanded U.S. agricultural exports in exchange for more U.S. imports of milk. Thus, if a change in dairy policy is to occur, it will have to arise out of greater consumer awareness of the costs of the programs, perhaps through court action or perhaps from an ideological conviction that regulation per se is bad.

Dale E. Hathaway

The first part of Professor Johnson's paper is an excellent review of historical policy development, and I can find no serious fault with it. It can be summed up by saying "even though policy makers consistently ignore economics and economic advice in the short run, somehow in the long run the policies for most products turn out to be pretty good." I would argue that this view summarizes the policy process as I see it, that is, it is a constant balancing of short-run pressures against what are perceived to be the long-run realities of world commodity economics.

The second part of Professor Johnson's paper has many of the characteristics of a congressional hearing. It tends to ask questions that implicitly begin, How could you be so stupid as to have done . . . ? I will respond, as officials typically respond to such questions, by a short statement obscuring the issue.

First, most of the points raised by Professor Johnson regarding loan levels, target prices, etc., become irrelevant if Dr. Schnittker is close to correct about the supply-demand balance for grains, oilseeds, and cotton in the 1980s.

Professor Johnson correctly observes that the major innovation of the last decade was the farmer-owned grain reserve. What he fails to acknowledge is that, if the reserve is operated wisely, it, not loan levels or target prices, will be the most significant policy variable in the coming decade.

Let me review what the various concepts really mean in the context of present and future program operations.

First, whereas loan rates historically determined the floor for market prices, the reserve release price now serves that function, as long as significant quantities of production are eligible for entry into the reserve. Thus, the loan rate may be important primarily as it determines the cash that a producer can realize for his crop while it is in the reserve. As the gap between the release price and the loan rate widens, the difference between the market price at which it pays a farmer to sell now and that at which it pays him to put grain in the reserve also widens. This also varies with the interest rate. This explains the support of the administration for a special higher loan rate for reserve grain, an effort that failed.

However bad the cost of production is for calculating key policy variables, it is unrealistic to assume that there is not some relationship between product prices, production costs, and political pressures regarding loan rates, target prices, and reserve release prices. Part of the reason sought by Professor Johnson for the apparently favorable treatment of the Great Plains crops—wheat, sorghum, and barley—relates to the relatively slower increase in yield for those crops, which, unlike corn, failed to offset a large portion of the increased production cost per acre by rapid increases in yield. This was the rationale for the differential changes in target prices and release and call prices. If the 1977 legislation had a flaw, it was that it did not deal adequately with adjustments in a period of severe inflation, a matter that has proved difficult at best.

Professor Johnson notes that the reserve program has been excessively refined and then goes on to suggest further refinements. The 1980 changes in the reserve program were made by and large with a view to making the program more effective and realistic, but such a program can become excessively complicated, so that administrators cannot manage it or farmers use it. I believe that is a real danger and, for this reason, we need to resist refinements of the type suggested by Professor Johnson.

The problems of the dairy program and the fact that they go well beyond the support program are obvious to the dairy industry as well as the government. It is clear that Congress will have to address these problems in the 1981 legislation.

The basic questions for the 1980s are these: (1) Are the market prices that have resulted or are likely to result from the current and prospective levels of the reserve operations too high in a market sense? (2) Will the resulting reserve levels be too large to provide reasonable stability for supplies and, thus, prices? (3) Will the result require large and expensive government programs to control excess production?

In my judgment, based on the best analysis we have available, the answer to all these questions is no. If that is the case, then I would agree with the adage "don't fix it," because I do not believe it is broken.

Professor Johnson seems to be saying that the general policy direction of the last four years has been correct and that it should be followed, with some modest modifications, in 1981 legislation. I concur in that conclusion and expect that Congress will too after considerable evaluation and debate.

A Note on the Book

The typeface used for the text of this book is
Times Roman, designed by Stanley Morison.
The type was set by
Maryland Linotype Composition Co., of Baltimore.
BookCrafters, Inc., of Chelsea, Michigan, printed
and bound the book, using Glatfelter paper.
The cover and format were designed by Pat Taylor,
and the figures were drawn by Hördur Karlsson.
The manuscript was edited by Carrie McKee and
by Gertrude Kaplan, of the AEI Publications staff.

Selected AEI Publications

AEI Associates Program